CREATION
AND
EVOLUTION

Dr Alan Hayward is a physicist and a Bible-believing Christian. He was a principle scientific officer at a Government research laboratory until 1977, when he retired early in order to devote more time to writing. He has published several books, including *Planet Earth's Last Hope, God's Truth* and *Does God Exist? Science says Yes!*

CREATION AND EVOLUTION

ALAN HAYWARD

BETHANY HOUSE PUBLISHERS
MINNEAPOLIS, MINNESOTA 55438

Originally published under the same title by SPCK, London
Bethany House Publishers edition published 1995

Published by Bethany House Publishers
A Ministry of Bethany Fellowship International
11400 Hampshire Avenue South
Minneapolis, Minnesota 55438
www.bethanyhouse.com

Printed in the United States of America by
Bethany Press International, Minneapolis, Minnesota 55438

Library of Congress Cataloging-in-Publication Data

Hayward, Alan.
    Creation and evolution / Alan Hayward.
       p.   cm.
    Includes bibliographical references and indexes.

    1. Creation. 2. Evolution—Religious aspects—Christianity. I. Title.
BS651.H38   1995
231.7'65—dc20   95–18994
ISBN 1–55661–679–1   CIP

Author's Note

This book touches upon many different fields of knowledge. It could never have have been written without the help and advice of numerous experts in subjects where my own knowledge is limited. I must therefore say a hearty 'Thank you' to all the people mentioned below, as well as to others who did not wish to be named here.

First, I am happy to mention the following who, although not known to me personally, were nevertheless quick to respond to my plea for assistance: Prof. J. Ambrose, Prof. R. J. Berry, Sir Robert Boyd, Prof. S. G. Brush, Sir Fred Hoyle, Mr G. R. Morton, Preb. E. K. V. Pearce, Dr R. Ritland, Prof. W. H. Rusch, Prof. W. R. Wharton and Prof. D. A. Young.

Among my own friends the following helped me greatly in their own specialist ways: John Bilello, Dallas Cain, Robert Clark, Rae Earnshaw, Wayne Frair, Ivan Stockley, Ken Walters, John Wenham, Harry Whittaker, my publishers and my son Jonathan.

Finally, two of my friends deserve a special mention. Dan Wonderly gave me an absolutely enormous amount of help with the geological and theological parts of the book, and his constant encouragement kept up my spirits throughout the long and arduous task. And Rita Dyson, with her usual efficiency and cheerfulness, typed the whole thing twice and bits of it several times. I thank God for friends and helpers like all these.

Above all, I must express my indebtedness to my wife. Her life was somewhat disrupted for a whole year by the writing of this book, but her help, her encouragement and her prayers never flagged.

Perhaps I should make it clear that none of these helpers is likely to agree with every opinion expressed in this book, and some of them might disagree with me considerably. Also, they are not to blame for any mistakes there might be in the book. I have taken pains to try and eliminate errors of fact – the first draft of every chapter has been checked by at least six people – but a few errors may still remain. There are probably few of them, and they are most unlikely to affect the validity of any of my conclusions; but be they few or many, the responsibility for any undiscovered errors is mine alone.

Contents

Illustrations

Introduction

===

The mystery of being, still unsolved
  By all our science and philosophy,
Fills me with breathless wonder.   R. L. F. Boyd[1]

One day in 1979 the unthinkable happened. Presidential candidate Ronald Reagan declared that he had creationist sympathies!

Whether this helped him to gain the Presidency of the United States we shall never know. But it certainly helped the whole western world to realize that, from now on, creationism would have to be taken more seriously.

Ever since then the public has been subjected to a barrage of books, articles and television programmes about evolution and creation. Those who have tried to follow the debate have frequently switched off in disgust. The subject is so technical, and attitudes on both sides are often so unreasonable and unhelpful, that the man in the street has often despaired of finding out what is going on.

SORTING OUT THE CONFUSION

Yet from the Christian point of view the controversy is too important to be ignored. No Christian who respects the Bible can afford to shrug his shoulders and say it doesn't matter whether Genesis is right or wrong. On the other hand, no Christian can afford to alienate most of the scientific community unless he is quite sure that this is necessary. Before taking up a position he needs to weigh the facts.

Unfortunately, the smoke of battle is so thick that it is difficult to see what the facts are. For one thing, from its very beginning the argument has been spiced with sarcasm and venom. When *On the Origin of Species* was published in 1859 the Bishop of Oxford started it all, with a famous crack about the apish ancestry of Darwin's staunch supporter, T. H. Huxley. A little later Huxley launched his own attack on the religious establishment when he declared that 'old ladies of both sexes consider it [Darwin's *Origin*]

I

a decidedly dangerous book'.[2] The schoolboy insults have never dried up, with a famous Darwinist in 1983 calling creationists 'a gang of ignorant crackpots'.[3]

News reporters are often as baffled as the general public, judging by the way they contradict each other. For example, the *International Herald Tribune* celebrated the centenary of Darwin's death on 19 April 1982 with a feature article by Philip Boffey stating:

> Virtually all [biologists] . . . say they are battling over subsidiary issues, not challenging the grand structure of Darwinian evolution.[4]

On almost the same day, readers of *The Times* found a similar feature article in which Christopher Booker said the opposite:

> The only trouble was that, as Darwin himself was at least partly aware, it [Darwin's theory] was full of colossal holes . . . A book which has become famous for explaining the origin of species in fact does nothing of the kind.[5]

In the scientific journals similar contradictions abound. At the time of the 1982 Centenary, editors carefully selected a batch of devout Darwinists to sing Darwin's praises. Sweeping assertions like the following popped up everywhere:

> Darwin's theses are no longer disputed by true scientists.[6]

> Darwin's theory is now supported by all the available relevant evidence, and its truth is not doubted by any serious modern biologist.[7]

Reading such statements you would never imagine that scientific books and journals are peppered with criticisms of Darwinism by eminent biologists. Yet, as chapters 1 to 4 of this book will show, such is the case.

But Darwinists do not have a monopoly of absurd and extreme statements. A creationist strip-cartoon for children begins like this:

> The monkey is pointing at a man who looks like a monkey. His name is Charles Darwin. He didn't want to believe that *God* created people. So he thought up a *big lie* instead. He said, 'People came from *monkeys!*' He called his big lie '*Evolution*'.[8] (Their italics.)

Somewhere behind all the rancour and rhetoric, all the overstatements and inaccuracies, there must be some vital information. This book will attempt the necessary – but far from easy – task of blowing away the smokescreen and exposing those underlying facts. In other words, my aim is to produce a kind of Plain Man's Guide to What is Going On.

The Middle Position

It is impossible for any writer to be entirely free from prejudice, so perhaps it may be helpful to state my own position here. I believe that truth in this field lies, as it does in so many areas, somewhere in the middle ground between the two hotly contested extremes.

This position holds both advantages and disadvantages. The main snag is that we live in an age when extremism is somehow regarded as noble, and moderation is often seen as a sign of weakness or unworthiness. Those who walk down the middle of the road are liable to be hooted at from both left and right.

The benefit of the central position is that it does enable one to see both sides. While not agreeing with either the dogmatic evolutionists or the extreme creationists, I can at least appreciate both their points of view. While both say many things that are questionable, both have a lot of useful things to tell us, too.

A QUESTION OF DEFINITIONS

Before we go any further it is necessary to clear up a little difficulty. *Different people use the word 'evolution' to mean quite different things.* Failing to realize this has caused endless confusion. The problem arises because three words are needed to specify three different concepts: 'succession', 'evolution', and 'Darwinism'. But because the three ideas are related the word 'evolution' is sometimes used for all three – and that is a recipe for mental chaos. So let us look at the three distinct notions, and the way these three words will be used in this book.

(1) *Succession*
Geologists studying the rocks that make up the earth's crust are rather like detectives examining the scene of a crime. By studying the traces left behind they attempt to reconstruct what might have happened long ago.

This leads them (rightly or wrongly) to conclude that the rocks were laid down bit by bit, over a period of more than three billion (thousand million) years, and that they can assign approximate ages to each layer of rock. Embedded in the rocks are countless millions of fossils. These are obviously the remains of plants, animals and fishes that have somehow been turned into stone.

When they classified these fossils according to the ages of the rocks where they were found, the geologists made a remarkable discovery. The oldest rocks contained the remains of nothing but lowly forms of life, like worms, snails and algae. Then, as time went by, more and more advanced forms of life appeared. Only after life had been developing for hundreds of millions of years did mammals arrive. Later still, just a few million years ago, the apes showed up. Last of all Man came on the scene.

This idea of the geologists, that life has been on earth for a long time and has gradually become more and more varied and more advanced, can be called *succession*.

(2) *Evolution*

If 'succession' has in fact occurred there are two alternative ways to explain it. And both explanations create problems.

One way is to suppose that some kind of Creative Power (or, as Christians would put it, God) has been at work for hundreds of millions of years, either continuously or on and off. Such a view is usually called 'progressive creation'. It invites the question: why should God spend all that time creating all sorts of wonderful living things, and then allow them to die out and be replaced by other species? To this there is no easy answer.

The other view is that all the living things of today are the direct descendants of earlier, rather different, living things; that these in turn were descended from still earlier forms of life; and so on, all the way back to the very first primitive organism – which itself probably sprang into existence through the interplay of natural forces. This idea is known as *evolution*. It is often defined by the brief expression: 'descent with modification'.

Some writers, especially in the USA, call this 'macro-evolution', to distinguish it from the small-scale variations – 'micro-evolution' – which occur within (or almost within) a species. In this book I think we can manage quite well without using these clumsy, half-Greek, half-Latin hybrid words.

The early Greek philosophers were probably the first thinkers to toy with the notion of evolution. Along with many other ideas from ancient Greece it reappeared in western Europe in the fifteenth and sixteenth centuries. By the late eighteenth century, even before Darwin was born, it was being widely discussed. And by the early nineteenth century, when geologists had produced a great deal of evidence for succession, the possibility of evolution was being treated very seriously indeed by advanced thinkers.

But one great difficulty stood in the way. Nobody – not even Lamarck, who made a brave attempt[9] – could explain convincingly how evolution could have taken place. Each species seemed to be fixed. There seemed no way in which one species could give rise to another.

(3) *Darwinism*

Darwin changed all that with his theory that the way evolution worked was by 'natural selection'. He proposed that small variations in each generation – the kind of natural variations that enable breeders to produce new varieties of dogs and cows and apples and roses – would eventually add up to very big differences, and thus, over hundreds of millions of years, could account for every species on earth.

The struggle for survival would act as the driving force behind evolution, he reasoned, by killing off most of the mediocre individuals in every generation and allowing only the prime specimens to survive. He called this principle 'natural selection', because it was Nature's counterpart to the deliberate selection practised by plant and animal breeders.

Darwin's original theory has been extended and modified in the light of recent discoveries. The commonest modern version of it is properly called neo-Darwinism. For the sake of simplicity the term *Darwinism* will be used in this book to cover all or any of the versions of Darwin's theory.

Why is it that the terms 'Darwinism' and 'evolution' are so often used (wrongly) as if they meant the same thing? Simply because it was Darwin who put the old idea of evolution on its feet. Before Darwin, evolution was regarded by most people as a wild, unbelievable notion. After Darwin, evolution seemed such a reasonable idea that the general public soon took it for granted.

Many people since Darwin's day have tried to find an alternative explanation of evolution, but none has succeeded. Just as when he first proposed it, Darwin's appears the only conceivable method of evolution. It still seems that Darwinism and evolution must stand or fall together. If Darwinism were to be proved wrong, evolution would once more become highly questionable – an idea without enough explanation to make it plausible.

CHRISTIAN ATTITUDES TO CREATION

Christians nowadays tend to view the subject of evolution and creation in one of three ways. These are illustrated in the logic diagram of Figure 1.

The problem begins with the idea of *succession*. As described above, this was developed in the early nineteenth century by geologists, who found evidence for a very ancient earth in which many extinct forms of life have succeeded each other through the ages.

Down the left hand side of the diagram is a chain of thought which has been followed by countless millions. It starts with 'succession' and ends with atheistic evolution – total unbelief.

The right hand side illustrates the three alternative ways in which Christians can break away from this chain.

(1) *Recent-creationists*
The most radical approach is that of the recent-creationists, who break away at the earliest possible point. They reject the whole idea of 'succession', and argue that geologists, physicists and astronomers are all mistaken in thinking the earth to be old.

By regarding 'succession' as a great mistake they are able to adopt the only possible alternative – a sudden, recent creation of the whole universe. This, they claim, is what Genesis teaches and consequently what every Christian ought to believe.

(2) *Ancient-creationists*
The middle ground is occupied by the ancient-creationists. They regard 'succession' as being so well supported by experimental evidence that it cannot be denied. But they reason that 'succession' is not necessarily due to evolution; it might just as well be due to successive acts of creation over a long period.

To justify their adoption of the second alternative they oppose evolution. They argue that Darwinism can be shown to be contrary to the evidence, and that evolution is therefore nothing more than an unsupported speculation. Genesis, they say, teaches creation, but not necessarily *recent* creation, and they use various ways of explaining the six days of Genesis 1.

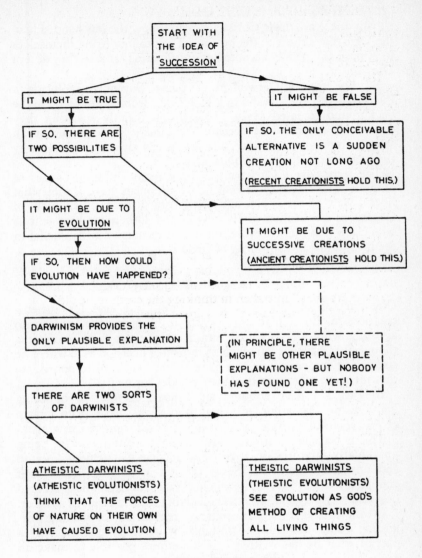

Figure 1. Logic diagram

(3) *Theistic Darwinists (Theistic Evolutionists)*

Finally there are those Christians who follow the left hand side of
the logic tree almost to the bottom. They cannot bring themselves
to oppose any widely accepted scientific ideas, and so they accept
Darwinism.

But not atheistic Darwinism, of course. Darwinian evolution to
them is merely the method by which God, keeping discreetly in the
background, created every living thing. Strictly speaking they
should be described as theistic Darwinists. Few people speak
strictly, however, and such folk are nearly always referred to by
the looser term, theistic evolutionists.

The term covers Christians holding many different shades of
opinion. The majority of theistic evolutionists have a somewhat
liberal view of the Bible, and often regard the early chapters of
Genesis as a collection of Hebrew myths. Others are evangelicals
who claim that theistic evolution can be reconciled with a belief in
the inspiration and authority of Genesis.

THE PLAN OF THIS BOOK

One purpose of this book is to present the case for ancient-
creationism. But I shall not attempt to bludgeon the reader into
agreeing with me. My first aim is to present facts, so that a
thoughtful Christian can reach an informed decision as to where he
stands. At the very least the book might help him to appreciate
that there are other points of view besides his own.

In Part I I have adopted an unusual method of opposing
Darwinism. My arguments and quotations have been drawn
exclusively from the writings of *evolutionists* who oppose Darwinism.

This is because creationist writings have a reputation for being
unscholarly mixtures of correct and incorrect statements, sound
and unsound arguments. Some are not at all like that,[10] but
enough are to have given the whole class a bad name. So it seemed
best to disregard all arguments emanating from creationist sources.

Creationists also have an unhappy reputation for making misleading quotations from evolutionist writers. By quoting only a
part of what he has written it is sometimes possible to make an
evolutionist sound like a creationist. I myself have seen some
frightful examples of this, and a number of evolutionists have been
angered at seeing their views distorted in this way.

I have tried not to make this mistake, and to be scrupulously fair
to all the writers quoted. Unfortunately it is not given to fallen
mankind to do anything perfectly, and I may not always have

succeeded in fulfilling this good intention. If so, I hope that anyone whom I might have misrepresented will write and tell me, so that the record can be put straight in any future edition.

Part II summarizes the scientific evidence that the earth is very old, and that 'succession' is practically a historical fact. It is my impression that many recent-creationists are quite unaware of most of this evidence, and they may find this uncomfortable reading. If so, let them take comfort from the thought that nearly all the leading Bible-believers from 1850 to 1950 were ancient-creationists.

In Part III the spotlight moves away from science and focuses on the Bible. Genesis and other parts of Scripture are examined to see what they really say about creation, and the pros and cons of the various Christian views of creation are discussed in the light of these Scriptures.

Finally, it might be as well to say that I have tried to use the same simple English as in my previous religious books. One minor consequence of this is that I have suppressed my personal preference for metric units in favour of old-fashioned English miles and so forth. Also, I have had to recognize that the traditional English use of the word 'billion' – a million million – is fast dying out; like most modern writers I now use the word only in its American sense – a thousand million.

A more serious problem is that it is not easy to write about profound scientific matters in non-technical language. At times I have had to oversimplify matters, and readers with a scientific background might think that some passages sound unscientific. When there has seemed a risk of this happening I have made free use of the notes and references at the back of the book to clarify the position.

A-level creationists and evolutionists may find these notes indispensable. But most readers will probably get along well enough without ever looking at them.

Part I

THE GENUINE SCIENTIFIC
OBJECTIONS TO DARWINISM

CHAPTER I

Wind of Change

=====

I am Sir Oracle,
And when I ope my lips, let no dog bark!   Shakespeare[1]

In the inner London suburb of South Kensington is an ornate Victorian building usually (but incorrectly) called the Natural History Museum.[2] In 1981, to mark its centenary, the Museum opened a splendid new exhibition on Darwinism – and thereby put the cat in the pigeon loft.

The first thing the visitor sees on entering the exhibition hall is a notice in flickering lights:

> Have you ever wondered why there are so many different kinds of living things?
> One idea is that all the living things we see today have EVOLVED from a distant ancestor by a process of gradual change.
> How could evolution have occurred? How could one species change into another?
> The exhibition in this hall looks at one possible explanation – the explanation first thought of by Charles Darwin.

To the majority of biologists this smacks of treason. Darwinism 'one possible explanation' indeed! Had they not been taught in college that Darwinism was the *only* possible explanation of evolution – and what's more, that it had been proved true?

As if to add insult to injury, a little further into the exhibition a poster actually admits:

> Another view is that God created all living things perfect and unchanging.

Such open-mindedness would have been unthinkable a few years ago. To many staunch Darwinists it is unthinkable still. One of the world's leading scientific journals, *Nature*, promptly ran an editorial headed, 'Darwin's death in South Kensington'.[3]

This quoted a phrase from the Museum's latest brochure, 'If the

13

theory of evolution is true . . .', as evidence of 'the rot at the museum'. The editorial went on to lament:

> The new exhibition policy, the museum's chief interaction with the outside world, is being developed in some degree of isolation from the museum's staff of distinguished biologists, most of whom would rather lose their right hands than begin a sentence with the phrase, 'If the theory of evolution is true . . .'

That did it. The poor editor was forced to publish the following letter, which was signed by no less than twenty-two of 'the museum's staff of distinguished biologists':

> Sir – As working biologists at the British Museum (Natural History) we were astonished to read your editorial 'Darwin's death in South Kensington' (*Nature* 26 February, p. 735). How is it that a journal such as yours that is devoted to science and its practice can advocate that theory be presented as fact? This is the stuff of prejudice, not science, and as scientists our basic concern is to keep an open mind on the unknowable. Surely it should not be otherwise?
>   You suggest that most of us would rather lose our right hands than begin a sentence with the phrase 'If the theory of evolution is true . . ' Are we to take it that evolution is a fact, proven to the limits of scientific rigour? If that is the inference then we must disagree most strongly. We have no absolute proof of the theory of evolution. What we do have is overwhelming circumstantial evidence in favour of it and as yet no better alternative. But the theory of evolution would be abandoned tomorrow if a better theory appeared . . .

DIE-HARDS VERSUS DOUBTERS

These extracts from *Nature* illustrate the dilemma facing the biological world just now. Despite the existence of many doubtful Darwinists there are still plenty of die-hards saying: 'There is no problem. Darwinism is true. End of story.' As long as anyone can remember many Darwinists have taken that hard line.

Yet, strange to relate, these same committed Darwinists are often found admitting that the evidence for Darwinism is sadly incomplete. Below are three examples from recent literature. All are from publications commissioned as part of the Darwin centenary celebrations in 1982.

True Believers Make Admissions

An article with the title, 'Darwinism at the very beginning of life' and the sub-title, 'Even before there was life there was natural selection', was written by Dr Leslie Orgel.[4] His claim was that the first living thing evolved in a Darwinian fashion from the chemicals lying on the earth's surface about four billion years ago. Yet despite his obvious confidence in his main conclusion, he slipped in these admissions:

> We must next explain how a prebiotic soup of organic molecules . . . evolved into a self-replicating organism. While some suggestive evidence has been obtained, I must admit that *attempts to reconstruct this evolutionary process are extremely tentative*.
>
> The origin of the genetic code is the most baffling aspect of the problem of the origins of life and *a major conceptual or experimental breakthrough may be needed before we can make any substantial progress*. (My italics.)

A second example is in Jonathan Howard's book, *Darwin*. He admits in the preface that he is a supporter of Darwin, and opposed to those he describes as 'Darwin's detractors'. Nevertheless, honesty compels him to make the following remarkable confession:

> All evolutionary reconstructions . . . rest heavily on *plausibility rather than evidence* to command assent.[5] (My italics.)

Then there is an article by Dr Brian Charlesworth, 'Neo-Darwinism – the plain truth'.[6] This title is evidently intended to mean that 'neo-Darwinism is plainly true', since the sub-title reads, 'Despite assertions to the contrary, Darwin's ideas about the origin of species hold good today.' Nevertheless, his scientific integrity compelled him to warn his readers:

> It is important to bear in mind, however, that *we are usually so ignorant* of the genetic structure of fossil populations and of the relations between environment, fitness and morphology *that we cannot provide explanations for any particular historical pattern of evolution*. (My italics.)

These three examples – which are absolutely typical – raise an interesting psychological problem. Why are orthodox Darwinists so sure of their conclusions, when they are ready to admit that the evidence is woefully incomplete? There is a simple answer to this question.

A Kind of Faith

It has often been pointed out that Man is a 'religious animal'. He has a psychological need to believe in *something*. In bygone days religion usually supplied that need. Nowadays many Europeans and Americans choose to believe in something other than the Christian faith of their forefathers. Witches, gurus, mediums and spoon-benders flourish. Modern man has had to adopt the word 'ideology', to describe the great political faiths that take the place of religion for millions.

One leading Darwinist has frankly admitted that evolution has become just such a faith. He wrote:

> The concept of organic evolution is very highly prized by biologists, *for many of whom it is an object of genuinely religious devotion*, because they regard it as a supreme integrative principle.[7] (My italics.)

Others have clearly implied it. For instance, in his Foreword to a new edition of Darwin's *Origin of Species*, Professor L. H. Matthews wrote:

> Belief in evolution is . . . exactly parallel to belief in special creation – both are concepts which *believers know to be true*, but neither, up to the present, has been capable of proof.[8] (My italics.)

Some Darwinists have objected to this tendency to make a kind of religion out of Darwin's theory. Nigel Calder, for example, complained:

> Neo-Darwinism has already showed signs of hardening into quasi-religious dogma . . . some of the critics of Kimura and Ohta [two Japanese biologists who dared to criticise Darwin] react like priests scenting blasphemy.[9]

Most revealing of all, a recent article by Dr Richard Dawkins on 'The Necessity of Darwinism'[10] was accompanied by a cartoon illustration. An ancient oak tree was shown with its largest branch broken off not far from the lower part of the trunk – and this broken stump was labelled 'GOD'. Growing out of the trunk above this was a splendid younger branch, soaring up towards the heavens, labelled 'DARWIN'.

Although some Darwinists are Christians the majority are agnostics or atheists. The fashionable way of life for such unbelievers is called Humanism, which they themselves have described as a 'religion without God'. And Humanists freely admit that Darwinism is their intellectual foundation. A lengthy book setting out the Humanist creed[11] uses the word 'evolution' six times on the very first page. The blurb on the dust jacket informs us in its opening paragraph:

> Evolutionary humanism . . . is emerging as the new system of thought and belief concerned with our destiny. Man is a natural phenomenon produced by the evolutionary process . . .

EXPRESSIONS OF DOUBT

There always has been an undercurrent of doubt among Darwinists. What is unusual about the present situation is that at last these doubts have come fully into the open. A few years ago biologists in many institutions would have been putting their careers at risk if they had criticized Darwinism openly. Now it has become almost fashionable to do so.

We even find a Darwinist reminding us that the first doubting Darwinist was Darwin himself! John Hedley Brooke quoted Darwin's admission 'that he was in a hopeless muddle: he could not believe that each detail of organic structure had been preordained; *nor could he think that the evolutionary process as a whole was the result of chance*.'[12] (My italics.)

Palaeontologists (fossil experts) have been among the most prominent doubters. David M. Raup spoke for many of them in a paper with the significant title, 'Conflicts between Darwin and Paleontology'.[13] He reckoned that only about a quarter of a million species of fossil plants and animals have yet been discovered. Yet evolutionists believe that at least a hundred times as many fossil species are still awaiting discovery. Hence, Raup warned, Darwinism appears to be based upon less than one per cent of the potential fossil evidence.

Biologist C. F. Robinow expressed similar misgivings in his own field:

> Dissatisfaction with the Darwinian theory of evolution continues to be felt by a fraction of professional biologists. It is surely better in the long run to recognize present limits to our understanding than to be lured into the acceptance of attractive, lucid solutions which are unrealistic.[14]

Punctuated Equilibria

This new spirit of doubt has led to the emergence of two new schools of biological thought, associated with the terms 'punctuated equilibria', and 'cladistics'. Their adherents have sometimes been portrayed in creationist writings as opposed to Darwinism, if not actually sympathetic to creationism. This is most unfair, and has led them to accuse some creationists of deceit.

The fact is that these new movements are more or less in harmony with the broad outline of Darwinism.[15] Niles Eldredge, one of the founders of the theory of punctuated equilibria, has actually written a book attacking creationism.[16] What he and his supporters oppose is the complacent, know-all attitude of orthodox Darwinists. Thus he wrote in 1982, in a book review with the sarcastic title, 'An Ode to Adaptive Transformation':

> I confess I cannot fathom the difference between [an orthodox Darwinist's] argument and the older [creationist's] argument from design: see this organ system; observe its intricacy! Only (God, natural selection) could have fashioned such a marvellous machine! There *is* a difference of course: God, as a supernatural being, does not belong to science, whereas natural selection patently does. But used in this inappropriate fashion, natural selection becomes a mere substitute for the Creator. It tells us nothing . . .[17]

Nevertheless, Eldredge and his many supporters insist that they are Darwinists. They want to see Darwinian theory overhauled, not scrapped. In particular, they think that Darwinists should pay more attention to the sudden way in which fossil species appear. As the other founder of the movement, Harvard's Professor Stephen Jay Gould, has said:

> For millions of years species remain unchanged in the fossil record, and they then abruptly disappear, to be replaced by something that is substantially different but clearly related.[18]

Many Christians would see this as evidence for periodic bursts of activity by the Creator, but the punctuated equilibrists have a different explanation. They point out that the geological record is so enormously long that, even if a species took a thousand years to evolve, it would still *appear* to arise in an instant – just as a large city appears as a tiny dot on a small-scale map. Gould argues that 'most species' arose within 'hundreds or thousands of years' – a time period that he calls a 'geological microsecond' – and then stayed unchanged for millions of years.[19]

This is in conflict with the orthodox idea that species evolved extremely slowly, through very large numbers of very small changes. Not so, say the punctuated equilibrists: evolution took place in short bursts, with long periods of rest between; what we must do now is to find a biological explanation of how it could possibly have happened.

The controversy is likely to go on for a long time, since both sides have at least one short suit. Orthodox Darwinism offers a plausible biological explanation for what might have happened, but is in conflict with the evidence of geology. And the alternative theory accepts the geological record, but cannot explain how species could arise so suddenly. To the outside observer it seems that both these versions of Darwinism are on shaky ground.

Cladistics

Cladistics is a fairly new method of classifying living things.[20] It is quite obvious that organisms can be divided into groups within groups. Men and apes together form a group known as primates. The primates are just a small part of a larger group known as mammals, and they in turn fall within an even larger group, the vertebrates (creatures with backbones). And so we could go on, all the way to the largest group of all, the animal kingdom.

Darwin saw this as evidence for his theory. The apes are our nearest cousins, he said, the other mammals our more distant cousins, and so on. This is why many books on evolution make great use of family trees, showing how various creatures are supposed to be descended from their fossil ancestors. The way in which living things are classified today is largely dependent on the shape of the evolutionary family tree.

And that, say the cladists, is where biology has gone wrong. We have made the tail wag the dog. We ought never to have allowed evolutionary *theory* to settle our classification scheme for us. We ought to begin again and classify living things anew, strictly on the basis of the observed biological *facts*.

At the Natural History Museum it was thought that this made sense, and the Museum began to reclassify its collection on cladistic lines. Sometimes the Museum's new scheme supported the accepted wisdom, and sometimes it conflicted with it. A leading member of the Museum staff, Dr Colin Patterson, stuck his neck out when he wrote:

Cladistics calls into question much of conventional evolutionary history.[21]

Despite the storm that has burst upon the Museum, Patterson is unrepentant. 'Is stability worth more than a century of conflict with evidence?' he asks.[22]

It is important to realize that cladistics is not evidence for creation. It is not even evidence that Darwin was wrong. The Museum's cladists stated their views on Darwinism in the letter reproduced earlier in this chapter: 'we have overwhelming circumstantial evidence in favour of it and as yet no better alternative. But the theory of evolution would be abandoned tomorrow if a better theory appeared.'

The real value of cladistics is that it cuts Darwinism down to size. Cladists believe that this badly needs doing: as Patterson said in a BBC broadcast, 'Biology is being carried out by people whose faith is in, almost, the deity of Darwin.'[23]

Cladists insist that Darwinism is still only an unproved theory which might well turn out to be true, but could possibly be false. Above all, cladism draws attention to what orthodox Darwinists – astonishingly – seem to have overlooked: that observed facts must always take precedence over an elegant theory.

CHAPTER 2

Biologists who Reject Darwinism

At any given moment there is an orthodoxy, a body of ideas, which it is assumed all right-thinking people will accept without question. It is not exactly forbidden to say this that or the other, but it is 'not done' to say it. George Orwell[1]

We saw in the previous chapter that many biologists nowadays have doubts about Darwin's theory, and think that it might have to be modified. But there are other biologists who go a great deal further, and think Darwinism is worthless.

These are not creationists. They are evolutionists who consider that Darwin's theory cannot be made to fit the facts, no matter how much biologists might modify it. Their view is that nothing less than an entirely new theory is needed to explain evolution. So far they have not managed to find one, but they are still looking.

There have long been quite a number of these folk about. And those I shall quote in this chapter are generally regarded as quite distinguished biologists, despite their unorthodox views.

CONTINENTAL BIOLOGISTS

Because English is fast becoming the international language of science, English-speaking scientists have little incentive to learn foreign languages. Unfortunately, this makes it easy for them to become inward-looking. They tend to forget that a great deal of valuable scientific work is still being published in foreign languages.

This probably explains how most British and American biologists acquired the curious – and incorrect – notion that 'practically everybody accepts Darwinism'. If they had paid a little more attention to what was going on in continental Europe they would have known better.

For instance, they would not have been so bewildered when a book by the Scandinavian biologist, Erik Nordenskiöld,[2] appeared in English translation in 1929. This stated that Darwin's theory of the origin of species 'was long ago abandoned. Other facts established by Darwin are all of second-rate value.'

When quoting these words in 1983, *New Scientist* dismissed them as merely 'reflecting the anti-Darwinian sentiments then current'.[3] As much as to say that the continentals have grown wiser since then!

Alas, nothing could be further from the truth. One of the greatest histories of science ever produced is a series of volumes written by various French scientists in the nineteen-sixties. This later appeared in English translation as *A General History of the Sciences*. In volume 4 the section on evolution[4] is written by one of France's most eminent biologists, Professor Andrée Tétry.

She discusses what she calls 'the two great theories of evolution', Lamarckianism and Darwinism, as well as some lesser theories, and dismisses them all as inadequate. Her conclusion is:

> In point of fact none of the theories we have been discussing provides an entirely satisfactory account of all the facts of evolution.

She is particularly hard on neo-Darwinism, which is sometimes called the 'synthetic theory' of evolution. Her description of it as 'the theory . . . which is favoured by British and American geneticists' is a clear hint that the rest of the world is a lot more sceptical of Darwinism than the Anglo-Saxons are.

She says it is 'hard to believe' that complex organs – and above all the human brain – could really have been produced by mutations, which are controlled by sheer chance. To do any good, she points out, a mutation must not only happen to be an exceedingly fortunate step forward – it must also 'adjust itself to the preceding mutation, and occur at precisely the right place and time.' In other words, for anything to evolve through a series of useful mutations, there would have to be a quite incredible succession of lucky chances.

After listing her objections she sums up:

> No wonder, therefore, that J. Kälin has called the synthetic theory [neo-Darwinism] a kind of 'synthetic euphoria'.

To read her attack on Darwinism, and her final conclusion that no alternative theory of evolution is any better, you might almost imagine her to be a creationist. In fact she ranks as one of France's leading evolutionists. But like many French biologists, she would rather say, 'We don't yet know how things could have evolved', than pretend that a bad theory is a good one.

And her words were written in the middle nineteen-sixties, when evolutionists all over the English-speaking world were loudly proclaiming, 'No respectable biologists doubt the truth of Darwinism.' It is no wonder that continentals sometimes accuse the British and Americans of arrogance and isolationism!

A French Botanist

In 1967 Dr Pierre Gavaudan, holder of the Chair in Botany and Cytology at the University of Poitiers, published a paper on evolution in the proceedings of a conference at an American university.[5] Its purpose was to inform the Anglo-Saxon biologists why he thought they were foolish to swallow Darwin's theory so uncritically. He called neo-Darwinism an 'ingenious romance', and compared it to an eighteenth-century French writer who was said to have 'exalted nonsense to the level of genius'. More plainly, he declared:

> The pretence of neo-Darwinism to be able to open on its own account the door to truth looks a little childish.

In support of this conclusion he gave various reasons drawn from his researches in botany. One of the most impressive was based on carnivorous plants, which trap insects and digest them. This ability to obtain airborne nourishment gives them a tremendous advantage, since they can flourish in very poor soils where other plants have a job to survive. So one might have expected large parts of the world to be overrun with carnivorous plants, quietly digesting their mosquito steaks. Yet in fact they are quite rare.

How did this extraordinary behaviour arise? The digestive systems of these plants are highly complex, and there seems no way they could have evolved in a multitude of small steps. And, if they really are a triumphant success of natural selection – 'the survival of the fittest' – why are there so few carnivorous plants around? He answers:

> The [Darwinian] theory is incapable of giving anything better than a highly fictional description of the origin of these remarkable arrangements.

Being a cytologist (cell expert) as well as a botanist, he then takes a look at plant and animal cells. Anyone wanting to learn all there is to learn would have to plough through 'many hundreds of kilometers' of paper, he says. And at the end he still would not know anything like enough to construct the simplest form of living cell!

He concludes that if the wisest men on earth could not even

begin to form a new cell, it is hardly likely that mutation and natural selection could do it.

Once more we have a distinguished biologist who writes rather like a creationist, but is actually an evolutionist. Having destroyed Darwinism he does not accept creation as the obvious alternative. Instead, he argues that there must be some mysterious property of living things that compels them to evolve along pre-determined lines.

But is that an explanation, or just another 'ingenious romance', with even less support than Darwinism?

A French Zoologist

Pierre-Paul Grassé is no ordinary evolutionist. Some years ago he was described by a famous American Darwinist as:

> The most distinguished of French zoologists, the editor of the 28 volumes of *Traité de Zoologie*, author of numerous original investigations and ex-president of the Académie des Sciences. His knowledge of the living world is encyclopedic . . .[6]

In his post as Director of the Laboratory of the Evolution of Living Beings, which is part of the University of Paris, he has been responsible for a great deal of research into the mechanism of evolution. Few men in all the world are better qualified to express an opinion about evolution.

In 1973 he published in French a major book on evolution, which appeared in English translation[7] in 1977. Its purpose was twofold. First and foremost, the book aims to expose Darwinism as a theory that does not work, because it clashes with so many experimental findings. As he says in his introduction:

> Today our duty is to destroy the myth of evolution . . . some people, owing to their sectarianism, purposely overlook reality and refuse to acknowledge the inadequacies and the falsity of their beliefs. (p. 8)

Then follow 200 large pages packed with evidence that Darwinism is on an entirely wrong track. Only after that does he turn to his second purpose, which is to offer a new theory of evolution to replace Darwin's.

His attack on Darwinism has many prongs, but its main thrust is aimed at the central idea of Darwinism: that evolution is due to the combined effect of (1) mutations, and (2) natural selection.

Mutations are the result of 'copying errors' in the genes. When a plant or animal reproduces, the new generation is usually almost exactly like the parents. The genes are extremely complex chemical substances in the germ cells, and they contain a sort of blueprint of the parents which is passed on to the next generation. If something goes slightly wrong when the genes duplicate themselves, the result may be a four-leafed clover, or the first copper beech tree, or a baby with twelve toes.

Such mutations give natural selection something to work on. Occasionally a mutant offspring is better equipped for survival than its normal brothers and sisters. When that happens the normal variety may die out locally, while the unusual one takes its place. And if that happens often enough, said Darwin, the outcome may be a new species. To summarize:

Mutation + natural selection = Darwinian evolution.

The only trouble is, says Grassé, that neither mutation nor natural selection works the way that Darwinists think they do!

Take mutation first. Grassé has studied this extensively, both inside his laboratory and in nature. In all sorts of living things, from bacteria to plants and animals, he has observed that mutations do not take succeeding generations further and further from their starting point.

Instead, the changes are like the flight of a butterfly in a greenhouse, which travels for miles without moving more than a few feet from its starting point. There are invisible but firmly fixed boundaries that mutations can never cross. As Grassé says:

> This text [a Darwinist book] suggests that modern bacteria are evolving very quickly, thanks to their innumerable mutations. *Now, this is not true.* For millions, or even billions, of years, bacteria have not transgressed the structural frame within which they have always fluctuated and still do . . . *To vary and to evolve are two different things*; this can never be sufficiently emphasized. (p. 6 – his italics.)
>
> Despite their innumerable mutations, *Erophila verna* [whitlow grass], *Viola tricola* [wild pansy], and the rest do not evolve. *This is a fact.* (p. 225 – his italics.)

He insists that mutations are only trivial changes; they are merely the result of slightly altered genes, whereas 'creative evolution . . . demands the genesis of new ones' (p. 217). Other biologists agree with this, he claims, and quotes an American geneticist[8] who has argued that 'big leaps in evolution required the creation of new gene loci with previously non-existent functions' (p. 218). But he offers no real explanation of how nature can 'create' new genes.

Turning to natural selection, he shows that this frequently does not work in a Darwinian fashion, either. For example, he asks why should goats and deer have developed scent glands that enable them to keep track of each other (a minor advantage) but which give them away to the carnivores that hunt them (a major disadvantage)? After a detailed examination of the way natural selection works, he concludes:

> Selection tends to eliminate the causes of a population's hetero-geneity and thus to produce a uniform genotype. *It acts more to conserve the inheritance of the species than to transform it.* (p. 119 – his italics.)

Things Wise and Wonderful

Although Grassé is a convinced evolutionist, he enthuses over the wonders of nature as heartily as any creationist. In particular, he mentions many organs and mechanisms in nature that will work only when they are complete. For Darwinism to suggest that mutation and natural selection could produce such things is sheer romancing, he insists.

One of his examples is the mechanism that causes blood to clot when it is exposed to air. This is essential to animal life: without it, a small scratch and we should bleed to death.

Yet the system only works because a whole collection of different, and highly complex, chemical substances act *together* to achieve the desired result. Remove just one of those vital chemicals, and the blood won't clot any more. How could natural selection create such a system, asks Grassé. Only if its action were 'prophetic', he answers! In other words, it couldn't.

Another of his many examples is the ant-lion larva. This remarkable insect lives in regions of dry sand or sandy soil, where it digs a pit about two inches deep and waits at the bottom for ants to tumble in. It has a delicate intruder-alarm system, sensitive to the slightest vibration. If a single grain of sand rolls into the pit the ant-lion springs to the alert, with its pincer-like mandibles gaping, ready to seize its prey. The underside of its body is provided with a set of horn-like anchors, so that it can grip the soil while struggling with its captive.

The ant-lion's mouth is quite extraordinary, being fastened almost shut with a complicated locking system. This makes it unable to eat solid food, but the mouth forms a kind of drinking straw, ideally suited to supping broth.

Having grabbed an ant, the first thing the ant-lion does is to inject a paralysing drug. Then it gives a second injection of digestive juices which gradually turn the ant's insides into a nourishing liquid, ready for the ant-lion to suck it out.

There is no drinking water in the hot, dry sandpits where ant-lions live. Most insects would soon die of dehydration in such an environment. But not the ant-lion. To begin with, he is provided with an impermeable skin which, like the aluminium foil around a roasting chicken, prevents his body moisture from drying up. And his digestive tract has a system for recycling the urine, as astronauts do in a spaceship, so that every drop of water can be used again and again.

For such a creature to have evolved along Darwinian lines, Grassé comments, it would have needed 'an avalanche of co-ordinated and mutually adjusted chance occurrences' (p. 163). The odds in favour of that, he declares, are 'infinitesimal' – a scientific way of saying that it is just not on.

Elsewhere he discusses the origin of the eye. He asserts that there is a better chance that dust blown by the wind might have produced Dürer's 'Melancholia' (a great sixteenth-century engraving) than that the eye was the result of copying errors in the gene. (p. 104.)

For reasons like these Grassé – who, remember, has been acknowledged as one of Europe's greatest zoologists – rejects Darwinism as demonstrably false. He calls it a 'pseudoscience' (p. 6) depending on frequent miracles (p. 103), and says that Darwinists only look at those facts that fit their theory (p. 50). They look upon chance as 'a sort of providence', which they do not name but 'secretly worship' (p. 107). Well might he ask:

> When is Darwinian doctrine going to be subjected to a thorough, critical re-evaluation? (p. 128)

Aware that he must sound at times like a creationist, Grassé makes it clear that he is not (p. 166). He also insists that he does not believe in vitalism, the idea that there is a mystical property of life which accounts for everything in nature (p. 216).

Having demolished Darwinism, what, then, does Grassé put in its place as an explanation of evolution? This is where Grassé becomes vague and unconvincing. He argues that living matter must contain some 'internal factors' that compel life to evolve along predetermined lines. These 'factors' are not mystical or magical, they are physical and should be discoverable by science, he reasons, and biologists should make a great effort to discover them.

Many Christians will be encouraged by this distinguished biologist's conclusion that something more than Darwinism is needed to account for the living world. And most of them will find it easier to believe in the creative activity of God, than in Grassé's elusive 'internal factors'.

ENGLISH-SPEAKING BIOLOGISTS

Until recently, anti-Darwinists have been a rare species in English-speaking countries. One of them, Professor C. P. Martin, of McGill University in Montreal, explained why this was:

> As to our fewness, it must be remembered that unless we command independent means of publication it is very difficult for us to obtain a hearing today.[9]

He went on to say why he and others believed in evolution, but not in Darwinism. His researches had convinced him that mutations are practically always harmful, and never creative. On the rare occasions when a mutation appears to be beneficial, it is really only undoing the harm done by a previous mutation – just as punching a man with a dislocated shoulder might possibly put his joint back into place. He concludes:

> Mutation is a pathological process which has had little or nothing to do with evolution.

The leaders of evolutionary thought, he says, are 'almost entirely devoid of a critical attitude'. This is true: it hits you in the face as soon as you open a typical evolutionary textbook. As the unortho-dox Darwinist, Professor G. A. Kerkut of Southampton University, has said. 'It seems at times as if many of our writers on evolution have had their views by some sort of revelation.'[10]

One of the few English-speaking biologists to attack Darwinism in the nineteen-fifties was Dr W. R. Thompson. A Fellow of the Royal Society, and director of a major research establishment, he was an entomologist (insect specialist) of world renown. In an introduction to a new edition of Darwin's *Origin of Species* in 1956 he warned the readers to take Darwin with a grain of salt. He wrote:

> Darwin in the *Origin* was not able to produce palaeontological evidence sufficient to prove his views . . . the evidence he did

produce was adverse to them; and I may note that the position is not notably different today. The modern Darwinian palaeontologists are obliged, just like their predecessors and like Darwin, to water down the facts . . . Thus are engendered those fragile towers of hypotheses based on hypotheses, where fact and fiction mingle in an inextricable confusion.[11]

A British Botanist

By any standards, J. C. Willis was a great botanist. Among the many distinctions conferred on him were Fellowship of the Royal Society and an honorary doctorate of science from Harvard University. The scientific establishment on both sides of the Atlantic felt obliged to honour him, even though he was a rebel. For throughout his life he poured out a stream of books and papers attacking Darwinism.

Because of his high standing the Cambridge University Press published his book, *The Course of Evolution*[12] – probably the only major attack on Darwinism handled by these sedate publishers within living memory. But orthodox Darwinists often suffer from tunnel vision: few of them have looked at Willis' publications, and a large number have never even heard of him.

According to Gavaudan[13], the objections raised by Willis have never been answered. There are scores of these, of which there is space to give only a handful here.

Take first his point that natural selection cannot possibly affect plants as powerfully as it affects animals. One plant species generally differs from its cousins[14] in quite small details, such as the shape of the leaves, or the arrangement of the leaves on the stem, or the layout of the veins in the leaf. It seems most unlikely that such features can have the slightest effect on the plant's ability to survive; how, then, can natural selection have produced them?

Climate is regarded by Darwinists as a major factor in natural selection. In a certain place the climate gradually gets wetter, with the consequence that new species of plants and animals evolve that can stand wetter conditions. But what happens when, halfway through this period, an altogether exceptional spell of weather causes a prolonged drought? The half-evolved water-loving animals might be able to survive by migrating temporarily to the nearest lake. But not the half-evolved moisture-adapted plants – they are rooted to the spot and will die there.

Thus Willis shows by example after example that 'the survival of the fittest' rarely applies in the plant world. With plants the more usual rule is 'survival of the luckiest'.

Again, Willis refers to an objection raised by Fleeming Jenkin,[15] that the effect of favourable mutations would soon be lost, through crossing with the parent species. Darwin described this as the biggest difficulty anyone had ever raised, and Darwinists have worked like Hercules to produce some ingenious answers to it. But, says Willis, those answers really don't work for the vegetable kingdom, where crossing cannot be avoided.

He also discusses many features of plants where no intermediate steps between two arrangements are possible. To give just one simple example, leaves are arranged on plant stems in two main ways. They may alternate as you go along the stem: left, right, left, right, and so on. Or they may be opposite each other in pairs. You cannot have a 'half opposite, half alternate' arrangement.

How, then, did one arrangement evolve into the other, when there cannot be any intermediate steps? And what possible survival value can one arrangement have over the other, anyway?

Again, Willis asks, why is it that so many arrangements in plants and their flowers are mathematically perfect? In the case of opposite leaves, for instance, they are always *exactly* opposite. Why is this? If natural selection were responsible for the arrangement, would it not have been content with 'more or less opposite', which would surely have served the purpose of survival just as well as 'precisely opposite'?

Giant Leap Forward

Willis cites the cases of climbing plants and parasitic plants. Because these are more specialized it is generally agreed that they must have evolved from their more ordinary relatives. But how?

Climbers differ in two ways from their upright relatives: they have weak, flexible stems, and they have tendrils, or some other climbing device. Which evolved first? If the weak stems came first, how did the floppy-stemmed plants escape being smothered by other vegetation while their tendrils were evolving? And if the climbing organs evolved first, what made such organs evolve when they were not yet needed?

Instead of roots, parasitic plants have suckers that can penetrate the outer skin of other plants, or even the bark of trees. How could a plant with roots evolve by gradual stages into a parasite? Willis claims that the only way a parasite or a climbing plant could have evolved is in a single, huge leap. The Darwinian idea of evolution by many little steps has never been properly thought through, he says. It simply does not fit the facts, so far as the plant world is concerned.

So he proceeds to list the evidence that evolution really has occurred in huge leaps. Most of this evidence is of too technical a nature to reproduce here. Much of it is mathematical evidence, being based on the statistics of plant distribution,[16] on which he was a world authority. It all adds up to an extremely strong case, which has never been refuted, and which has been accepted by quite a number of botanists.

If his case really is unanswerable, why has it not been accepted more widely? Largely because of his breathtaking conclusion. The mutations that we see occurring today are all very small, producing creatures that differ only slightly from their parents. But the mass of evidence found by Willis pointed to occasional gigantic mutations, or 'differentiations' as he called them.

These must have created, in one generation, not just new species, but also new genera (groups of species), and even new families (groups of genera). Thus the seed of a grass might bring forth a sugar cane or a bamboo; or translating Willis' ideas to the animal kingdom, a chimpanzee might have a litter of human beings – or vice versa.

He offered no suggestion as to how such huge, creative steps could occur. While he expressly ruled out the idea of any divine activity, all he could offer in place of it was this:

> It is an inspiring thought that so great and complex a process as evolution has not been a mere matter of chance, but has behind it what one may look upon as *a great thought or principle* that has resulted in its moving as an ordered whole, and working itself out upon a definite plan . . . there is a general law, probably electrical, at the back of it.[17] (My italics.)

It is intriguing to read the great botanist's conclusion that there must be 'a great thought or principle . . . at the back of it'. But what did Willis really discover? Evidence for a splendid new theory of evolution? Or evidence that there must surely have been a Creator at work?

Another English Botanist

In 1961 the Botanical Society of Edinburgh sponsored a survey of botanical knowledge, complete in one volume.[18] The whole field was divided into eight sections, and eight eminent botanists were asked to write papers on the areas where they were expert.

The paper entitled 'Evolution' was written by Professor E. J. H. Corner, FRS, of Cambridge. It is a remarkable paper in many ways, not least because Corner speaks much more favourably of Willis than of Darwin! This distinguished anti-Darwinian has sometimes been portrayed as a creationist, because he said:

> I still think that, to the unprejudiced, the fossil record of plants is in favour of special creation. (p. 97)

This, however, is unfair, because the rest of the page gives a rather different picture of Corner's views. What he is really saying is that some of the available evidence seems to support evolution, whilst some – the evidence from fossils – appears to support special creation. And later in the paper Corner makes it clear that he does indeed believe in evolution.

But not in Darwinian evolution. He rejects Darwinism as a 'temple' where believers 'worship'. And most of them, he charges, 'would break down before an inquisition'. He summarizes his views on Darwinist writings in one terse sentence: 'Textbooks hoodwink.' (p. 97)

In his 'Conclusions' he states:

> This evolution can be likened to a piece of clockwork which, once wound up, proceeds in a set manner . . . It will take much research, I fancy, to discover how this clock was wound up. (p. 113)

So we can safely add Corner's name to the growing list of distinguished biologists who think Darwin was completely wrong. Like most of the others who feature in this chapter, his view is that evolution followed some pre-ordained path, and that it must have worked by some totally unknown means.

That is not the same as asserting that the evidence points to the existence of a Creative Power. But it does seem to be only one step short of it.

CHAPTER 3

Other Evolutionists with Serious Doubts

Man's most valuable trait is a judicious sense of what not to believe. Euripides[1]

There are other professionals besides biologists who are in a position to express doubts about Darwinism. Mathematicians, physical scientists, philosophers of science and others have studied the subject in depth, too.

In some ways they are better qualified to pass judgement on Darwinism than biologists. They can look at the subject from a fresh viewpoint, and they do not always have the same inbuilt prejudices as most biologists. So they have a better chance to see whether the whole broad scheme of evolution makes scientific sense.

MATHEMATICIANS

The French atheist Jacques Monod described Darwinism in the phrase, 'Chance and necessity'. Mutations are due to chance; natural selection is a process governed by the laws of nature, and so is a matter of necessity.

Another unbeliever, Stephen Jay Gould, has spelt it out in more detail:

The raw material for evolutionary change – and the raw material only – arises by a process of random mutation. Natural selection then enters for the second part, and it acts as a conventional, deterministic, predictable directing force.[2]

In other words, Darwinism implies that every new development in nature – both good and bad – is produced purely by chance. Natural selection then sorts them out. The majority of new variations are useless, and natural selection destroys these. The occasional useful ones are preserved, and in time many small steps add up to a major advance.

Thus the only *creative* force in nature, according to Darwinism, is chance. All that natural selection does is to pick the winners

33

from the many candidates that chance has thrown up. Chance creates; then selection selects.

Ever since Darwin's day this has presented a big problem. Is it reasonable to attribute such fantastic creative powers to chance? Could chance mutations really have created all the complex forms of life that exist?

Intuitively, a great many people – both scientists and laymen – have felt, 'No, it's altogether too unlikely.' But this sort of gut feeling is not good enough for science. Fortunately, there is a branch of mathematics known as the theory of probability which enables us to calculate the odds against certain unlikely events happening. In recent years it has been applied to Darwinism – with devastating results.

The Origin of Life

There is one big snag about probability theory. Mathematicians can only apply their calculations to fairly simple situations. But real life is astonishingly complex. So before a mathematician can start crunching numbers he usually has to make some simplifying assumptions about the problem.

Computer programmers have a favourite saying, 'Garbage in, garbage out!' In other words, if the mathematician starts with silly assumptions he will end with a silly answer. Consequently, if you do not like the conclusions of a particular piece of probability analysis, you can always evade them by challenging the basic assumptions. This is why there is at present quite a hot debate between staunch Darwinists and many mathematicians, who have calculated that Darwinism is so unlikely as to be impossible.

The arguments begin with the question of how life started. Darwin dismissed this quickly, by assuming that either God or natural forces produced a primitive organism or two in some warm little pond when the earth was young. To him, the only problem worth discussing in detail was how all other species evolved from the first creature.

Nowadays, however, evolutionists are very much concerned with how that first living creature came into existence. A whole new area of science, called 'chemical evolution', or 'pre-biotic evolution', or 'abiogenesis', is concerned with this question. The trouble is that we now know that the simplest living creatures are vastly more complex than Darwin realized, and their evolution from ordinary chemicals takes a great deal of explaining.

The simplest self-sufficient living things are single-celled creatures such as bacteria.[3] Each one is a complicated chemical factory in miniature. It contains many specialized chemicals known as nucleic acids and enzymes; these are such complex substances that a single molecule contains thousands of atoms, all joined together in a precise order.

Various scientists have tried to calculate the probability of such substances coming into existence by the chance interactions of chemicals.[4] The most eminent of these is perhaps the astronomer and mathematician, Sir Fred Hoyle, who is an evolutionist (though not a Darwinist) and an agnostic.

He began by assuming that the very first living thing contained much smaller and simpler enzymes then any present-day bacteria. But the likelihood of even one of these very simple enzymes arising at the right time in the right place, he calculated, was only 1 chance in 10^{20}. (This is mathematical shorthand for a 1 with twenty zeros behind it: thus, to a mathematician, $10^2 = 100$, $10^3 = 1,000$, and so on, including $10^{20} = 100,000,000,000,000,000,000$.)

Clearly, this is a very slim chance indeed. But wait. There are thousands of different enzymes, and they all work in different ways. To put together the simplest conceivable living creature you would need enzymes that can absorb energy and use it, enzymes that can produce a cell wall to hold the whole thing together, and many others. Altogether, Hoyle reasoned, about 2,000 different enzymes are needed – and each one tailor-made to do a particular chemical job.

And what are the chances that all these different enzymes 'just happened' to appear, through natural movements of molecules? Hoyle[5] made it 1 chance in $10^{40,000}$ – a number so enormous that it would fill a whole chapter just to write it out in the usual way!

Everybody agrees that such a small probability amounts to total impossibility. But evolutionists regard that as a most unhappy conclusion, and so they either dispute Hoyle's finding or dismiss him airily as a highly unorthodox scientist. The calculation itself is hard to fault. One bitter critic of Hoyle grudgingly admits that the figure of 1 in $10^{40,000}$ is 'probably not overly exaggerated'.[6]

His answer to Hoyle is that this is not how Darwinians think life originated. 'The enzyme system of the cell is thought to have evolved from simpler systems', he asserts. But how? He does not say.

Another of Hoyle's critics attempted to describe such a 'simpler system'. H. N. V. Temperley, an emeritus professor of mathematics, claimed in 1982 that one enzyme (or at the most, a pair of enzymes) could have formed the first living thing.[7] The chance of two simple enzymes occurring together is only 1 in 10^{40}, which is just – though only just – within the bounds of possibility. (Mathematicians generally regard anything with a probability of less then 1 in 10^{50} as totally impossible.)

However, the idea that a mere pair of simple enzymes could have formed a living being is, according to Hoyle and many others, quite ridiculous. Those two molecules would have had to possess the power to absorb energy and 'do things' with it, and the power to reproduce themselves. Above all, if they were to evolve, they would have to possess the 'skill' to select the right chemicals from their environment and assemble these into other 'living molecules' more complex and even more wonderful than themselves.

Everything that chemists know about molecules goes against such ideas. To attribute such fantastic powers to molecules flies in the teeth of all existing scientific knowledge. It is almost like believing in magic.

Hoyle claims to have many supporters in the scientific community. He writes:

> Quite a number of my astronomical friends are considerable mathematicians, and once they become interested enough to calculate for themselves, instead of relying upon hearsay argument, they can quickly see the point.[8]

So, agnostic though he is, Sir Fred Hoyle is driven to the conclusion that 'there is an enormous intelligence abroad in the universe.'[9] This notion, he says, is 'palatable to most ordinary folk but exceedingly unpalatable to scientists'. Why? 'Because of course scientists delight in seeing themselves as the only Johannes Factotums in the whole Universe.'

Another leading mathematician and astronomer, Professor Chandra Wickramasinghe, shares Hoyle's views and has stated the mathematical facts as he sees them:

> The chances that life just occurred on earth are about as unlikely as a typhoon blowing through a junkyard and constructing a Boeing 747.[10]

Probability and the Origin of Species

Hoyle went on to make a detailed examination of the evidence in favour of Darwinism. He and his colleague Wickramasinghe published their findings in 1981, in a book[11] with the forthright contention:

The general scientific world has been bamboozled into believing that evolution has been proved. Nothing could be further from the truth. (p. 87)

In a chapter entitled 'The evolutionary record leaks like a sieve', they compiled a formidable list of purely biological objections and claimed, 'These conclusions dispose of Darwinism.'

But their most weighty arguments are the mathematical ones. To keep the calculations manageable they concentrated on the development of various complex chemicals needed by living things. For instance, they considered the origin of haemoglobin, which is the basis of animal blood, and also occurs in peas and beans. Taking into account the known rates of mutation they showed that there simply has not been nearly enough evolutionary time for this to develop in peas and beans. Its existence there remains a mystery.

More fundamentally, they dealt with the origin of genes. Their calculations showed that useful mutations just don't occur often enough to account for all the hundreds of thousands of fundamentally different genes there are.[12] To give point to their mathematics they cite the absurdity of thinking that chance mutations could ever produce 'genes which were to prove capable of writing the symphonies of Beethoven and the plays of Shakespeare'. Unbelievers though they are, there is only one possibility they can accept: that those genes were created by some superior intelligence from outside our planet.

Professor H. S. Lipson is a distinguished member of the Institute of Physics. He, too, has interested himself in the mathematical probability that Darwinian evolution has occurred. And he has been driven – most reluctantly, so he says – to the conclusion that it has not.

In a series of communications to *Physics Bulletin* in 1979 and 1980[13] he briefly stated his reasons for concluding that many organs in nature simply could not have evolved. He went on to say:

We must go further than this and admit that the only acceptable alternative is creation. I know that this is anathema to physicists, as indeed it is to me, but we must not reject a theory that we do not like if the experimental evidence supports it.

Yet Lipson is clearly not a creationist in the usual sense of the word. It was not the Bible that led him to speak of creation, for in another journal he wrote:

It seems to me that in our present state of knowledge, creation is the only answer – but not the crude creation envisaged in Genesis.[14]

Mathematicians and Darwinists in Debate

When I first came across the title of a book, *Mathematical Challenges to the Neo-Darwinian Interpretation of Evolution*[15], I assumed it was a piece of creationist propaganda. But I could hardly have been more wrong. It was the proceedings of a high-level international conference, where some of the world's greatest Darwinists and a number of mathematicians met to discuss whether Darwinism made mathematical sense.

The mathematicians present were not merely eminent in their own fields. They were invited because of their specialist knowledge of biology, many of them having done mathematical research related to one of the life sciences. Even so, the conference proceedings make rather sad reading. The two groups seemed unable to find much common ground: instead, they kept restating their opposing points of view.

A good illustration of this occurs on p. 29. Dr S. M. Ulam had just given a paper where he showed, mathematically, that it seemed virtually impossible for the eye to have evolved in a Darwinian fashion. Now he was facing a barrage of criticism from the evolutionists. One of these, Sir Peter Medawar, complained:

> I think the way you have treated this is a curious inversion of what would normally be a scientific process of reasoning. It is, indeed, a fact that the eye has evolved; and, as Waddington says, the fact that it has done so shows that this [Ulam's] formulation is, I think, a mistaken one.

This remark is pure *Alice Through the Looking Glass*. Ulam had produced mathematical evidence that the eye could not have evolved by random mutations and natural selection. Medawar retorted that it was *a fact* that the eye had evolved, and therefore Ulam simply must have got his sums wrong!

The extraordinary thing is that the evolutionist Medawar even accused Ulam of '*a curious inversion* of what would normally be a scientific process of reasoning'. Medawar's reaction was like that of a man who had been standing on his head for so long that he thought the rest of the world was the wrong way up.

Another prominent evolutionist, Dr Ernst Mayr, was equally irrational. He dismissed Ulam's mathematics by saying:

Somehow or other by adjusting these figures we will come out all right. We are comforted by knowing that evolution has occurred. (Page 30)

'Knowing', indeed!

Throughout the conference this sort of situation recurred. The Darwinists took as their starting point that their opinion was fact. 'Please don't confuse us with your evidence', was their entrenched attitude.

Perhaps the most impressive argument of all was that raised by Professor Murray Eden, of the Massachusetts Institute of Technology, on page 9. He pointed out that the human genes contain about a billion nucleotides. (A nucleotide is the smallest unit of information in our genes – like a letter in a chemical alphabet. Groups of nucleotides convey messages to the developing embryo: messages such as, 'This white rat shall have pink eyes', or 'This child shall be left-handed like its Dad.'[16]) He went on to show that, however you made the calculations, you ended up with the same conclusions: the length of time life has been on earth was not nearly long enough for all those nucleotides – all that information – to have been generated by chance mutations.

The question of creation was kept out of the discussion practically all the time, because the conference was to be conducted on an entirely scientific basis. Nevertheless, occasionally it was impossible to keep it completely under wrappings. At one point Professor Schützenberger, Professor of Mathematics at the University of Paris, was vigorously pressing his deep objections to the biologists' glib acceptance of Darwinism. The Chairman, Dr Waddington, challenged him by saying, 'Your argument is simply that life must have come about by special creation.' Dr Schützenberger replied, 'No!' The record of the discussion adds that a number of voices from the body of the hall cried out, 'No!'

Evidently the kind of objections that the mathematicians were raising were such as believers in divine creation might have voiced. Yet the mathematicians were at pains to deny the charge of creationism. They stoutly maintained that their thinking was purely scientific. Whatever bias they might have had was not a creationist bias.

PHILOSOPHERS

The trouble with modern science is that there is so much of it. To stay among the leaders of research a scientist is forced to specialize in an extremely narrow area. This frequently means that he becomes unable to see the forest for the trees.

Philosophers of science refuse to fall into this trap. They stand well back from the day-to-day affairs of science and take a broad view of the whole scientific field, or perhaps of a large section of it. Because of this breadth of vision, and because of their independent stance, their views on controversial topics are always worth hearing.

Arthur Koestler wrote several books attacking the scientific establishment, which he regarded as hidebound, arrogant and unreasonable. Although he believed in evolution, for many years he had grave doubts about Darwinism. As long ago as 1971 he could say:

> There is a considerable proportion, perhaps even a majority, of eminent biologists inside the scientific Establishment, who . . . feel that while the Darwinian theory of natural selection operating on random mutations answers *some* of the problems posed by evolution, it leaves the most important ones unanswered.[17] (His italics.)

More recently he drew attention to what he regarded as the four greatest fallacies in popular scientific thinking, which he dubbed 'the four pillars of unwisdom'. The first of these is the very foundation of Darwinism, and the second and third are closely connected with it. These are the first three of Koestler's four great pieces of 'unwisdom':

(1) That biological evolution is the result of *nothing but* random mutations preserved by natural selection.
(2) That mental evolution is the result of *nothing but* random tries preserved by reinforcements.
(3) That all organisms, including man, are *nothing but* passive automata, controlled by the environment. (His italics.)[18]

Another Sceptical Philosopher

Professor E. W. F. Tomlin has held various senior positions, including the Chair of Philosophy and Literature in the University of Nice. For many years he has made a special study of the philosophical implications of biology.

A few years ago he was asked to write a paper for publication in

The Encyclopedia of Ignorance.[19] This encyclopedia was intended to survey the frontiers of modern knowledge, by drawing attention to what is still unknown. But this was not enough for Tomlin. He entitled his paper, 'Fallacies of Evolutionary Thinking', and used it to expose the ignorance of Darwinists, who have an answer to the riddle of evolution – but the wrong one! As he says on his first page:

> The truth is that evolution *was an hypothesis which hardened into dogma before it had been thoroughly analysed*. Hence it mothered a number of fallacies. (His italics.)

Then he goes on to explain the two most important of these 'fallacies'. His first complaint need not detain us long, because other writers have also made it: mutation and natural selection are largely negative, destructive, influences, which do not possess anything like enough creative power to account for all the marvels of the living world.

It is his second complaint that makes his paper important. Darwin's theory, he says, caught on because it met a need. Many intellectuals in the mid-nineteenth century had already adopted the idea that 'existence lacked purpose'. Darwinism appealed to them because it provided a way to justify their belief. According to Darwin there was no purpose in anything; it all 'just happened' according to the whim of natural selection.

But this, argues Tomlin, is just wishful thinking. There *is* purpose in Nature, lots and lots of it, and you have to be wilfully blind not to see it. Take the human brain and nervous system, he says. 'To ascribe their development to the play of blind forces is to suspend rational judgement and to betray the cause of science.' A little later he goes further and says it is – literally – 'crazy' to do so.

In the Summary at the end he presents his main finding:

> A *positive evolutionary principle* at work, even at the sub-human level, is an inescapable conclusion. (My italics.)

His readers are left wondering what Tomlin means by 'a positive evolutionary principle', which has to account for the purpose that seems to underlie the existence of Nature's many wonders. Is he hinting at some mysterious creative power in Nature itself? Or is he a secret believer in some kind of Creator?

Either way, his views provide cold comfort for evolutionists.

A SCIENCE WRITER

Francis Hitching is best known for his television documentaries on unexplained natural phenomena. But he is also a science writer of the first rank, as readers of his books will be aware.

In 1982 he published one of the most penetrating books on the evolution controversy ever to appear.[20] It is written from the standpoint of a convinced evolutionist: 'Evolution is a fact', he asserts on page 12.

Yet he is an evolutionist with an altogether unusual flexibility of mind, and a willingness to look at all sides of the question. Although he thinks creationists are totally wrong in their conclusions, he presents their case with remarkable fairness and thoroughness before rejecting it.

Then he applies this same fairmindedness to a detailed examination of Darwinism. His conclusion? That Darwin's theory is almost as certainly wrong (though not quite!) as creationism is.

His first chapter concentrates on the fossil evidence for evolution. This is really much weaker than the public have been led to believe. He says:

> The curious thing is that there is a consistency about the fossil gaps: *the fossils go missing in all the important places.* (p. 19 – his italics.)

In other words, Darwin has been let down by the rocks. Darwin admitted that there was a shortage of fossil evidence in support of his ideas, but he was confident that the proof he needed would turn up as the earth's crust was further explored. But it hasn't. All the vital pieces of evidence obstinately refuse to appear.

For example, the oldest layer of rocks where fossils are found in abundance is the Cambrian, which is roughly half a billion years old. It appears that there were no land animals then, but the seas were teeming with life. Millions of fossils from that period have been found, including snails, octopuses, starfish, sea urchins, sea lilies, and hosts of others.

Yet in the layers beneath the Cambrian there are hardly any fossils at all. And those few that have been found beneath the Cambrian are fossils of small, primitive organisms such as algae.[21] The expected ancestors of the Cambrian sea-creatures evidently do not exist.

Evolutionists rule out the obvious solution, of a great burst of activity by the Creator at the start of the Cambrian period. But they have no alternative explanation. The astonishing lack of pre-Cambrian fossils is a major weakness in Darwinism.

Those Missing Links are Still Missing

Hitching stresses the almost total absence of 'major transitional' fossils – that is, fossils of creatures that were half-way through a really big evolutionary change. Their absence, he says, is all the more surprising in view of the abundance of fossil evidence for minor changes, such as the presumed evolution of *Eohippus* (a small, primitive horse-like creature) into the modern horse.

But where are the fossils showing how fishes evolved into amphibians? Or how reptiles evolved into mammals? Or reptiles into birds? Missing, all missing, says Hitching.

'Not so!' cry the Darwinists, indignantly. 'Look at *Archaeopteryx*. That is half way between a reptile and a bird.'

Hitching is ready for them. He presents a great deal of evidence that *Archaeopteryx* is not an intermediate at all. Although *Archaeopteryx* was formerly believed to have lived long before birds appeared, this is not so. A fossil was found in Colorado in 1977 of a true bird which could not have been descended from *Archaeopteryx*, because it lived at the same time. Moreover, it now appears that *Archaeopteryx* had such excellent wings that it should have been able to fly very well. It was a genuine bird, although rather an odd sort of bird. You might as well call the penguin an intermediate between a bird and a fish, he says, as to call *Archaeopteryx* a link between dinosaurs and birds.

Then Hitching discusses the Darwinian notion that reptiles evolved into mammals. Not only is there a total lack of intermediate fossils, but it is hard to see how it could possibly have happened. How, he asks, did mammals evolve their jaw and their ear? For all reptiles have a lower jaw made up of at least four separate bones on each side, and a single bone in each ear. But every known mammal, alive and extinct, is the opposite: it has a one-piece jawbone, and three bones in the ear. All these bones fossilize readily, yet there is not a single fossil species with two bones in the ear or with two or three bones in the jaw.

Nor has any Darwinist offered a plausible explanation *why* these changes should have occurred, or *how* they might have happened. If these intermediates ever existed, how did they survive with jaws and ears that were neither one thing nor the other, and which would certainly not have worked well even if they worked at all?

Hitching quotes a few orthodox Darwinian answers to these

questions, and shows how unconvincing they all are. For instance, in *The Origin of Vertebrates*[22] N. J. Berrill says:

> There is no direct proof or evidence that any of the suggested events or changes ever took place . . . In a sense this account is science fiction, but I have myself found it an interesting and enjoyable venture to speculate . . .

By way of contrast Hitching quotes the supremely confident words of David Attenborough in *Life on Earth*[23], the book of the famous TV series:

> Important changes also took place among the proto-fish . . . The creatures had acquired jaws. The bony scales in the skin which covered them grew larger and sharper and became teeth. No longer were the backboned creatures of the sea lowly sifters of mud and strainers of water. Now they could bite. Flaps of skin grew out of either side of the lower part of the body, helping to guide them through the water. These eventually became fins. Now they could swim.

This sort of language is typical of popular books on evolution. *But it is entertainment, not science.* It explains nothing. It is just about as meaningful and as realistic, says Hitching, as the patter of a conjurer crying, 'Abracadabra!' as he brings a rabbit out of a hat.

The Mysterious Whale

Another of Hitching's examples is the question of the whale's origin. As everybody knows, the whale is not a fish although it lives in the sea as if it were one. It is a warm-blooded, air-breathing mammal, specially adapted for life in, and mostly under, the water. Darwinists rarely mention the whale because it presents them with one of their most insoluble problems.

They believe that somehow a whale must have evolved from an ordinary land-dwelling animal, which took to the sea and lost its legs. That sounds simple enough until you stop to think of all the other changes that had to take place before a land animal had become a whale. Here are some of them.

1. The body of a land mammal ends in a pelvis, which supports a relatively flimsy tail. This always moves from side to side, and is used mainly as a fly swish. A whale has no pelvis; instead it has an entirely different bony structure that supports a large

flat tail, which moves up and down so that it can be used for propulsion under water.

2. So that it can keep cool in hot sunshine a land mammal has a skin full of sweat glands. The whale does not need these, but instead his skin is lined with a thick layer of blubber (fat) to keep him warm in cold water. Moreover his skin has a strangely fashioned outer surface which helps to streamline the flow of water.

3. An eye that is used for seeing under water has to be built quite differently from one that is used for seeing in air. That, of course, is why underwater swimmers have to wear goggles or face masks. Needless to say, the whale has an underwater eye.

4. Land animals communicate by air-borne noise, conveyed between their vocal systems and their ears. Whales, on the other hand, have an underwater system of communication that is entirely different, being closely similar to the sonar system of submarine detection used in the navy.

5. It would be difficult for a land mammal to feed under water without drowning itself, but whales are so constructed that they can do this easily. Many of them eat very small fish, which they catch in a kind of sieve of whalebone in their mouths, a device which is perfectly suited for its purpose.

6. A land mammal giving birth in the water would immediately drown its infant, and there is no way in which it could suckle its young at sea. But whales have no problems because they are built to an entirely different plan which enables them to bear and nurse their offspring in deep water.

A land mammal that was in process of becoming a whale would fall between two stools – it would not be fitted for life on land or at sea, and would have no hope of survival. And to make the difficulty even worse, the fossil evidence shows that all these incredible changes had to happen within a timespan of five to ten million years – just a fraction of one per cent of the time that life is supposed to have been on earth. It is not surprising that zoology textbooks carefully avoid discussing the evolution of the whale in any detail.

Once more, it must be remembered that these powerful objections to Darwinism do not come from a creationist. Hitching is an evolutionist, who has taken a close look at both creationism and Darwinism and cried, 'A plague o' both your houses!'

ANOTHER SCIENCE WRITER

Gordon Rattray Taylor, one-time Chief Science Adviser to BBC Television, was another science writer of high standing. The last of his many scientific books, *The Great Evolution Mystery*,[24] was published posthumously in 1983. Its opening sentence indicates the message of the book:

> Darwin's theory of evolution by natural selection, which has stood as the one great biological law comparable with the laws of physics for more than a century, is crumbling under attack.

He then proceeded to mount his own onslaught on Darwinism, which must be one of the most devastating ever to appear in print. Although Darwinists claim to have explained the great mystery of nature, Taylor demonstrates that nature is actually teeming with problems that Darwinists cannot solve. Here are just a handful of his hundreds of examples.

(1) *Under-development*

There are many organs, says Taylor, that seem to have defied Darwin by stopping short in their development. The best-known example is perhaps the sting of the bee, which is barbed so that it sticks in the body of the animal that is stung. Then, when the bee tries to fly away, the sting is torn out by the roots, leaving the bee so mutilated that it usually dies. Is it really a great aid to survival to have a weapon which is suicidal to use, like a nuclear arsenal? If the wasp could evolve a nice smooth sting which he could use time after time with careless abandon, why could not the bee?

Darwin himself wrestled with this problem. A century later his disciples seem to be no nearer a solution.

(2) *Over-development*

Then there is the opposite problem, which Taylor calls 'overshoot'. He invites us to consider a number of examples, including the extinct Irish elk. The most Irish thing about this animal is its name, since it was actually a Siberian deer of moderate size. Why on earth should even an *Irish* elk have evolved gigantic antlers, twelve feet across and weighing more than a quarter of a ton, which must have been about as helpful as a twenty-foot, hundred-pound riot stick would be to a normal-sized policeman?

Again, was it really natural selection that gave the peacock an enormous tail, which greatly slows it down when it is trying to escape predators? Darwinians argue that the beautiful tail assists the mating process. But most other birds manage to conduct their courtships quite happily without such a potentially fatal encumbrance, so where, asks Taylor, is the Darwinian advantage in such an overgrown organ?

(3) *Bone*

The earliest creatures, like amoebae and jellyfish, had no skeletons at all. Then came a host of others like beetles and snails, with their skeletons in the form of a horny skin or shell. Advanced forms of life did not become possible until Nature made a breakthrough by inventing bone.

And what an invention! Taylor shows that there is a great deal more to bone than meets the eye. It has an extraordinary lattice-like structure when seen under the microscope; this gives it the property of lightness combined with strength, as in the lattice girders of the Eiffel Tower. This structure is composed partly of mineral matter and partly of living tissues, working together in harmony. The whole is criss-crossed by blood vessels; there are internal factories where bone cells are constructed, and marrow cavities for the manufacture of blood cells. Where bones meet there are well-fitting joints, complete with a protective capsule of cartilage and an elaborate lubrication system. Taylor remarks:

> It is obvious that the creation of bone required not one but a whole burst of mutations, all integrated to a single end – *an incredible thing to happen by chance.* (p. 57, my italics.)

(4) *Feathers*

Evolutionists are baffled by bone because it had to be invented *before* there was any need for it, so that afterwards an entirely new kind of animal with a skeleton could arise. Similarly, the problem of the origin of feathers is that they had to be invented in advance so that, later on, birds could use them to fly.

Evolutionists make light of this difficulty. Feathers were originally in the form of down, and were invented to keep animals warm, they argue. These primitive feathers are supposed to have served an evolutionary purpose at the time; only later did the first birds turn these eiderdowns into wings. Taylor demolishes this argument by showing that wing feathers are entirely different from the downy variety, because they are provided with thousands of microscopic hook-like fasteners. These allow the wing to fold when not in use, and engage when the wing is stretched out ready for flight, thus turning the whole assembly into a continuous sheet to catch the wind. With withering sarcasm he tells us:

> The downy feathers which are designed to conserve heat (Designed? Perish the thought: let us say, 'which by pure chance serve to conserve heat') lack the hooks. (p. 67)

Darwinism has no explanation for complex structures (of which bone and feathers are just two of many examples) which had to arise before there were any creatures that could utilize them. Their existence indicates that there must be an overriding purpose behind them.

(5) *Eggs*

According to Taylor a bird's egg is just as big a miracle – and just as much of a problem to Darwinists – as its wings. The egg of a fish, which is supposed to have evolved first, is contained in nothing more elaborate than a blob of jelly. That is adequate for water-dwelling creatures, but a land animal needs something more: the nucleus of her egg must be packaged in its own private pool of liquid.

So the precious yolk where the new life develops is surrounded by the white, which sustains the developing infant. The yolk is attached to the shell with a shock-absorbing suspension of elastic threads, while the shell that contains it all is a masterpiece of engineering. It has to be of exactly the right strength: hard enough to stay in one piece when the bird sits upon it, but soft enough to let the chick peck its way out when the time comes. It has to be waterproof, and yet porous to air so that the chick can breathe.

Evolutionists have no idea how the bird's egg could have evolved. All they can tell us is that the reptile egg is similar to it and is supposed to have appeared first. This, of course, only throws the problem back one stage. They cannot even say *when* the evolution of the egg might have happened; Taylor laments that, 'as usual, the fossil record is blank just when we most need it.'

(6) *The Eye of the Trilobite*

The trilobite was a small marine creature which has long been extinct. There is nothing quite like it alive today; it was something like a cross between a shrimp and a woodlouse. And although some species of trilobite were blind, others had an extraordinary eye – so extraordinary that Taylor calls its first appearance 'the most incredible event in the history of evolution.'

The remarkable part of this eye was its lens. Unlike the lenses of our own eyes, which are flexible so that we can change their shape to focus on objects at various distances, the trilobite eye was rigid. The upper half of the lens was made of a mineral substance, calcite, with its crystals stacked in a special way. As a result, beams of light entering this lens from almost any distance were automatically in perfect focus. Taylor asks:

> By what conceivable chance could the trilobite have accumulated the one material in the universe – namely calcite – which had the required optical properties, and then imposed on it the one type of curved surface which would achieve the required result? . . . We are still reeling at the improbability of this. (p. 98)

For good measure, Taylor explains that the lower part of the lens is a substance of animal origin, chitin. This has optical properties which harmonize perfectly with those of the mineral calcite. Thus the combination lens is made free from what opticians call 'spherical aberration', a fault which affects all lenses made of a single material. And all this optical wizardry in the eye of a primitive water-bug!

Baffled Evolutionist

Throughout most of his book Taylor sounds almost like a creationist. Yet, he was, in fact, every inch an evolutionist. 'The fact that an evolutionary process occurred is not in doubt', he insists (p. 2). But not a Darwinian process, for 'evolution takes place in spite of natural selection rather than because of it' (p. 159).

Like other writers quoted in this book, he is driven to the conclusion that there are directive forces at work. 'The most prominent thing about evolution is that it is going somewhere', he observes (p. 163).

Taylor never even considers the possibility of divine control; to him, Nature herself is responsible for all her own wonders. 'Life as we know it created the conditions for its own existence, an occurrence more allied to purpose than to chance' (p. 206). Further development was the result of 'some inner necessity, some built-in, primordial necessity (p. 207).

The final conclusion of Taylor's book is remarkable for its humility. He admits he is baffled, and implies that, if other evolutionists were honest, they too would admit, 'We are in no position to say that we understand the mechanism of evolution.' (p. 245)

In his closing paragraph he goes even further, and speaks of 'the probability that some things will never be understood'. He concludes that 'there are forces at work in the universe of which we have as yet scarcely an inkling.'

What a pity that this profound thinker could not take the last, short, logical step to becoming a believer in divine creation.

ANTHROPOLOGY TODAY

Strictly speaking, anthropologists do not really belong in this chapter. As a class they seem to be completely loyal to Darwin. I have not been able to find a single instance of an eminent anthropologist attacking Darwinism.

This raises an interesting question. Why is it that, of all the disciplines concerned with evolution, anthropologists remain the only group solidly committed to Darwinism?

There seems little doubt about the answer. Anthropologists, it appears, have so few facts to go on that they deal mostly in opinions. With such a background they naturally have no cause to question the truth of Darwinism.

Anthropologists themselves sometimes admit how little they really know. Only a few years ago one of them wrote:

The origin and beginning of man remains a subject for myth.[25]

Now myths are all very well so long as people don't take them too seriously. Unfortunately, some anthropologists have a habit of taking their subject (and themselves, sometimes) much too seriously.

For example, in 1981 the anthropologist Richard Leakey put on a TV series, *The Making of Mankind*. In this he made so many dogmatic assertions that the TV critic Chris Dunkley soon took him to task:

Leakey has a proselytizing zeal which can slide over into arrogance . . . When, with only circumstantial genetic evidence and no 'proof' from his own fossil records, he asserts of chimpanzees 'There can be no doubt that we share a common ancestor' he is simply wrong. Not only can there be doubt, but some of it is manifested by men who command at least as much respect as Leakey. Nor is this a lone example; he resorts with disappointing readiness to such words as 'unquestionably'.[26]

Only five months later a paper by Cherfas and Gribbin[27] made a similar complaint about anthropologists in general: 'They still talk of *Ramapithecus*, 14 million years ago, as the first hominid [man-like creature], and they continue to believe that Man's split from the apes took place some 20 million years ago.' Yet, Cherfas and Gribbin protested, there was clear biochemical evidence from as long ago as 1967 that Man, chimpanzee and gorilla shared a common ancestor as recently as 5 million years ago. When, they wondered, were anthropologists going to wake up?

A few months later Leakey provided an answer. He told a distinguished audience at the Royal Institution that his TV series was 'probably wrong' in a number of crucial areas. With surprising candour he admitted:

> I am staggered to believe that as little as a year ago I made the statements that I made.[28]

This sequence is fairly typical of the march of progress in anthropology. First, a lot of dogmatic assertions; then, 'long and often acrimonious debate'[29]; then a sudden, violent change of opinion; and then the whole cycle repeats itself.

Evidence in Short Supply

The reason for this curious way of going on is not surprising. It is simply the consequence of the great shortage of evidence. As recently as 1982 it was reported in a scientific journal:

> The main problem in reconstructing the origins of man is lack of fossil evidence: *all there is could be displayed on a dinner-table.*[30] (My italics.)

The previous year the anthropologist John Reader made a similar point:

> Judged by the amount of evidence upon which it is based, the study of fossil man (palaeoanthropology) hardly deserves to be more than a sub-discipline of palaeontology or anthropology. The entire hominid collection known today would barely cover a billiard table.[31]

A senior research fellow at the Zoological Society of London has written of the consequence of this lack of evidence:

> In recent years several authors have written popular books on human origins which were based more on fantasy and subjectivity than on fact and objectivity. At the moment science cannot offer a full answer on the origin of humanity.[32]

John Reader has frankly admitted this:

Ever since Darwin's work inspired the notion that fossils linking modern man and extinct ancestor would provide the most convincing proof of human evolution, *preconceptions have led evidence by the nose* in the study of fossil man.[33] (My italics.)

The shortage of evidence is particularly serious because of the nature of anthropology. In other areas of science experiments can be repeated; this means that when a pioneer scientist makes a mistake, other workers can soon discover it. But when an archaeological site has once been 'dug', much of the scientific evidence is lost for ever. Later workers are entirely dependent on the anthropologist who makes a find for his description of the site conditions. If he is careless, or prejudiced, or just unlucky, he may make a vital mistake that will never be exposed unless similar bones are found elsewhere.

The shortage of evidence applies to other areas of anthropology, too. Much has been made of cave paintings, and yet, as another anthropologist has admitted:

One of the major problems – then as now – was the inability to date directly images painted on a cave wall.[34]

Even when the evidence is extensive, the conclusions based upon it can be highly questionable. Practically all the 'missing links' in Man's supposed ancestry have been reconstructed from a few small fragments of bone. The one outstanding exception is *Australopithecus afarensis*, which is based upon a practically complete female skeleton found in Ethiopia in 1974. It is known to the learned as AL 288-1, and to the rest of us as Lucy.

Much was made of Lucy by her finder, Don Johanson, and others. He assigned her a date of around three million years ago, and claimed that she represented the earliest known ancestors of the human race. Books and magazines began to publish imaginative drawings of Lucy and her family, looking almost as human as the nudists on Brighton beach.

Then in 1983 two American anthropologists, Stern and Susman, rather spoiled the artists' fun.[35] They published the results of a re-examination of Lucy's skeleton, which had led them to very different conclusions. Many of her bones were more like chimpanzee bones than those of a human. She probably did not walk upright like a woman, but in a slouched position like an ape. And she probably spent much of her time climbing trees, since her skeleton was better suited to that than to walking.

So what really was Lucy? A forerunner of the human race, or

just an extinct species of ape? The short answer is that there is no way of knowing.

This, it seems, is also true of most of the questions relating to the ancestry of man. Opinions abound, and are expressed with the utmost confidence. But they change from year to year, and from anthropologist to anthropologist.

And all because facts are in such short supply in this field of science.

CHAPTER 4

The Design Argument Stages a Comeback

Every formula which expresses a law of nature is a hymn of praise to God.
Maria Mitchell[1]

In the middle of the nineteenth century every little choirboy must have heard of Paley's watch. In those days it was the No. 1 reason for believing in God. All educated people were expected to know about it: at least one university offered a whole paper on Paley in its entrance examination.

In his *Natural Theology*, Paley argued like this. Look at a watch. Every part in it fulfils a purpose. None is any use on its own, but the whole assembly forms a useful machine. It would be ridiculous to assume that any watch ever came into being by accident. Somebody must have *designed* it, to do its job. The existence of a watch indicates the existence of a watchmaker. And similarly, the harmony we see in the wonders of Nature implies the existence of a Great Designer – God.

Then along came a number of atheistic philosophers, building on Darwin's foundation. Design in Nature, yes, they said. But there is no need to assume a divine Creator. Natural selection explains the make-up of every living thing. Natural selection is the unseen Watchmaker, not God.

But now the wheel is turning full circle. Sir Fred Hoyle and his colleague, Professor Wickramasinghe, although they are both outspoken agnostics, have recently admitted:

It is ironic that the scientific facts throw Darwin out, but leave William Paley, a figure of fun to the scientific world for more than a century, still in the tournament with a chance of being the ultimate winner.[2]

TAKING STOCK

It will be useful at this point to sum up the findings of the previous three chapters – in other words, to list the scientific facts that, according to Hoyle and Wickramasinghe, have 'thrown Darwin out'. There are three main objections.

First, there is the evidence that the history of life on earth has not been one of slow, continuous progress. There have been long periods of standing still, interspersed with sudden advances. Instead of moving steadily like a determined snail, life has progressed like a half-hearted grasshopper, taking long rests between leaps.

This evidence comes mainly from the fossil record, but according to some leading botanists it is strongly supported by evidence from living plants. It is so convincing that a whole new school of thought – 'punctuated equilibria' – has arisen, which hopes to modify Darwinian theory to take account of these huge leaps.

The leaders of another school of thought among biologists – 'cladistics' – are sufficiently disturbed by the fossil evidence to put Darwinism on one side with the label 'not proven'. It might turn out to be right, partly right, or wrong; the evidence is so incomplete that it is impossible to tell. So the thing to do for the present, they argue, is to leave Darwinism out of account. They have started reclassifying living things on the basis of what they *are*, not what they are supposed to have evolved from.

The second big problem for Darwinists is that mutations do not appear to bring progressive changes. Genes seem to be built so as to allow changes to occur *within certain narrow limits*, and to prevent those limits from being crossed. To oversimplify a little: mutations very easily produce new varieties within a species, and might occasionally produce a new (though similar) species, but – despite enormous efforts by experimenters and breeders – mutations seem unable to produce entirely new forms of life.

The third big objection to Darwinism is its sheer improbability. All that natural selection does is to destroy the unfit; the 'fit' have to be produced by mutation, which is known to be the result of pure chance. And the idea that chance could create all the manifold wonders of nature is preposterous – so preposterous that a great many mathematicians, as well as quite a few biologists, have rejected Darwinism on statistical grounds. A theory that requires an endless succession of mathematical miracles cannot be right, they say.

The situation today has been aptly summarized by the cell biologist, Professor Jack Ambrose of London University:

> A creative view of the origin of life and species no longer needs to be defended against evolutionary arguments. It is the reductionist evolutionist who is now in retreat.[3]

THE EVOLUTIONARY ALTERNATIVES

I have kept my promise not to use creationist arguments to oppose Darwinism. All the anti-Darwinists whose views appeared in the previous chapters can be termed evolutionists. They accept that the fossils provide evidence of succession, and they think that the best explanation of succession is that life must have evolved – somehow. But how?

They are mostly vague about the alternative to Darwinism. Yet, despite this vagueness, there is a remarkable similarity about their views. To re-quote just a few of the numerous statements of the same kind from the two previous chapters:

Gavaudan speaks of evolution occurring according to '*a general plan* in nature'.[4]

Grassé says that '*immanent finalization* is an intrinsic property of all living creatures',[5] which causes them to evolve along predetermined lines.

Tomlin insists that '*a positive evolutionary principle* at work . . . is an inescapable conclusion.'[6]

Willis claims that there must be in Nature 'what one may look upon as *a great thought or principle* that has resulted in its moving as an ordered whole . . . *a general law*, probably electrical.'[7]

Corner's idea is that 'evolution can be likened to *a piece of clockwork* which, once wound up, proceeds in a set manner.'[8]

All of which amounts to the same thing. Evolution is such an extraordinary thing to have happened that we simply cannot account for it along the lines of existing scientific knowledge. There must be a mysterious, undiscovered *something* in nature that, against all the odds, has forced evolution to occur.

They all leave it an open question as to what that 'something' might be. None of them suggests it might be the Christian God. But nothing that they or anyone else have said rules out that possibility, either.

Non-Biblical Creationists

Some of the other anti-Darwinists are more outspoken. Although they do not accept the authority of the Bible, and hence are not creationists by any normal definition of the term, they are not afraid to use the term 'creation'.

Professor Lipson, for instance, is convinced that 'creation is the only answer.'[9]

Hoyle and Wickramasinghe also say their view 'is anti-Darwinian and is in a sense a return to the old concept of special creation'.[10] But their idea of 'special creation' is a far cry from the Bible's. They express their idea of gods (for they believe in many) in a row of mathematical symbols, and finally equate the ultimate Supreme Being with the universe itself.

Somewhere in remote space, they suggest, one of these deities has long been busy, creating genes and lowly forms of life, such as bacteria. He makes these by the billion and broadcasts them into space. Eventually some of them drift down to Planet Earth. The bacteria cause new diseases, but the space-borne genes somehow become incorporated in existing creatures, and thus new species appear.

Another agnostic, Francis Crick, the Nobel prize-winning biologist, has an even more startling theory.[11] He recognizes that the chance of life starting on earth by natural processes is exceedingly remote. But given the whole universe to play with, he reasons, there is a much better chance that life would have started spontaneously somewhere.

Perhaps life began on some far-off planet and evolved into a highly advanced civilization, says Crick. If the inhabitants of that world wanted to bestow life on some other solar system – ours, for instance – what would they do? Obviously, they would load a spaceship with deep-frozen seeds of life, and shoot it in our direction! And that, suggests Crick (in a book which is supposed to be serious science, not science fiction) is probably how life on earth began.

The New Biology

According to Hitching,[12] many anti-Darwinists are now beginning to talk about 'the new biology', as something that is about to supersede Darwinism. They don't yet know where they are going, but they are sure the journey will be fun. As one of them said to him:

The language of the new biology, when it is properly formulated, will be rigorous, scientifically and mathematically, but it will have a totally different flavour from contemporary biology.

Hitching describes a recent conference in America where new views about evolution were discussed. He quotes several speakers there, and the two following quotations of his give some slight idea of what the 'new biology' is about:

Evolution could be viewed as the expression of an inherent playfulness of an always intelligent universe. (Elise Boulding.)
Life appears no longer as a phenomenon unfolding *in* the universe – the universe itself becomes increasingly alive. (Erich Jantsch.)

If this is the best that New Biologists can offer as a replacement for Darwinism, it is not hard to see why the Darwinist old guard stands firm. What sort of science is it that solves impossible problems by resorting to 'an intelligent universe' – a universe that 'becomes increasingly alive'?

This does not look much like a new biology. It has all the marks of the old theology, but newly dressed in scientific language. Like the theory of Hoyle and Wickramasinghe, it looks like a version of Creationism for Unbelievers.

PALEY REHABILITATED

Thus it seems that Paley's design argument really is a force to be reckoned with once again. Darwin's theory is now regarded by many biologists as unsatisfactory. It simply does not explain the marvels of the living world. And *there is no better scientific explanation in sight*. As one deeply disturbed Darwinist has recently admitted:

The neo-Darwinian process, *for all its flaws and abuses*, remains the only viable framework within which to view life.[13] (My italics.)

Darwinism begins to look more and more like a huge maze without an exit, where the world has wandered aimlessly for a century and a quarter. Although biology has made enormous progress in that time, the central problem is as real today as it was in 1850. All the complex organs of living things were evidently designed to fulfil a purpose. If a Creator didn't design them, what did?

But it is not only in biology that the design argument carries weight today. Within recent years exciting discoveries have been made in cosmology (the study of the universe and its origin). These provide powerful supporting evidence for the existence of a Creator, who appears to have designed the universe itself with almost unbelievable precision.

The cosmologist Paul Davies, who holds the chair of theoretical physics at Newcastle-upon-Tyne, admits that he is not a religious man. Yet he has written in a recent newspaper article:

> Something strange is happening to the universe. In the words of the astronomer Fred Hoyle, it is as though somebody has been monkeying with the laws of nature . . .
>
> A once-popular argument with theologians was to point out how astonishingly well ordered the universe is, how harmoniously its components dovetail together. All this, it was reasoned, must be the result of design, and therefore evidence of a Great Designer. Yesterday's theologians would have been delighted with today's discovery of just how delicately balanced that cosmic order turns out to be.[14]

The Speed of the Big Bang

It has been known for more than half a century that our universe is expanding. This fact soon led many astronomers to believe that the universe had a spectacular beginning at some point in time – probably at least 10 billion years ago.

At that moment of creation, they suggested, all the matter and energy in the universe would have been concentrated in one spot. Then a sort of king-sized atomic explosion occurred, and everything blew apart with enormous violence and at fantastically high temperatures. As the expansion continued things gradually cooled down, until eventually galaxies of stars were able to form.

Recent mathematical studies have shown that this is almost certainly what must have happened. These calculations are based on data obtained in atomic energy laboratories as well as astronomical data. They have led to the surprising conclusion that this 'Big Bang', as cosmologists call it, must have been a real touch-and-go affair.

For if some sort of 'big bang' is to produce a habitable universe, then the explosive power has to be exactly matched to the power of gravity. If the bang that formed our universe had not been quite big enough, the expanding matter would soon have collapsed back on itself. In that case the universe would have ceased to exist, long before any planets suitable for supporting life could have formed.

On the other hand, too big a bang would have caused the universe to expand so much that it would have contained nothing but gas: stars and planets could never have formed then, either.

And there is practically no margin of safety. As the radio-astronomer, Sir Bernard Lovell, has explained:

> If at that moment the rate of expansion had been reduced by *only one part in a thousand billion*, then the Universe would have collapsed after a few million years . . . Conversely, if the rate had been marginally greater, then the expansion would have reached such magnitudes that no gravitationally bound system (that is galaxies and stars) could have formed.[15] (My italics.)

Commenting on this and other strange features of the universe, Professor Paul Davies remarks in a recent book:

> It is hard to resist the impression of *something* – some influence capable of transcending spacetime and the confinements of relativistic causality – *possessing an overview of the entire cosmos* at the instant of its creation, and manipulating all the causally disconnected parts to go bang with almost exactly the same vigour at the same time, and yet not so exactly coordinated as to preclude the small scale, slight irregularities that eventually formed the galaxies, and us.[16] (My italics.)

To use Davies' own phrase, 'it is hard to resist the impression' that here is an unbeliever going to great lengths to avoid using the word 'God' – even though he is aware that the scientific facts point that way.

The Four Basic Forces

There appear to be just four basic forces holding everything in the universe together, from the smallest atomic particles to the greatest galaxies. Physicists call them the gravitational force,[17] the electro-magnetic force, the strong nuclear force and the weak nuclear force. Each of these has a characteristic strength that physicists have measured.

If we ask, why do those forces have those particular strengths, there seems to be no answer. One might as well ask why a certain pebble picked from the beach happens to weigh 594 grams, or why the shell beside it is 35 millimetres long. It seems that they just happen to have those values – Nature, so to speak, arbitrarily decided to make them like that.

But now suppose that, instead of picking up a pebble, we pick up a large, hollow sphere of stainless steel. We put it on a balance and find that it weighs 99,984 grams.[18] This, again, looks at first as if it has no significance – as if somebody just happened to make it that weight, for no special reason.

Then we measure its volume, and find that, at a temperature of 0°C, it occupies exactly 100 cubic decimetres. This immediately gives significance to that value of 99,984 grams, because the sphere has precisely the same density as distilled water at its freezing point. One gram heavier and it would sink in it; one gram lighter and it would float. Evidently somebody must have taken great pains, making that sphere with a precision of one part in 100,000, so that it has neutral buoyancy in freezing distilled water.[19]

Now it has been discovered recently that the universe itself is rather like that sphere – only more so. Something (or Somebody) has evidently tailored the values of those four fundamental forces of nature, so as to give the universe precisely the properties it needs if life is to exist in it.

To give just one example of the way these forces are matched, take the relationship between gravity and the weak nuclear force. It is the perfect balance between these two that has caused the universe to keep expanding at a comfortable, steady rate. To achieve this, according to Paul Davies, the two forces have to be tuned to each other with the astonishing accuracy of one part in ten thousand billion billion billion billion![20]

If they became mismatched by this minute amount in one direction, then, says Davies, 'the expansion of the universe would be explosive, and it is doubtful if galaxies could ever have formed against such a disruptive force.' With the same amount of mismatch in the other direction, 'the explosion would be replaced by a catastrophic collapse of the universe.' He concludes:

It is truly extraordinary that such dramatic effects would result from changes in the strength of either gravity, or the weak nuclear force, of less than one part in 10^{40} [a one with forty noughts behind it].

More recently, he has said that in the very earliest moments of the 'Big Bang' the accuracy of tuning would have to be one part in 10^{60}. This, he explains, is the accuracy a marksman would need if he wanted to hit a one-inch target at the other end of the universe – twenty billion light years away.[21]

What makes it even more extraordinary is that this fantastically well-controlled expansion of the universe is absolutely uniform, in all directions.[22] All this, says Davies, provides 'compelling evidence that something is "going on" '.[23]

Creation of the Elements

It appears that only the two lightest of the hundred-or-so chemical elements, hydrogen (including its isotope, deuterium, or 'heavy hydrogen') and helium, were formed in the white heat of the Big Bang. Of these elements, the important one is hydrogen. This provides the atomic fuel for our sun and all the other stars. It also is necessary for the formation of water, which is the basis of all life.

Yet it is only by another of those extraordinary cosmic coincidences that any worthwhile amount of hydrogen was formed. The easy thing to form in a big bang is helium, and it is most surprising that all the atomic nuclei did not turn into helium, leaving nothing to produce hydrogen. Why did they not? Because, once again, the values of Nature's basic constants were exactly right. As Sir Bernard Lovell has put it:

> If the proton+proton reaction had been only a few per cent stronger, then all the protons would have formed into helium in the first few million years of the Universe, and once more, a universe would have evolved which could never be comprehended by any form of intelligent life.
>
> It seems that the chances of the existence of man on Earth today, or of intelligent life anywhere in the Universe, *are* vanishingly small. Is the Universe as it is, because it was necessary for the existence of man?[24] (His italics.)

Lovell's book leaves that question unanswered. Like Davies, he leads his readers right to the point of seeing that the universe has been exquisitely designed for its purpose – and then stops short of suggesting that there must be a Great Designer.

If only hydrogen and helium were formed in the Big Bang, where did all the other elements come from? They were formed, it seems, by slow cooking in the interiors of stars, and afterwards were scattered through the universe when some of those stars exploded, as some types of stars are wont to do from time to time.[25]

This discovery helps to answer the question that has puzzled many Christians: if God is mainly interested in our little planet, then why did He create this whole vast universe? Apparently it is all there for a purpose. Many of the elements in our own bodies were probably created in some long-vanished star, in a remote corner of the galaxy, thousands of light years away.

What concerns us now, however, is that the formation of the heavier elements is yet another of those almost miraculous happenings. Carbon and oxygen, for example, are two elements that all living things require in abundance. Yet they are formed abundantly inside stars only because their nuclei both happen to be exactly 'in tune' with the energy supply of the star.

Hoyle and Wickramasinghe[26] have estimated that the chances against this 'tuning' being a lucky accident are about a thousand to one. In another publication Hoyle comments on this 'coincidence':

> A commonsense interpretation of the facts suggests that a superintellect has monkeyed with physics, as well as chemistry and biology, and that there are no blind forces worth speaking about in nature.[27]

But it is not enough for these essential elements to be formed inside stars. It is equally essential that in due course the star should explode, in such a way as to disperse those elements without destroying them. And that, too, is something that only happens because the weak nuclear force has just the right value. As Davies has put it:

> If the weak interaction were much weaker, the neutrinos would not be able to exert enough pressure on the outer envelope of the star to cause the supernova explosion. On the other hand, if it were much stronger, the neutrinos would be trapped inside the core, and rendered impotent.[28]

Our Sun – Designed for Its Job?

There was a time when scientists fondly imagined there might be millions of planets with life on them, scattered all over the universe. But not nowadays. As the title of an article in *New Scientist* put it, 'Space is lonelier than we thought.'[29]

For one thing, planets have to be exactly the right distance away from their sun. This article estimated that if we were 1 per cent farther out, the earth would be a frozen waste; 5 per cent closer in, and the seas would have turned to steam.[30]

Moreover, very few stars possess the right combination of radiation and gravitational pull to support a life-bearing planet. To be any use, a star must be of the same type as our own sun, and within a few per cent of the size of our sun. Many stars are either blue giants or red dwarfs, and neither of those types could possibly support life.

Yet it is only by still another incredible 'accident' of nature that *all* stars are not of those useless varieties! To quote Davies again:

> If gravity were *very* slightly weaker, or electromagnetism *very* slightly stronger, (or the electron slightly less massive relative to the proton), all stars would be red dwarfs. A correspondingly tiny change the other way, and they would all be blue giants.[31] (His italics.)

Astronomers have always had a sense of awe, when they contemplated the majesty of the universe. Until recently this was largely because of its sheer size and age.

But now they have a better reason to be overwhelmed. All this new evidence of meticulous design has evidently made a deep impression on astronomers and cosmologists.

How do they explain it? Since most of them appear to be unbelievers, they shy away from the obvious explanation. There is no place in their science for the Creator of Christian theology.

Their suggested alternatives are pathetically unconvincing. Hoyle and Wickramasinghe freely admit that the facts point clearly to the existence of a creator. Then they feebly suggest that perhaps the universe itself is intelligent enough to be that creator.

Others admit that the odds are many millions to one against the universe being the way it is by sheer chance. But, they add, the most improbable things can happen if you wait long enough. *Somebody* has to win the top prize in every sweepstake.

So, they say, perhaps there are an infinite number of separate universes, all with properties fixed at random – and ours just happens to be the one lucky one, with the right properties to support life!

Yes, perhaps. But how long has science been in the business of making wild, unsupported, mind-bending guesses? Doesn't it make better sense to believe in the Christian God, for whose existence there is a great deal of evidence, than in an infinite number of mighty universes, for whose existence there is not a particle of evidence?[32]

CONCLUSIONS

As we are now coming to the end of Part I, it is time to take stock and see what we have learned. As we do so, bear in mind that all the authorities who have been quoted so far are evolutionists, and most of them are unbelievers. And they are all, without exception, eminent men in their fields. So they cannot be airily dismissed as either creationists or cranks.

It is obvious that Darwin's theory no longer has the standing it had a few years ago. A small but significant minority of biologists have rejected it entirely, and are looking for a better theory of evolution to put in its place. So far, though, they have failed to find one.

A larger number have grave doubts about Darwinism, but are not prepared to scrap it altogether. They hope that it can yet be made to fit the facts, with the aid of some necessary modifications. The only problem is that they at present have no real idea how to doctor it.

In these circumstances, the most optimistic verdict possible about Darwinism is, 'not proven'. A more realistic assessment would be, 'a very questionable theory'.

On the other hand, the case for the existence of the Creator is stronger today than it has ever been. In every branch of science there is a growing body of evidence that the universe and its contents have been *designed* – that things just could not be the way they are as the result of chance. This evidence has so much weight that even some eminent scientists who are unbelievers have had the courage to face it, although they take refuge in the notion of a Creative Universe. The most reasonable answer to the question: Creation? is surely: Yes – creation of some sort.

But what sort of creation? That question will be considered in Part III, where I shall try to bring science and theology together. Meanwhile, we must make a lengthy digression in Part II, to see what science has to tell us about the age of the earth.

Part II

THE AGE OF THE EARTH

CHAPTER 5

Another Wind of Change

The suppression of uncomfortable ideas may be common in religion or politics, but it is not the path to knowledge.

Carl Sagan.[1]

It is only within the past couple of decades that the age of the earth has become a subject for debate in English religious circles. When I was a young Bible-believing Christian around nineteen-fifty, the matter was regarded as settled.

There was only one creationist society in Britain in those days, the Evolution Protest Movement, and its leading members all accepted without question that the earth is very old. I must have rubbed shoulders with hundreds of ancient-creationists, but I only remember ever meeting one recent-creationist before 1960. Young-earthists were as rare as flat-earthists in Britain in those days.

The pendulum began to swing in 1961. In that year J. C. Whitcomb and H. M. Morris published their recent-creationist classic, *The Genesis Flood*,[2] and it took a substantial part of the evangelical world by storm. In a surge of enthusiasm several new creationist societies were formed in the USA in the nineteen-sixties, and a couple in Britain in the nineteen-seventies. The majority of these were formed to promote recent-creationism, and the others were prepared to accommodate it. By the time the Evolution Protest Movement changed its name to the Creation Science Movement in 1980 it, too, was revealing recent-creationist tendencies in its publications.

Recent–creationism is now seen by many evangelical Christians as the only reasonable alternative to Darwinism. Ancient-creationists in America have found themselves becoming an unfashionable minority, with the trend in Britain following not very far behind.

What gave rise to this remarkable change in attitudes? And to what extent is it justified by new discoveries in the past quarter of a century?

To tackle these questions we must first set these recent events in their historical context, and that will mean going back more than two thousand years.

ANCIENT CONFLICTS BETWEEN SCIENCE AND CHRISTIANITY

Some of the Greek philosophers who lived during the six centuries before Christ knew a surprising amount about the universe.[3] For example, Aristarchus of Samos knew enough to argue that it is the earth that revolves around the sun, and not vice versa. He never convinced many people of this, but his views spread far enough to be recorded in a number of books, some of which Copernicus read seventeen centuries later, with world-shaking results.

One thing these ancient Greek philosophers were quite clear about was that the world was not flat. They not only knew it was round, but by combining astronomical observation with geometry they calculated the earth's diameter, more or less correctly. They also worked out the distance from the earth to the moon fairly accurately, and also – though less accurately – the distance to the sun.

But this Greek wisdom did not go down too well with some of the Fathers of the early Church. Rather than examine for themselves the experimental evidence that the earth is round (for example, the way a ship far out at sea can be seen from a cliff-top, but not from the beach), they preferred to dismiss the idea as 'unscriptural'. Even the great Augustine joined the attack:

> But as to the fable that there are Antipodes, that is to say, men on the opposite side of the earth, where the sun rises when it sets to us, men who walk with their feet opposite ours, that is on no ground credible . . . For Scripture, which proves the truth of its historical statements by the accomplishment of its prophecies, gives no false information; and it is too absurd to say, that some men might have taken ship and traversed the whole wide ocean, and crossed from this side of the world to the other, and that thus even the inhabitants of that distant region are descended from that one first man.[4]

Augustine, of course, believed that he was demolishing bad science with Scripture. In fact, he was unsuccessfully opposing good science with *his own incorrect deductions from Scripture* – a mistake which has been repeated all through history.

The Sixteenth-Century Battle

The rhetoric of those sincerely mistaken early Fathers could not blind men's eyes for ever. By 1492 it was generally agreed, at least by the educated classes, that the world was a globe with a circumference of something like twenty thousand miles. That was why Columbus sailed west, in search of a short cut to China and India.

In the sixteenth century a new battle broke out between science and religion, a battle which continued until well into the next century. It began when Copernicus revived Aristarchus' idea that the earth rotates every 24 hours while orbiting the sun once a year. Opposition came from both Catholics and Protestants; for instance, Martin Luther said:

> People gave ear to an upstart astrologer who strove to show that the Earth revolves, not the heavens or the firmament, the sun and the moon . . . This fool Copernicus wishes to reverse the entire science of astronomy; but sacred Scripture tells us that Joshua commanded the sun to stand still and not the earth.[5]

It is interesting to see how Luther was repeating Augustine's mistake, by putting too much confidence in his own *deductions* from Scripture. The Bible did not say, 'The earth is fixed and the sun and moon revolve around it every 24 hours.' Luther *deduced* that this notion was implied in the verses which read:

> Joshua said to the Lord in the presence of Israel:
> 'O sun, stand still over Gibeon,
> O moon, over the valley of Aijalon.'
> So the sun stood still, and the moon stopped, till the nation avenged itself on its enemies.[6]

Another Old Testament passage on which Luther and his contemporaries based this conclusion is this piece of poetry:

> In the heavens he [God] has pitched a tent for the sun,
> Which is like a bridegroom coming forth from his pavilion,
> Like a champion rejoicing to run his course.
> It rises at one end of the heavens and makes its circuit to the other,
> Nothing is hidden from its heat.[7]

It is understandable that they should make this mistake. Those passages really do look as if they teach that the sun makes a daily trip around the earth. It is only too easy for us, with the benefit of hindsight, to say, 'Luther and Co. ought to have been more humble. They should have said, "We think our interpretation is correct, but we admit that other interpretations are possible. Maybe those Scriptures do not intend to describe things as they really are, but only as they *appear* to be from our viewpoint." '

But the fact is that their kind of behaviour has been very common amongst enthusiastic believers of all ages. If we had been in his shoes, many of us would probably have fallen into the same trap as Luther and thumped our Bibles as we denounced Copernicus. And if we are not careful we might easily fall into a similar trap today.

The Clash with Geology

By the end of the seventeenth century that conflict also was resolved in favour of science. The turning point was Galileo's construction of the first powerful telescope; for a while people could ignore what the telescope revealed, but eventually the experimental evidence was bound to triumph over blind prejudice.

Yet no sooner was this second great controversy settled than a third one blew up. For many centuries it had been believed that the world was only a few thousand years old, and the Reformers considered that they could date it from Scripture as being less than six thousand years. It therefore shook the world when eighteenth-century geologists discovered evidence that the earth's crust is very much older than that.

It is important to note that it was in the *eighteenth* century that this first happened – well before Darwin was born. The pioneer geologist James Hutton, for instance, wrote that he could see 'no vestige of a beginning' to the earth's history[8] – and he died in 1797.

Recent-creationists usually ignore this historical fact. Their literature abounds with incorrect statements like this:

Why, then, do geologists say the rocks are hundreds of millions of years old, when they may only be thousands of years old? The answer is that *they are trying to agree with the theory of evolution* that needs enormous lengths of time to explain all the forms of life we know today.[9] (My italics.)

Such unfounded accusations are grossly unfair to all the early geologists. Not only did they reach their conclusions many years before Darwin launched his theory of evolution, but many of them were Bible-believing Christians and creationists.

Among them were William Buckland and Adam Sedgwick.

Buckland held the chair of geology at Oxford in the early nineteenth century, while Sedgwick was his counterpart at Cambridge. Both were leading churchmen, and both preached the plenary inspiration of Scripture and argued in favour of special creation. In their early years they held that some geological features, and especially the fossil-rich deposits found in caves, were relics of the Biblical Flood. After a while Sedgwick came to see that even this limited version of 'Flood geology' did not fit the facts, and strongly denounced it. Eventually Buckland abandoned it, too.

Buckland maintained close links with Sedgwick and the famous French geologist, Baron Cuvier, another Bible believer who spoke out against atheism and evolutionary speculation. The three of them were in their heyday while Darwin was a small boy. They did much to persuade the early nineteenth-century church that the earth was extremely old, and that such views could be harmonized with the teaching of Genesis.

A generation later, the most famous Christian geologist of the mid-nineteenth century was probably Hugh Miller. A presbyterian of the Free Church and a leading religious journalist, he witnessed extensively to his belief in the inspiration and accuracy of all Scripture. His brilliant field research on the geology of the Western Highlands gained him the presidency of the Royal Physical Society of Edinburgh. He wrote a number of best-selling books on geology as viewed by a Bible-believing Christian, with titles such as *The Testimony of the Rocks*, and *Footprints of the Creator*.

During the same period Edward Hitchcock was the president of Amherst College in Massachusetts. He also held the chairs of natural theology and geology there, and was highly regarded as a conservative theologian and as a scientist. His lectures on the age of the earth were famous. But it took some time to overcome the opposition, for in about 1840 he wrote of a small minority who were still dragging their feet. His message is clear enough, despite his quaint 'question and answer' technique.

Problem
Some maintain that the fossiliferous rocks were deposited by the deluge of Noah.

Refutation
1. That deluge must have been for the most part violent and tumultuous in its action on the globe: for the ocean must have flowed over the land in strong currents; and when it retired, urged on as it was by a wind, similar currents must have

prevailed. But a large proportion of the rocks were evidently deposited in quiet waters.

2. If deposited by that deluge, the materials and entombed organic remains of the rocks ought to be confused and mingled together; whereas in both these respects they are actually arranged with great regularity into groups.

3. The period occupied by the Noachian deluge was vastly too short for the disposition of rocks seven miles in thickness,[10] and with a great number of entire and distinct changes in their nature and organic contents.

4. The organic remains in the rocks do not correspond to the animals and plants now living on the globe. But this deluge took place since the creation of the present races; and, therefore, by this hypothesis, they ought to be found in the rocks. Hence they were deposited before that event.

Rem(ark)

An apology is due to the geological reader, for introducing a formal refutation of an hypothesis, which, to him, appears so entirely absurd. The apology consists in the fact, that many intelligent men are still found maintaining this hypothesis.[11]

Even if he did make terrible puns, Hitchcock and the other Bible-believing geologists eventually won their case. By the middle of the century almost all educated Protestants were content to reconcile Genesis with geology. (The discussion of how they did so must wait until Part III.) In the language of today, they had become ancient-creationists. And this third great peace treaty between Christianity and science was made *well before* Darwin published his *On the Origin of Species* in 1859, and so launched the fourth great battle.

THE IMPACT OF EVOLUTION

It is now a matter of history that within a few years Darwin changed the thinking of the whole world. And this was despite the fact that, at the time, most of the world's scholars and scientists were still professedly Christian. No other scientist, before or since, has ever achieved such a triumph. How did Darwin manage it?

A number of factors were operating, of which the following were perhaps the most important.

(1) Darwin was a brilliant and a hard-working man, who had spent half a lifetime doing his homework thoroughly. The result was

a highly plausible theory. It had its weaknesses – many of them – but they were not easy to spot at the time.

(2) At that time science was riding the crest of a wave. Exciting new discoveries were being made every year, many of them incontrovertible. The public had become conditioned to accepting new scientific ideas without asking too many questions.

(3) The church did not resist Darwinism for long, because it was beginning to be affected by the so-called 'Age of Reason'. There was a widespread tendency to prefer scientific explanations to supernatural ones, in every field of knowledge. So it was easy for theologians to accept Darwin's ideas, and then to start explaining even the Bible and Christianity on evolutionary lines.

(4) Finally, there is an important principle of psychology. When somebody has once made one big concession, it becomes easier to persuade him or her to make another. Within living memory Christianity had conceded, for good reasons, that it had been wrong about the age of the earth. This made it much easier for the church to concede it was also wrong about the origin of species and of man – even though the reasons for this second concession were nothing like as good.

Nineteenth-Century Opposition to Darwinism

By the end of the nineteenth century fundamentalists had become a despised minority, almost an object of ridicule. There were only a small number of scholars left who believed whole-heartedly in the authority of Scripture, though most of these continued to maintain an ancient-creationist position.

The one important exception was Philip Gosse, a distinguished marine biologist who was also a prominent member of the Plymouth Brethren. Alone among the Christian scholars of the later nineteenth century, he stuck to his lifelong belief in a recent creation. As a scientist he was well aware of the evidence for an ancient earth, and he could see only one way to deal with it. This led him to write the extraordinary book that brought him fame. It is called *Omphalos* – the Greek word for 'navel'.

When Adam was newly created, reasoned Gosse, he would not look like a day-old babe. He would have been created as a fully grown man. (Indeed, he might well have been created with a navel – hence the title of the book.) To all appearances, he had taken the usual twenty years or so to grow up. But appearances would have been deceptive: Adam must have been created with an appearance of an age that he did not possess.

Then Gosse took a huge leap of the imagination. What applies to Adam applies also to the rest of creation, he argued. Every other living thing was created full-grown, with an appearance of being days, weeks or years old. The earth's crust also was created with an appearance of age: in an instant great gorges were formed that *looked* as if they had been worn away over millions of years by the rivers running through them; in an instant beds of rock that *looked like* sediment several miles thick were created, complete with millions of fossils that *looked like* the remains of long-dead creatures. Gosse cheerfully agreed that geology had found much evidence of a great age for the earth. But it was not the earth's *real* age that geologists had discovered, only its *apparent* age, he claimed.

As readers of Sir Edmund Gosse's classic biography, *Father and Son*, will be aware, Philip Gosse was a diehard. He stuck to his ideas despite being unable to carry many of his fellow believers with him, and despite being widely ridiculed. Yet in a strange sort of way his influence lingers on today, as we shall see in Chapter 6.

Earlier Twentieth-Century Creationism

Creationism was at its lowest ebb during the first quarter of this century. There was only a little scholarly witness in America to the inspiration of Scripture and the doctrine of creation, and next to none in Europe.

Between the two world wars there came the first stirrings of a profound change in British theological circles. A strong movement emphasizing the infallibility of Scripture had sprung up in the universities, and gradually affected a large number of educated Christians.

In parallel with this movement back to the Bible came a revival of creationism. The Evolution Protest Movement was launched in London in 1932, with the physicist Sir Ambrose Fleming, the 'father of modern radio', as president. The first secretary was the versatile Douglas Dewar. He took a first in the Natural Sciences Tripos at Cambridge before turning to the law, and subsequently combined a career in the Indian Civil Service with research on Indian birds, for which he became internationally recognized. (Sadly, there has never since been another biologist of comparable standing in the entire creationist movement.)

During the late forties and early fifties the leading lights of the Evolution Protest Movement were Dewar and L. Merson Davies, who was awarded two doctorates for his research in geology. In their hands the EPM became the world's main centre of creationism, pouring out a stream of books and papers of high scientific quality.

Dewar, Davies and their colleagues had no doubts about the age of the earth. They based their creationist arguments on an unreserved acceptance of historical geology. There was never any doubt amongst them that Genesis and geology must be harmonized. To them, the only question was how best to expound Genesis so as to produce such a harmony.

The situation was not quite the same in America, where recent-creationism had never completely died out. Although the bulk of American creationists accepted the geological evidence of a great age for the earth, a minority believed otherwise. It is doubtful, however, whether any of the American recent-creationists of that period were professional geologists. And it must be remembered that minority groups have always flourished in America. A recent magazine article there reported that the International Flat Earth Research Society had 1500 members, 'many of whom are doctors, lawyers and other professional and educated people'![12]

But in mid-century Britain, at any rate, the situation was clearcut. The creationist movement then was led by men with a good grounding in biology and geology. And it was still a solidly *ancient*-creationist movement, just as it had been for the past hundred years.

THE REVIVAL OF RECENT-CREATIONISM AND ITS CONSEQUENCES

It was mainly the Seventh-Day Adventist author, George McCready Price, who kept recent-creationism alive in the USA during the early twentieth century. He wrote several books including *The New Geology* (1923) and *The Modern Flood Theory of Geology* (1935).

Few of his fans knew enough geology to realize that there was nothing 'new' or 'modern' about Price's geological ideas. They were merely a return to the old ideas of the early eighteenth century, when it was generally believed that the Flood could account for the earth's geological structure. Outside his own church Price had only a little following in America and practically none in Britain.

Recent-creationism did not take off as an organized movement until 1963, two years after Whitcomb and Morris published their famous book, with the founding of the Creation Research Society in America. Numerous other organizations with a recent-creationist emphasis have come into being in the USA since then, including the Bible-Science Association, the Creation-Science Research Center and the Institute for Creation Research, as well as the Biblical Creation Society, in England.

In recent years some American recent-creationists have entered the political scene. In some states they have had enough power to promote legislation, permitting or compelling schools to teach creation along with evolution. Although an Act of this sort was thrown out by the state of Arkansas in 1982, following a sensational court case, the controversy about legislation continues in various parts of the USA.

These recent-creationist pressure groups have sometimes exercised their power in an intolerant way. For example, the ill-fated Arkansas 'Act 590 of 1981' contained the following definition of 'creation-science':

SECTION 4. Definitions. As used in this Act:
(a) 'Creation-science' means the scientific evidences for creation and inferences from those scientific evidences. Creation-science includes the scientific evidences and related inferences that indicate: (1) Sudden creation of the universe, energy, and life from nothing; (2) The insufficiency of mutation and natural selection in bringing about development of all living kinds from a single organism; (3) Changes only within fixed limits of originally created kinds of plants and animals; (4) Separate ancestry for man and apes; (5) *Explanation of the earth's geology by catastrophism, including the occurrence of a worldwide flood*; and (6) *A relatively recent inception of the earth* and living kinds. (My italics.)

This narrow definition upset many ancient-creationists, who saw themselves as being squeezed out by it. Taxed with this, leaders of the recent-creationist movement have expressed their regrets. They say they did not really intend to exclude other versions of creationism, and will try to be more liberal in any future bills they promote.

Meanwhile, the harm has been done. Their political activities have stirred up a hornet's nest of opposition, both from atheists[13] and from Christians[14] who do not share their particular view of creation.

A Personal Confession

When I received an unexpected invitation to write a book about 'the creation/evolution debate', I was nonplussed. One side of me was keen to accept, because the subject fascinated me.

Yet I was, frankly, scared of the job. I knew that it would be impossible to do it without revealing what I knew of the case against recent-creationism. And this I was reluctant to do, because I knew it would hurt. Why should I write a book that would hurt those I regard as my friends?

It took me ten months of prayerful uncertainty before I finally said 'Yes'. And even then I said it regretfully, like a father signing his consent to a painful operation on his child. I agreed because Providence seemed to be urging me in that direction. The job needed doing, and I thought of the biblical character, Esther, when she was faced with a far worse task. She was told that God would no doubt use somebody else if she 'held her peace' – but that she herself would suffer for her cowardice.[15]

In the next few chapters I shall be obliged to oppose the notion that the earth is young. But I shall not *attack* it; one does not attack one's own friends. If we must use a military metaphor, I hope my allies will view me as exhorting them rather than attacking them. I am appealing to them to stop using the strategy and weapons of a bygone age in our common fight against unbelief.

For recent-creationists *are* my friends and allies. Let there be no mistake about that. The things we have in common are much more important than those on which we differ. We share a belief in an inspired Bible. We agree that Darwin was mistaken, and that God is the Creator of every living thing. Compared with this, the question of the age of the earth pales into insignificance.

Why Argue About the Earth's Age?

Why, then, do I think it necessary to put the case for an ancient earth? Partly, I suppose, because I care about truth, for its own sake. It seems a pity that many people should cling to a belief in a young earth simply because they have been shown only one side of the argument. Some of them might well be glad of the chance to see the other side.

But there is much more to it than that. My main reason for opposing the notion of a young earth is this: those who advocate it are damaging the cause of Christ without realizing it.

Think of the historical parallels mentioned earlier in this chapter.

The early Fathers thought they were defending the Bible when they argued that the world must be flat. But in fact they were only defending their own wrong interpretations of the Bible. And in the long run they harmed their own cause, by giving people the impression that Christianity was opposed to the scientific method of seeking knowledge.

Luther and his contemporaries also meant well when they opposed Copernicus and Galileo because 'the Bible said' the sun goes round the earth. But they, too, had mistaken their own interpretation for Bible teaching. Thus they, too, made many people think that Christians were prepared to hide their heads in the sand.

There are many indications that history is in danger of repeating itself, when well-meaning creationists argue that the earth is only a few thousand years old. On the one hand, as we shall see in Part III, Genesis does not say whether the earth is young or old. It is simply one particular *interpretation* of Genesis that provides the foundation for recent-creationism.

On the other hand, the scientific evidence for an ancient earth is overwhelming. As a recent editorial in *Science* said:

> The creationists also state that the age of the earth is between 6,000 and 10,000 years. In taking this stance they are in conflict with data from astronomy, astrophysics, nuclear physics, geology, geochemistry, and geophysics. In these disciplines an enormous mass of observational and experimental data has been accumulated bearing on the age of the earth and of the universe. Many independent approaches whose results buttress each other are in agreement that the age of the earth is much greater than 10,000 years.[16]

It is one thing to say, as ancient-creationists have been saying for a hundred years, that Darwin got it wrong. That may not be easy for a scientist to accept, but it is not impossible. And, as the previous four chapters have shown, it is getting easier every year.

But it is quite another matter for recent-creationists to argue that the astronomers, the astrophysicists, the nuclear physicists, the geologists, the geochemists and the geophysicists are all on the wrong track, too! When they have had time to ponder the implications, how many educated young people will accept such a sweeping dismissal of so large a part of science? And what will happen when they finally turn and reject it? Is there not a danger that many of them will swing to the other extreme and reject the Bible altogether?

There is no doubt that the case for a young earth is weaker than the case for creation. Leaders of the recent-creationist movement are well aware of this. Henry Morris, for instance, wrote in 1982:

> The critics of the creation movement commonly focus their attacks not on creation in general, but on *recent* creation [his italics] . . . I have frequently found in debating the subject of creation versus evolution that the evolutionist prefers to attack the concept of flood geology or the idea of recent creation.[17]

One cannot blame the critics. It is standard debating practice to attack your opponent at his weakest point. By tying up the weak case for a young earth in the same package as the strong case for creation, recent-creationists are almost asking to be defeated.

This was illustrated at the recent Arkansas 'creation trial'. The creationists paid for Britain's Professor Chandra Wickramasinghe to come and testify for them as an expert witness. As we saw in Chapter 3, Wickramasinghe is an unbeliever, and so his rejection of Darwinism is particularly significant. So is the fact that, although he does not believe in any recognized god, he thinks that the origin of life must be the work of some kind of supernatural creative being.

Yet it was reported that his potentially powerful witness for creation carried little weight with the court. The judge found himself 'at a loss to understand why Dr Wickramasinghe was called on behalf of the plaintiffs'. Why? Largely because other creation witnesses were arguing for *recent*-creation – and Wickramasinghe told the court that 'no rational scientist' could believe in an earth less than a million years old.[18]

Although the above is taken from a biased account of the trial in an anti-religious journal, an account by one of the creationists involved in the hearing makes a broadly similar admission:

> The inclusion of points 5 and 6 (catastrophism and young earth) is an unnecessary red flag for those opposed to the Act . . . *In view of the actual irrelevance of long time periods to the basic arguments for creation, it is ill-advised to wave unnecessary red flags in front of the evolutionists.*[19] (My italics.)

I couldn't have put it better myself.

CHAPTER 6

The Witness of the Sedimentary Rocks

One may not doubt that somehow, good
Shall come of water and of mud.   Rupert Brooke[1]

As we saw in the previous chapter, there was enough geological evidence by the middle of the last century to convince the educated world that our planet is millions of years old. Since then discoveries have gone on piling up at a tremendous rate, until today the case is overwhelming.

It is therefore curious to find the foremost recent-creationist, Dr Henry Morris, stating as recently as 1982 that there are only a 'handful of indicators of an old origin'; and only 'three or four processes that can be interpreted to yield ages old enough to allow for evolution.'[2] These enthusiastic statements are doubtless encouraging to those whose minds are made up already. But as we shall see, they are not in accordance with the facts.

In this chapter and the next I shall present just a little of the mountain of data pointing to a great age for the earth. Brief though this selection will have to be, it will show that there is a far stronger case to answer than Dr Morris realizes. Then, in chapters 8 and 9, we shall look at the 'scores of evidences of young age'[3] tabulated by Dr Morris, together with other evidence presented by him and his colleagues, and we shall see how weak the case for a young earth really is.

SEDIMENTARY DEPOSITS

The rocks making up the earth's crust can be divided into three main classes: igneous, sedimentary and metamorphic.

Igneous rocks – the name comes from the Latin *ignis*, fire – are produced when molten magma wells up from beneath the solid crust. Sometimes the molten material is ejected on the surface, as in the case of a volcano. Often, however, the molten rock merely forces its way through layers of existing rock and congeals far below the surface. When this happens geologists call the resulting rock formation an 'igneous intrusion'.

It is usually easy to identify igneous rocks because, like most materials that have solidified from a molten mass, they contain distinctive crystals. Sometimes, as in granite, the crystals are large and cannot be missed. In other rocks, such as basalt, the crystals are small and difficult to see without a microscope. There are usually no fossils in igneous rocks.

Sedimentary rocks, on the other hand, have been formed without heat. As the name suggests, many of them were formed from sediments – mud, and suchlike – that long ago settled on the beds of seas, rivers and lakes. But the class also includes rocks that were formed from sand dunes in deserts or on seashores, rocks formed by minerals precipitating from solution, and coral reefs and other formations built up by living creatures and plants. Many sedimentary rocks contain an abundance of fossils – that is, traces of living things which somehow have been preserved or have left their imprint in the rock.

Metamorphic rocks are those that have been 'metamorphosed' (Greek for 'changed in form') deep within the earth's crust, by a combination of extreme pressure and high temperature. Fossils are usually altered or destroyed by Nature's pressure-cooking, and crystals are often formed by it, so that beginners can easily mistake metamorphic rocks for igneous rocks.

For a quick mental picture of the earth's continents, think of a coating of (mostly) sedimentary rocks about a mile thick, sitting on top of what geologists call the 'basement' of igneous rock. But that one-mile thickness is only an average. The actual thickness varies enormously. In a few places the sedimentary coating has been scoured away completely, to expose the basement; in many places it is much less than a mile, and in other places it is a great deal more.

The greatest thicknesses occur near the mouths of large rivers. For instance, in regions around the delta of the Mississippi, geologists working for oil companies have measured the thickness of the sedimentary covering as more than seven miles. Other measurements have shown that in this area the crust is slowly sinking at a rate of about an inch per year – presumably under the weight of the two million tons of sediment per day that the river deposits there. The surface level remains about the same, however, since the sinking and the build-up are roughly in balance.[4]

It is rather obvious that this enormous stack of sediment could not possibly have been laid down by the Mississippi in a few thousand years. This becomes even more certain when we take into account the way the river mouth has moved around during geologic time, over a distance of many hundreds of miles, leaving thick deposits wherever it has been. Clearly, millions of years must have been needed for that amount of deposition.

There is no way that the Flood can be held responsible for these massive deposits. It is stretching the long arm of coincidence much too far, to suggest that there *just happened* to be a vast hole in the ocean bed seven miles deep near the mouth of the Mississippi; and that the Flood *just happened* to fill that hole with sediment, while leaving nearby areas of the Atlantic unfilled; and that similar coincidences *just happened* to occur around the mouths of all the world's great rivers.

CORAL REEFS

A coral reef is an enormous underwater structure built by countless generations of a strange kind of shellfish, the coral polyp. Instead of building himself a detached house like a normal shellfish, the coral prefers to live in a huge apartment block. So he builds his tube-shaped house of calcium carbonate firmly anchored to the reef. Further generations go on building upwards, while the remains of other kinds of shellfish and the skeletons of some forms of algae also become incorporated. And so the reef grows and grows.

Nature imposes strict limits on the growth rate of a reef. The coral polyp has to extract his building materials from the sea, and since there is only a very little calcium carbonate in seawater it is a slow process. The hollow, branching tubes of coral built by the former occupants are quite brittle, and so the lower levels of the reef have to turn into solid, hard limestone before they can support the weight of new growth above. This means that a great deal more calcium carbonate has to precipitate from the seawater and cement everything into a solid mass – another slow process.

The living corals face many hazards. Storms can break off the growing tips and wash them away. A thin film of mud can kill the polyps. Predators like the crown-of-thorns starfish can multiply and wipe out whole colonies. When the reef reaches the surface it can go no higher, unless and until the sea level rises or the seabed sinks. And if the water becomes more than about a hundred feet deep, the coral again finds itself out of its element and cannot thrive.

There are many living coral reefs in the world's warmer seas, and some of them are immensely thick. Holes drilled in the Eniwetok reef in the Pacific have revealed a depth of 4,600 feet.

Now if the world is only 10,000 years old, and that reef began growing on Creation Day 5, it would have had to develop at an *average* rate of five and a half inches a year.

But a great deal of research has been done on the growth rates of coral reefs, and such rates have been shown to be quite impossible. Under *ideal* conditions a growth rate of about half an inch a year would be good going.[5] And because of earthquakes, tidal waves, giant hurricanes and so forth, ideal conditions never continue for any length of time. Moreover, the test borings at Eniwetok showed a number of discontinuities in the reef, when growth evidently stopped altogether. Great quantities of fossil pollen at various depths in the reef show that on several occasions the sea must have receded, so that land plants and trees could colonize the reef surface for a while.

There is plenty of scope for debate as to just how old the Eniwetok reef is. But one thing seems beyond dispute: it must be hundreds of thousands of years old, at the lowest possible count. And it is pointless for the recent-creationist to suggest that perhaps growth rates were very much faster before the Flood than now. For growth rates are limited by fundamental laws of physics and chemistry, and there is no reason to think that those laws were changed in Noah's day.

Ancient Buried Reefs

A hundred years ago prospecting for oil was a simple business. You followed a hunch and drilled a deep hole, to see if oil would gush up. If it did, you barrelled it; if it didn't, you went away and tried your luck somewhere else.

Nowadays the oil industry employs whole regiments of geologists and other scientists to do the job more methodically. First they make what they call a 'seismic survey': this involves firing explosives to send vibrations far into the earth's crust, and then analysing the echoes that come back. Thus they can build up something like an X-ray map of what lies at various depths.

Afterwards they make test borings, sometimes using a special kind of drill which is vaguely reminiscent of an apple-corer. It brings up 'cores' from various depths; these solid samples of rock are examined for structure and chemical composition, and any fossils present can be identified. In this way a fairly complete 3-D picture has been formed of the top few miles of the earth's crust, in oil-bearing areas. And a fascinating picture it is, too.

We know now that formerly the oilfields of Alberta, Texas and the Great Lakes area were all beneath the sea. There was a period when thousands of feet of sedimentary rock were deposited there, and the fossils these rocks contain bear witness to their marine origin. Then a number of coral reefs grew on top of the sedimentary deposits, and these reefs eventually became fossilized into limestone.[6,7] (Some of them are not coral reefs, strictly speaking, because the salt-water creatures that built them are not actually classified as coral polyps. But they are similar in their reef-forming habits, and so we can safely ignore this rather technical distinction.)

Some of these reefs are massive, being about a thousand feet thick and many miles long, and must have taken many thousands of years to grow. We know that they grew in their present sites, because a coral reef has a clearly defined 'top' and 'bottom', and an equally distinct 'ocean side' and 'lagoon side'. And these reefs are all the right way up and the right way round, so they cannot possibly be made of boulders that were formed somewhere else and then heaved into position by waves, currents, or earthquakes.

Finally, the reefs were all covered by many more layers of sediment. In most cases these have buried the reefs to a depth of several thousand feet.

Thus we have evidence here of a 3-stage process which must have occupied a great deal of time. Enough time was needed:

(1) For the lower layers of sediment to be deposited, complete with fossils, and then to harden into rock. (The latter is essential, because coral does not grow on seabeds of thick mud.)
(2) For the coral reefs to grow on top.
(3) For the upper layers of sediment to bury them.

Orthodox geology can explain these remarkable sandwich formations, because it recognizes that great periods of time were occupied by these processes. But the recent-creationist theory of 'Flood geology' is quite unable to explain them at all. This is because 'Flood geologists' believe, for reasons which will be discussed in chapter 8, that practically all fossil-bearing rocks were laid down by the Flood. But if the Flood deposited the rocks beneath the reefs, how did the reefs have time to grow, and what laid down the thousands of feet of sediment that buried them?

The Bahama Banks

The Bahama Banks are underwater mountains of sedimentary rock, sitting on the floor of the Atlantic. Their highest peaks break surface to form the Bahamas Islands. Although the Banks are not in an oil-bearing region, two very deep test wells have been drilled into the Great Bahama Bank. Many seismic surveys have also been made, and the exposed surfaces around the edges of the Banks have been closely examined.

As a result of all this work we now know that the Bahama Banks are made of limestone and a modified limestone known as dolomite[8], right down to the foot of the deepest borehole, which penetrated nearly 18,000 feet. The whole massive structure, from top to bottom, was found to be one tremendous stack of fossil material. Some of it has been ground down by forces such as wave action so that the original form of the fossils has been destroyed, but there remains an enormous number of fossils that are still easily identifiable. And these are all of organisms, including coral and many others, that live only in shallow water.

Evidently we have here a sort of king-sized coral-type reef, which slowly grew upwards as the seabed gradually sank. There appears to be no other conceivable explanation. The Banks cannot be made of fossil material that grew somewhere else and was deposited in a great underwater heap, because they have *steeply sloping sides*. Anyone who tries building an underwater sandcastle with steep sides will soon see for themselves the force of this argument! And there is, as always in a fossil reef, so much 'right way up' material that the 'grew in place' explanation is obviously correct. Moreover, the limestone in the Banks is remarkably pure, with none of the contaminating mud that is always deposited by floods.

Estimates vary of how long these enormous Banks took to grow. But all run into millions of years, since it is inconceivable that they could have grown in a short period of time. The present rate of growth, which is not necessarily the same as past rates of growth, is about one inch in a hundred years.[9]

ROCKS RESEMBLING TREE-RINGS

Shale and claystone are rocks which were formed from clay, deposited on the bottom of some ancient lake or sea. In some places these rocks are made up of many thin layers, which sometimes alternate between lighter and darker colour.

The English name for these alternating bands is 'varves', which comes from a Swedish word meaning 'layers'. The Germans, however, call them *Jahresringe* – 'year-rings', or, as we would put it, 'tree-rings'. This name is obviously appropriate, because varves do look somewhat like the grain in a piece of wood that has been sawn at right angles to the rings.

But the appropriateness does not stop there. Varves, like tree-rings, are annual growth bands. When geologists in the nineteenth century studied the clay settling to the beds of lakes, they found that often it was one colour in summer, and another in winter.[10] This led them to conclude that varves were yearly growth layers. Were they right?

Modern studies of microfossils in varves, and especially of the fossil pollen which is found in the summer layers but not the winter ones, have shown that they undoubtedly were. This means that we can tell how long it took a varved deposit to form, in just the same way as we can tell the age of a cut-down tree – by counting the total number of growth bands.

Some of these deposits are very thick and have hundreds of thousands of varve couplets. (It usually takes two layers to make one annual growth band, or varve: one summer, and one winter.) The current world record is held by the Green River shale deposits in Wyoming, Utah and Colorado, where there are up to several million successive bands. A typical couplet here consists of a layer of clean clay particles followed by a layer impregnated with organic material, including pollen and spore particles. The thicknesses vary from year to year, with maximum thicknesses occurring about every 11½ years, every 50 years, and every 12,000 years. The 11½-year cycle corresponds to that of the sunspots, and the 12,000-year cycle to the precession of the equinoxes; both these astronomical cycles affect rainfall, which in turn affects the amount of clay washed into lakes.[11]

Once again we have an indication of great age that simply cannot be explained away. There is no possibility that a great flood – or any other catastrophe, for that matter – could have produced *millions* of paper-thin bands of alternating light and dark colour in an extensive deposit of shale. Above all, there is no way that pollen could have found its way into the darker bands, and *only* the darker bands, unless they were produced at yearly intervals over a vast epoch.

Evaporite Varves

As everybody knows, seawater contains dissolved salts – around three per cent on average, though there is more than this in the tropics and less in the Arctic and Antarctic. Not all of this is ordinary salt, sodium chloride, although the bulk of it is. There is also a little calcium carbonate and calcium sulphate, plus minute quantities of a great many other substances that we can afford to ignore for the present.

If a glass beaker of seawater is left in a warm room to evaporate slowly, what happens? Nothing, at first, except that the water level gradually falls and the concentration of salts in the water increases. When about half the water has evaporated the remaining water can no longer hold the original amount of calcium carbonate in solution, and this will begin to settle out as a solid film on the glass. By the time the volume is down to one-fifth of the original, most of the calcium carbonate will have been precipitated, and the calcium sulphate will start to come out. At one-tenth of the original volume there will not be much calcium sulphate left in solution, and the sodium chloride will just be starting to settle out.

If all the water is allowed to evaporate there will eventually be three layers of salts on the bottom of the beaker: first, a thin layer of calcium carbonate; then a thin layer of calcium sulphate; and finally a much thicker layer of sodium chloride. Between the layers there will generally be a very thin borderline zone where the two salts appear as a mixture.

This sort of process can be observed happening in a big way in certain shallow tropical lagoons and mudflats, especially in the Persian Gulf region. Layers of calcium carbonate, calcium sulphate and sodium chloride are laid down from time to time, depending on what the concentration of the seawater happens to be at the time. Sometimes the calcium carbonate is converted to dolomite, if enough magnesium happens to be present and the conditions are favourable. In regions where the seawater rarely becomes concentrated enough to deposit sodium chloride, the resulting 'layer cake' builds up very slowly, at a small fraction of an inch per year, because of the low concentration of calcium carbonate and calcium sulphate in seawater.

Minerals that were formed by the evaporation of seawater are called 'evaporites'. The term includes both the varved deposits described in the previous paragraph, and the massive deposits of sodium chloride that are formed when whole seas dry up.

Petroleum geologists know a great deal about evaporite deposits deep in the earth's crust, because oil is often found beneath them. One such deposit is in the Delaware basin, among the oilfields of west Texas. There is an enormous buried reef here, the Capitan reef, which once must have enclosed a vast ocean basin about ninety miles across and a hundred and sixty miles long. Part of the reef has eroded away, but there is still about three-quarters of the complete loop remaining. It is mostly well over a thousand feet thick.

Over a large area of the enclosed basin a huge deposit of calcium carbonate/calcium sulphate varves was laid down. There are about 200,000 of these varve couplets, with an average total thickness of about 1,300 feet over much of the basin. They are so clearly distinguishable that some of the varve sequences can be identified like fingerprints. In this way some of the individual varves have been traced from oil-well to oil-well over a total distance of about forty miles.

There seems only one way to explain these facts. At one time the seawater in this vast enclosed basin became sufficiently concentrated for some of the dissolved salts to start crystallizing. Each summer, evaporation would cause the salt concentration to increase, precipitating first the carbonate layer and then the sulphate. Sometimes the water in the basin became concentrated enough for sodium chloride to be precipitated also, but not often. Usually the winter rains would fall and often some fresh sea-water would find its way into the basin, diluting the contents before the sodium chloride could crystallize, and causing the carbonate/sulphate cycle to start again the next summer.

Needless to say, this sequence of events would not happen with clockwork regularity, every year for two thousand centuries. In practice the cycles were no doubt interrupted from time to time by cold, wet summers or, more seriously, by a catastrophic breach in the reef, or by other geological events. So the idealized picture, of one pair of varves per year, leading to 200,000 years for the entire deposit to form, is over-optimistic. What it does is to give the minimum possible time for the 200,000 varve couplets to be formed. The actual time was probably longer.

And if the reader is still dubious, let him reflect that the precipitation of 1,300 feet of these evaporites would necessarily have involved the evaporation of a million feet of seawater, and work out how many summers that would have taken. (Bear in mind that the Dead Sea, which is in one of the hottest places on earth, only evaporates about 10 feet of water a year.)

Hot springs of volcanic origin could not possibly account for such vast deposits of such great uniformity. Volcanic springs produce irregular, chunky deposits – not wafer-thin layers of alternating carbonate and sulphate with relative thicknesses corresponding to the proportions of the two salts in seawater. Nor could they have generated the organic microlayers that occur between many of the varve couplets. Geologists who have researched the Delaware basin evaporites are all agreed that evaporation of seawater is the only possible explanation for them.[12]

It is impossible for the Flood to have produced anything like the Delaware basin evaporites. There are thousands of feet of fossil-bearing rocks below the evaporites, and many more fossil-bearing layers above them. So, according to the advertised principles of 'Flood geology', the whole evaporite mass – several thousand square miles in area, well over a thousand feet thick, and composed of 400,000 separately identifiable layers – should all have been laid down part-way through the year-long Flood.

What a hope!

THE MUD ON THE OCEAN FLOOR

One of the most remarkable features of the living world is that the majority of living organisms are too small to be seen with the naked eye. Thanks to the invention of the microscope, we are in a far better position to marvel at the Creator's handiwork than our ancestors.

A shovelful of garden soil contains millions of invisibly small creatures. Even more amazing, so does a bucketful of seawater drawn from near the surface in mid-ocean. Many of these tiny marine organisms – tens of thousands of species have been identified already – are miniature, floating 'shellfish', of two main kinds.

The Foraminifera and coccolithophores have shell-like skeletons of calcium carbonate. In regions where their shells (officially described as 'tests') accumulate on the seabed in large quantities they form what is called 'chalk ooze', which can eventually solidify to produce chalk. The chalk hills and cliffs of south-east England are composed almost entirely of Foraminifera and coccolith microfossils.

The other group consists of the Radiolaria and diatoms, which both have shells of silica (silicon dioxide). These form a brown substance on the seafloor, known as 'siliceous ooze'. When this solidifies (the proper geological term is 'lithifies', from the Greek *lithos*, stone) it can form a flinty kind of rock, known as chert.

These two types of ooze cover a large part of the deep ocean beds. The ooze on a huge area of the Pacific Ocean floor, some two thousand miles wide and over five thousand miles long, has an average thickness of 1,200 feet. Elsewhere it is usually thinner – but is still quite thick. In some areas very fine clays washed off the land and carried far out to sea play a role on the ocean bottom, too. So does the debris from submarine volcanoes.

But the commonest of all these materials is chalk ooze, which has been found covering about a third of the entire seabed. It occurs even on the tops of underwater mountains where the depth of water may be only a mile or so, instead of the several miles which is more usual in the great oceans. This shows that the minute shells have settled where they first fell, since avalanches don't slide upwards!

Oceanic geologists have done much research in the hope of finding out how long these chalk oozes have been accumulating. Measurements of the present-day rate have been made and it is extremely small, amounting to only about one inch in a thousand years. Nobody supposes that the growth rate has always remained the same, but it is worth noting that at the present rate it would take a good ten million years to accumulate a thousand feet of ooze.[13]

To compress the period of growth into a few thousand years, it would be necessary to assume that growth rates in the past were *thousands* of times faster than nowadays. But marine biologists know that this cannot possibly have been the case, because of the natural limits on growth rates.

The growth of Foraminifera, as with larger members of the animal kingdom, is limited by the supply of the coccolithophores and other food they consume, and this in turn is limited by the amount of solar energy those organisms can absorb. They have to compete for their nourishment with countless other marine creatures. They also need copious supplies of oxygen and calcium carbonate – but the ability of seawater to hold these in solution is measured in parts per million. If the population density becomes too high, they are liable to choke in their own 'sewage'. Many of the Foraminifera and coccolithophores do not survive long enough to die of old age, but are eaten by their competitors. And, finally, the shells of those that do die cannot all reach the ocean floor, since many of them disintegrate and dissolve on the way down.

Juggle the figures how you will. With an effort we might be able to bring that figure of ten million years down to one million, but there is no way of reducing it to ten thousand – or anything like it. The stern laws of Nature forbid it.

ROCKS FORMED THROUGH HEAT

Geologists have learnt a lot about age by studying large igneous intrusions. These are great masses of formerly molten rock that were once injected upwards into the earth's crust, like insulating foam being injected into the wall cavity of a house. Just as that foam is always of more recent date than the brick walls surrounding it, so an igneous intrusion is bound to be younger than the sedimentary rocks which it once forced apart and infiltrated.

The mathematical laws of cooling of hot bodies are well known, and have been confirmed by countless experiments. Consequently, it is not difficult to calculate how long it must have taken an igneous intrusion to cool. The first step is to determine its chemical composition and hence its melting point; this gives the *minimum* temperature it must have had when it was intruded. Then the dimensions must be measured, especially the thickness, and its thermal properties. Finally, the dimensions and the thermal properties of the surrounding sedimentary rocks must be ascertained. Then the actual calculation can safely be entrusted to a computer.

Davis Young[14] has listed the computed *minimum* cooling times of a number of igneous intrusions, thus:

The small Palisades sill, near New York –
'a few hundred' years.
The large Muskox intrusion, N.W. Canada –   7,000 years.
The Stillwater igneous formation, Montana –   50,000 years.
The Busveld complex, S. Africa –   nearly 200,000 years.
The granitic batholith, Southern California –   1,000,000 years.

Needless to say, these figures are only estimates and are only as accurate as the data and assumptions upon which they are based. But they are unlikely to be very wide of the mark. And it must be remembered that, for the reasons already given, the surrounding fossil-bearing rocks are undoubtedly older than the igneous intrusions.

The Metamorphic Rocks

Although it is more than a quarter of a century ago, I still remember the excitement that one day rippled through the establishment where I then worked. Colleagues in our new high-pressure laboratory had just succeeded in producing some synthetic diamonds!

Since then, all sorts of minerals have been made in high-pressure laboratories for research purposes. Geologists wanted to learn how Nature turns sedimentary rocks into metamorphic rocks, and by doing it themselves they were able to find out what temperature and pressure were needed in various cases.

The results of all this work make fascinating reading, but there is space here for only one example. There are some metamorphic rocks in New England which have been studied intensively.[15] Although most of the fossils they once contained are now unrecognizable, enough fossils remain (albeit in a rather tatty condition) to prove conclusively that these were originally sedimentary rocks.

To produce similar rocks in the laboratory researchers had to take the appropriate sedimentary rocks and heat them to about 600°C, while putting a pressure of about 30 tons per square inch upon them. *No lesser combination of temperature and pressure would do the job.*

Now the only way that Nature can apply 30 tons per square inch to a rock formation is to bury it under a great weight of other rocks. If there are no sideways movements in the crust, this necessitates at least ten miles of rocks pressing down; with sideways movements, it might be possible to knock off a mile or two. The exact depth may be a subject for discussion, but one fact seems absolutely undeniable: most of the earth's metamorphic rocks must have been produced several miles down in the earth's crust.

Yet many metamorphic formations are found today upon the surface. To reach this position they must have had a history something like this:

(1) First, the original sediment was deposited, and afterwards turned into a sedimentary rock, complete with fossils.

(2) This was then buried by the accumulation of further layers of sediment, totalling several miles in thickness. In some places, volcanic activity might speed up the burial process somewhat.

(3) As the weight of overlying rocks became sufficient to reach the necessary pressure, and the heat from the earth's interior raised the rocks to the necessary temperature, the metamorphic changes took place.

(4) Finally, the combined effect of earth movements and erosion

would eventually bring the metamorphosed layer right back to the earth's surface again.

The mind boggles at the prospect of estimating how long all this must have taken. Yet it appears that there is no alternative explanation of the metamorphic rocks on offer. So far as I am aware, no recent-creationist has yet suggested that the Flood could have subjected sedimentary rock formations to temperatures of 600°C and pressures of 30 tons per square inch, simultaneously!

EARTH'S SPEED OF ROTATION

Recent research has shown that the days and nights are getting longer. Because of friction, mostly that of the tides, our spinning earth is gradually slowing down. The rate of deceleration has been measured against atomic clocks, and it averages 0.000 015 seconds per day per year at present, although there is reason to think that over long periods in the past the slightly higher figure of 0.000 020 would be more appropriate. So a million years ago the days would have been about 20 seconds shorter than nowadays.

But measurements indicate that the length of the *year* is not changing. This is what might be expected. There is no appreciable friction in outer space to slow down the forward motion of the earth as it orbits the sun. These two facts together – a lengthening day and a constant year – mean that the number of days in a year must gradually decrease so as to balance the books.

Now let us go back in our imagination to the Devonian period, which geologists believe was about 400 million years ago. The days then would have been about 400×20 seconds shorter than they are now, which would make them about 21·8 hours long. But the years then would have contained 365¼×24 hours (= 8766 hours), just as they do today.

So if we divide the number of hours in the Devonian year, 8766, by the number of hours in the Devonian day, 21·8, we arrive at an estimate of the number of days in the Devonian year. It comes to just over 400 days.

Surprising though it may seem, we have ways of seeing whether this really was so. Certain living species of coral and of shellfish not only have annual growth bands like tree rings; they also exhibit *daily* growth bands. With experience, researchers can pick out about 365 of the daily growth bands between the yearly ones.

Fortunately (or should we say, providentially?) certain fossil corals and fossil shellfish from the Devonian period display the same phenomenon.[16] And in both the corals[17] and the shellfish[18] there are about 400 daily bands between the annual ones.

This provides an unexpected and striking confirmation that the conventional geological date for the Devonian period is reasonably correct.

This brief selection of evidence from the sedimentary rocks illustrates the truth of Dan Wonderly's summary of the geologist's case:

> We are by no means in a position of having to struggle to find evidence for great age in the earth. There is a veritable avalanche of such evidence.[19]

CHAPTER 7

More Evidence of Age

Behold the height of the stars,
how high they are!
          Eliphaz the Temanite[1]

The nineteenth-century astronomers were not far behind the geologists in concluding that the universe was far older than people had thought. England's greatest astronomer of the age was the German-born Sir William Herschel. By 1800 he had calculated the distances of many remote galaxies, though by modern standards his values were of rather poor accuracy. He realized that the light from these galaxies must have taken very much more than 6,000 years to reach our own planet. In 1802 he wrote:

> A telescope with a power of penetrating into space, like my 40 feet one, has also, as it may be called, a power of penetrating into time past . . . Almost two millions of years ago, this object must already have had an existence in the sidereal heavens, in order to send out those rays by which we now perceive it.[2]

Eleven years later he said in a conversation with Thomas Campbell:

> I have looked further into space than ever human being did before me. I have observed stars of which the light, it can be proved, must take two millions of years to reach the earth.[3]

Herschel's argument was quite straightforward. Earlier astronomers had already made rough measurements of the speed of light, and found it to be in the region of 190,000 miles per second. (The true value is close to 186,000.) It was a simple matter to combine this with Herschel's own mathematical estimates of distance, and so to find how long the light from these distant objects had spent in travelling to the earth.

But Herschel's figures remained highly questionable until 1838. Until then, the only distances that had actually been measured had been within the solar system, with a maximum of a few hundred millions of miles. The method of measurement is called 'parallax'; it is the astronomical equivalent of the method of triangulation used by surveyors and mapmakers, with the width of the earth's orbit being the base line. (See Figure 2.)

In the eighteen-thirties Friedrich Bessel, using new and improved instruments, applied this method to measuring the distance of an object *outside* the solar system, the star 61 Cygni. In 1838 he reported that it was the equivalent of 64 million million miles away, which meant that its light must take more than 10 years to reach us. And this is one of our nearest neighbours; the most distant stars had already been shown to be many thousands of times more distant than the nearest ones. Immediately, this showed that Herschel's estimates of distance were on the right lines.

Further measurements by other astronomers followed fast. By 1850 most educated Bible-believers accepted that the case was proved. For example, in that year the Christian writer John Pye Smith concluded in his book, *On the Relation Between the Holy Scriptures and Some Parts of Geological Science*, that:

> These views of the antiquity of that vast portion of the Creator's works which Astronomy discloses, may well abate our reluctance to admit the deductions of Geology, concerning the past ages of our planet's existence.[4]

Since that time astronomers have developed a number of ingenious new methods of measuring distances, which are too technical to discuss in detail here. These have been checked against each other, and – for the nearer stars – against direct measurements by the parallax method. They all lead to the conclusion that light

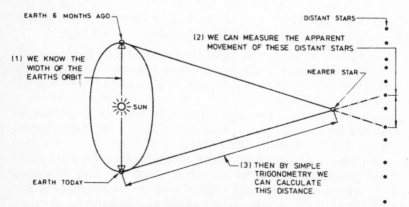

Figure 2. Basis of the method of parallax.

from the most distant objects in the heavens must have taken about ten *billion* years to get here.

It is as well to treat this conclusion with caution. New facts may yet come to light that would make it necessary to scale it down a bit. Nevertheless, there seems no prospect of it ever being reduced to anything like ten thousand years. It is difficult for anyone who has studied the astronomical evidence to doubt that the universe is many millions of light-years big, at the very least.

RECENT-CREATIONIST RESPONSES

Why, then, do recent-creationists not accept this powerful evidence that the universe is millions of years old? Partly, no doubt, because most of them have never studied astronomy in enough depth to appreciate the strength of the case. It is all too easy to dismiss evidence that you have never examined closely, especially when it leads to an unpalatable conclusion.

Those few recent-creationists who have gone into the subject thoroughly are aware that they have a problem. They have two favourite solutions to offer.

The first is the solution of Gosse, the nineteenth-century creationist who thought that God created fossils to give the earth an 'appearance of age'. In the same way, Gosse argued, when God created the stars he must have created vast beams of light at the same moment, stretching all the way across space from the stars to the solar system.

A similar solution was offered by Henry Morris, who did not deny that the stars really are millions of light-years away. He wrote in 1972:

If the stars were made on the fourth day, and if the days of creation were literal days, then the stars must be only several thousand years old. How, then, can many of the stars be millions or billions of light-years distant since it would take correspondingly millions or billions of years for their light to reach the earth?

This problem seems formidable at first, but is easily resolved when the implications of God's creative acts are understood.

. . . Why is it less difficult to create a star than to create the emanations from that star? In fact, had not God created 'light' on Day One prior to His construction of 'lights' on Day Four? It is even possible that the 'light' bathing the earth on the first three days was created in space as *en route* from the innumerable

'light bearers' which were yet to be constituted on the fourth
day.[5]

Another suggestion, which amounts to the same thing, is that
God first created the world with a velocity of light that was infinite
and then slowed it down to its present value. But if you work
through the physics of such a process, it is apparent that this
would have involved God in changing the entire structure of the
universe immediately after he had made it! Not only does this
seem unlikely, but there is no evidence whatever that such an
enormous change has occurred. This is an even more unlikely-
sounding version of Gosse's idea than the straightforward version,
that perhaps God created the light beams separately from the
stars.

And why not? The Almighty certainly *could* have done that if
he had chosen to do so. Is there any reason to believe that, in
fact, he did not? Yes, there is a very good theological reason – so
good that it has even led many recent-creationists to reject Gosse's
suggestion. But a discussion of that must wait until the next
chapter.

Meanwhile, I shall content myself with making one observation.
If Gosse was right, then most of the world's astronomers might
as well look for other employment, and stop wasting their time!
For the overwhelming majority of the heavenly bodies are very
much more than ten thousand light years distant. This would
mean that (on the Gosse hypothesis) in most cases the astronomers
are not studying the stars themselves, but only the beams of light
that were specially created on the same day as the stars.

If they followed Gosse, astronomers would be bound to think:
'What guarantee do we have that the physical reality behind these
beams of light corresponds to the light beams? Indeed, how do
we know that there actually *is* any physical reality there? If
Gosse's principle of 'appearance of age' means that God created
the 'appearance of stars', then there would be little point in God
creating the actual flaming bodies that we thought we were
observing. When Genesis said, 'He made the stars also', it must
mean that he made those long beams of light – and not necessarily
the multitude of sun-like bodies that we thought we were seeing.
The whole universe may be only a sort of cosmic film-set. Let's
go home!'

It is not surprising that most recent-creationists nowadays look
for a better solution than Gosse's. They think they have found
one in the notion of curved Riemannian space, which has been

popularized by Dr Harold Slusher[6] and other writers. It deserves
a close look.

Can Curved Space Rescue the Young Universe Theory?

Slusher introduces his curved space theory by saying:

> In connection with the time it takes for light to get here from
> the stars, a very important work was done by Parry Moon of
> the Massachusetts Institute of Technology and Domina E.
> Spencer of the University of Connecticut. This work was
> published in the *Journal of the Optical Society of America*,
> August, 1953. This work is significant particularly in the matter
> of the age of the universe as well as it is to cosmology and to
> electrodynamics.

Soon after, Slusher's readers find themselves led into a discussion
of Einstein's theory of relativity and a mathematical argument
which most of them cannot understand. Eventually Slusher comes
to the sensational conclusion reached by Moon and Spencer:
because of the suggested curvature of space, light could take a
kind of 'short cut' through 'Riemannian space'. Consequently, if
space really is like that, light could cross 100 light years as if it
were a mere 14.7 light years, or 1,000 as if it were only 15.6, and
an *infinite* distance as if it were only 15.71 light years.

Needless to say, this is sweet music to a recent-creationist's
ears. And because of the impeccable antecedents of Moon and
Spencer, it appears to be a part of soundly-based, orthodox
science. Unfortunately, things are not always quite what they
seem. Let me try to put the Moon and Spencer suggestion in its
real setting.

Like a codfish hopefully laying a million eggs, creative research
scientists throw out lots of suggestions, many of which never get
anywhere. The dustbins of science are bulging with the many
unsound suggestions made by geniuses, whose relatively few good
ideas won them knighthoods or Nobel prizes. Usually they nurse
each good idea carefully and present it to the world in a lengthy,
thoroughly worked-out paper. If the idea is a rather wild, specu-
lative one, then they might just set it out briefly, to see what
happens.

This is what Moon and Spencer did. Most of their paper[7]
consists of a discussion of the evidence for and against Einstein's
special theory of relativity, of which they disapproved. (This was
1953, and the evidence for special relativity then was not so

overwhelming as it is today.) Having reached the conclusion that
Einstein could not be faulted, they turned in their last couple of
pages to their revolutionary suggestion.

In effect, they asked the question: 'Is it possible to conceive of
any kind of a universe where Einstein's theory would appear to
be true, when it was actually false?'

Yes, it is, they concluded. *If* there were two quite different
kinds of space co-existing, superimposed on each other,
(1) ordinary space and (2) curved Riemannian space (the latter is
a curious mathematical abstraction); and *if* the stars were posi-
tioned in the ordinary space while light travelled through the
Riemannian space; and *if* the Riemannian space (which in theory
could have any curvature that you might like to assign to it) just
happened to have a radius of curvature of 5 light years – *if* space
were like that, then nobody could prove Einstein wrong.

Another odd consequence of such a universe, they pointed out,
would be that light could travel right across it by travelling only
5π (15·71) light years.

Such a universe, of course, is nothing more than a figment of
a mathematician's imagination. There was not in 1953, and still
is not today, a shred of evidence that the real universe is anything
like that. Far from regarding their own suggestion as 'a very
important work' (Slusher's phrase), Moon and Spencer seem to
have regarded it as a mere mathematical curiosity. Having slipped
it into that paper they let the matter drop and never returned to
it again. And the world of science showed no interest in it, either
– until recent-creationists rescued it from limbo, dusted it off,
and started using it as if it proved their point.

Faced with this obvious misuse of the Moon and Spencer paper,
papers by several writers have recently appeared, setting the
record straight. In particular, D. J. Krause points out that
experimental work by Brecher in X-ray astronomy in 1977 has
now shown that Moon and Spencer's suggestion is 'invalidated'.[8]
The astrophysicist Dr Perry Phillips has also cited a number of
recent reports of experimental work which, he says, proves
conclusively that the Moon and Spencer speculation cannot be
right.[9]

Hence, what might have been an alternative explanation turns
out to be no alternative at all, and we are left with an unanswerable
testimony to the age of the universe. The most distant parts of
the universe are so far away that their light takes millions or
billions of years to reach us. It is hard to resist the conclusion that
they have been there for a very long time.

OTHER ASTRONOMICAL EVIDENCE

The stars in our galaxy are not just scattered about at random. Many of them occur in local groups, which astronomers call 'clusters'. Much research has gone into the study of star clusters, and this has revealed evidence that some of them are quite a bit younger than the universe itself. There are many vast clouds of gas scattered about the universe, and it appears that from time to time one of these condenses and forms a star cluster.

How do we know this? It is a long story and a detailed one, of which I can only give a brief summary here. It stems from the fact that astronomers have developed well-proven techniques for determining the temperature, the mass, the composition and the energy output of stars. These have shown that, in general,[10] the larger the star, the hotter it is, and the faster it is burning up its store of energy. These techniques have enabled astronomers to work out the life span of each particular kind of star. They have found, for example, that the hottest and brightest blue stars were endowed with only enough energy to keep them going for a few million years, whereas the coolest red stars have a life span of many billions of years.

With this background in mind, we must now take note of a most remarkable fact about the star clusters. The stars of different life expectancies are distributed among the clusters in a completely systematic way.

Some clusters contain stars of all life spans, from the shortest to the longest. Some contain all except the very shortest-lived types. Some contain all except very short-lived and fairly short-lived types. And so on, all the way to those clusters where only the long-lived types are present.

But *never* do we find a cluster without a selection of the long-lived types. The missing ones are always from the shorter end of the range. We can look at the data for each cluster and say, 'This particular cluster contains only those types of stars with life spans greater than *x* years', where *x* has a different value for each cluster.

What are astronomers to make of this? They believe that there is an obvious reason for it. Originally each cluster contained stars of every type. But now the clusters without any stars of the shorter-lived types are like that because those types of stars have already burned themselves out. Consequently, a cluster with stars of all life spans above, say, 500 million years, but *without* any of the star types having life spans *below* 500 million years, has evidently been 'using up' its short-lived stars for the past 500 million years, or thereabouts. To generalize, the figure of 'x years' in the previous paragraph is the approximate age of each cluster. Those clusters that have so far been examined by this technique appear to range from less than ten million years old to more than a billion.[11]

Since this conclusion is based upon a great mass of experimental data it seems inescapable, unless we are prepared to write off the extraordinary distribution of star types in clusters as a mere coincidence. And the odds against that have been calculated to be countless millions to one.

Exploded Stars

Every so often a star explodes. When this happens it rapidly becomes millions of times brighter than it was before, stays like that for a few weeks or months, and then fades until it is considerably fainter than it was at first. All that is left of it then is a small, dense remnant of the star, surrounded by a great cloud of expanding gas.

Most star explosions, or 'supernovae' as the astronomers call them, occur in other galaxies and so can be observed only in telescopes. Very occasionally one occurs in our own galaxy and can be seen with the naked eye. Chinese astronomers recorded such an occurrence in a particular region of the sky in AD 1054. In the place where they saw it there is now the Crab Nebula – an expanding gas cloud with a small remnant star at its centre.

Measurements of the size and expansion rate of this cloud have been made, and have enabled the date of the explosion to be calculated. The result is in good agreement with the recorded Chinese date of the supernova appearance.

Many other supernova remnants have been discovered, most of them with larger and less dense gas clouds than the Crab Nebula. Measurements on these have led to ages of thousands or tens of thousands of years, although in such cases there are obviously no historical records to check them against. One of particular interest is called the Cygnus Loop, whose size and expansion rate show that the initial explosion took place approximately 60,000 years ago.

This is very young by comparison with the estimated age of the universe, of course. But it does afford a direct measurement of age that can hardly be faulted. And it is clearly at variance with the recent-creationist claim that the heavens were created not more than about 10,000 years ago.

OCCURRENCES OF RADIOACTIVE SUBSTANCES IN NATURE

Although there are only about a hundred chemical elements in existence they all have several isotopes, which are similar chemically but differ somewhat in atomic structure. Thus there are several hundred 'species' of atoms; these are known collectively as the 'nuclides'.

A small number of nuclides can be generated naturally on the earth or the moon, either by the radioactive decay of heavier nuclides or (very rarely) by cosmic or nuclear radiation. The majority can be generated by Nature only in the conditions existing in the interior of stars. All this is known from laboratory experiments, where some of the star-interior conditions can be reproduced.

For most nuclides, therefore, we have only two possible modes of origin. Either they were created by God in some unknown way (and recent-creationists will want to add, 'a few thousand years ago'). Or, as cosmologists believe, they were formed in some cosmic process, such as the big bang itself, or, more probably, in the interior of some star that exploded before the solar system was formed with the aid of its fragments – an event that might have happened some four or five billion years ago.

Now it so happens that there is a way of deciding between these two main alternatives. This is because all radioactive substances follow the same law of decay: exactly half of the quantity of radioactive material is transformed into something else (the 'decay product') in a fixed interval of time (the 'half-life').

By way of example, consider one gram of a substance with a half-life of one year. A year later there will be only half a gram left. After another year half the remainder will have gone, leaving a quarter of a gram. After a third year we shall be down to an eighth of a gram, and so on. After ten half-lives (ten years in this example) we are always reduced to about one-thousandth of the original amount; twenty half-lives takes us down to a millionth, thirty to a billionth, and so on.

It follows that materials with short half-lives soon disappear completely – or, to be more precise, they decay to such a low concentration that we cannot possibly detect them. No matter whether the solar system is 10,000 or 5 billion years old, we should not expect to find on earth any nuclides with half-lives below, say, a hundred years (except the ones that are being generated here), and we don't.

But if the earth is only ten thousand years old we certainly should expect to find radioactive nuclides in Nature with half-lives between, say, 1,000 and 50 million years old. *But we don't* (except for the six that are naturally generated here). There are forty such nuclides that can only be made in star-interior conditions, and *every one* of them is absent from the earth's crust.

On the other hand, there are seventeen radioactive nuclides with half-lives above 80 million years – and *every one* of them does occur naturally. This is exactly what we should expect if they and the solar system are about four or five billion years old.

Stanley Freske has calculated[12] the odds against this distribution 'just happening' to occur, by pure chance. They are worse than a million billion to one. This means that the distribution of the radioactive nuclides provides a positively overwhelming argument for an ancient earth. Even a young-earth creationist has admitted that 'on this point uniformitarian theory fits the facts better than [recent-] creationist theory as currently formulated.'[13]

THE DATING OF ROCKS BY RADIOACTIVITY

Traces of radioactive substances occur in many igneous rocks, and often these can be used to determine the approximate date when the molten rock solidified. In general, radioactivity cannot be used to date sedimentary rocks directly.[14] But because igneous rocks are often found in close association with sedimentary rocks, the latter can be dated indirectly from the radiometric measurements on the igneous rocks.

The whole subject is too complex to describe here in any depth.[15] Briefly, the methods depend on measuring the extent to which some radioactive substance in the rock – the 'parent' substance – has decayed into another substance – the 'daughter'. Numerous methods are in use, including those that involve the decay of potassium-40 into argon-40; the decay of rubidium-87 into strontium-87; the decay of uranium-238 into lead-206; and the decay of thorium-232 into lead-208.

With any of these methods the geochronologist ('rock-dater') begins by measuring the amounts of parent and daughter elements in the rock. To convert these data into an estimate of age, however, he also needs to know:

(1) The half-life of the parent element, and whether this half-life has remained the same throughout the history of the rock.

(2) How much of the daughter element (if any) was present in the rock at the time it solidified.

(3) How much (if any) of either daughter or parent element has leaked out of the rock, or has found its way into the rock, since it solidified.

At first sight this seems a tall order. How can a geochronologist possibly know the answers to those questions? In fact, it is not so difficult as it sounds. To be sure, there are many circumstances where the answers cannot be obtained, and when he comes across such a case the geochronologist either turns to another method or looks for a better sample of rock. But in many circumstances he can be reasonably confident that he does know the answers.

The first question no longer poses any problem. All the necessary half-lives have been measured rather accurately in the laboratory, and our knowledge of the structure of the atom indicates that half-lives are most unlikely to vary by more than a small amount.

Moreover, radioactive atoms of various types differ enormously in their structure and the way they decay. Consequently, if some undiscovered factor had caused decay rates to change, it would be bound to have produced different changes in different types of atom. In that case, dating methods based upon different types of atom would not agree with each other. But the different methods actually give results that agree very well with each other, and this shows that half-lives cannot have changed enough to have caused major errors.

Geochronologists have their techniques for dealing with the second question, too. These vary with the method of dating concerned. The easiest to understand is that used in the potassium-argon method. Argon is a gas, and provided that the molten rock is exposed to low pressures before it solidifies, the argon is released like the gas in depressurized mineral water. The conditions where any initial 'daughter' argon can become trapped in the rock are well understood, and geochronologists only use the potassium-argon method when they are fairly sure that the answer to question (2) is, 'None'.[16] Sometimes they slip up and use the method when they should not have done; but their mistake usually soon reveals itself by results that do not agree with each other or with other data.

In each of the other methods there is generally a quantity of daughter element present at the start. But techniques for evaluating that quantity are available, and have been proved useful and reliable.

Geochronologists have struggled with the third question for many years. Their experience has enabled them to draw up rules for selecting rock samples, so as to avoid rocks where leakage (in or out) of parent or daughter is likely to have occurred. Having selected his sample, the geochronologist can then test it for leakage. He measures the amounts of parent and daughter in many different regions of the sample, and then plots the results on what is called an 'isochron' diagram. If there has been leakage, the points on his graph paper will be scattered about; if they lie along a straight line, this shows that leakage is most unlikely to have occurred. Once in a while the points *might* happen to form a straight line by sheer coincidence – just as you *might* drop a handful of peas on the kitchen floor, and find them ending up in a line. But it won't happen very often!

Is Radiometric Dating Reliable?

With these points in mind we can turn now to the key question: how accurate is radiometric dating? Before attempting to answer the question, perhaps it is worth mentioning that for years I happen to have made a special study of how the accuracy of scientific measurements can be estimated, and have published a book on the subject.[17]

One of the fundamentals of this subject is as follows. If a scientist wants to be really sure of his results he needs to measure the same quantity many times over. Moreover, he must employ several entirely different methods, each involving different principles and assumptions. Then, if the results given by the different methods are in close agreement, he can have great confidence in the accuracy of the measurements.

It seems to me that these requirements are adequately met in the case of radiometric dating. The various methods are so different in their nature that they can safely be used to check each other. And such excellent agreement has been obtained that good accuracy seems to be clearly indicated.

But this is not all. The Victorian geologists had already divided geological history into periods, long before radiometric dating was invented. They knew that the Precambrian rocks were the oldest, because these occurred right at the bottom of the geological column – but they did not know how old. They knew the rocks of the Cambrian Period were a bit younger – but they could not say how much younger. Then came the Ordovician Period, the Silurian Period, the Devonian Period, and so on, all the way up to the Recent. These could all be put in a relative order of age, but could not be given absolute ages in the nineteenth century.

Then along came the twentieth-century geochronologists with their radiometric methods, to provide the missing figures. And the agreement between these new *absolute* ages and the previously established *order* of ages is quite striking. Such agreement is either the result of another fantastic coincidence, or else the radiometric dates are at least in the right order.

Unless . . . unless the modern geochronologists cooked their results, like so many cheating schoolboys, to *make* them agree with the earlier geological data. Some recent-creationists are so worried about the facts that they actually have hinted this might be so. But that would imply a large-scale conspiracy by thousands of scientists, and, knowing how individualistic scientists are, I find such a suggestion ludicrous. My own experience, based on a working lifetime in research laboratories, is that some scientists do cheat – but not many. When the occasional piece of scientific dishonesty comes to light, sensation-hunting journalists (and some axe-grinding creationists) make far more of it than the facts warrant.

And what Christian, mindful of his Master's warning, 'Judge not, that ye be not judged', would want to accuse scientists of wholesale deceit, anyway?

The Recent-Creationist Objections

Recent-creationists respond to this massive pile of evidence by criticizing all three of the assumptions noted above. But when examined carefully their criticisms are seen to be superficial. Here are a few examples.

In his monograph, *Critique of Radiometric Dating*, Harold Slusher attacks the first assumption, that half-lives do not vary significantly.[18] He quotes a non-creationist, H. C. Dudley, as stating in a book that the belief 'that radioactive decay rates are constant' is an 'erroneous conclusion'.

This seems powerful stuff. However, if you read on, through a highly technical discussion of Dudley's views, you find just two examples of varying decay rates reported by Dudley. One varied by 0·1 per cent, the other by 3·6 per cent.

Slusher avoids mentioning what those figures imply. An increase in decay rate of 0·1 per cent would bring a measured age of one billion years down to 999 millions; 3·6 per cent would reduce it to about 965 million years. One wonders why Slusher bothered to spend four pages discussing Dudley's ideas.

So did Dudley. When it was pointed out to him what use had been made of his book he clarified his own position by stating:

> Since laboratory findings indicate that the maximum observed alterations of *any* decay rate, *to date* is approximately 10 per cent, usually less, the figure of 4·5 billion years for the earth's age seems to be a good ball park figure.[19] (His italics. 'Ball park figure' is scientists' slang for 'approximation'.)

Neither Slusher nor, so far as I am aware, any other recent-creationist writer points out that, to bring a figure of a billion years down to ten thousand years, decay rates would have to be speeded up a *hundred thousand* times. Still less do they mention that such an increase would have released energy a hundred thousand times as fast, thus turning the planet into a molten inferno![20]

When Radiometric Dating Goes Wrong

Geochronologists are well aware that radiometric dating is not infallible. This is because the second and third assumptions (known initial conditions; no leakage in or out) can sometimes be invalidated. Geochronologists are naturally keen to avoid these problems, so as to ensure accuracy. A great deal is already known about the possible causes of error and how to avoid them, and progress in this area continues. Research workers frequently publish papers showing how false data can be obtained, and what precautions must be taken to prevent this.

Two consequences follow from these publications. The first is that geochronologists are constantly learning how to avoid errors, and the value of radiometric dating is increasing all the time. The second is that recent-creationists take this literature and misuse it woefully.

For example, a group of geochronologists warned:

> Processes of rock alteration may render a volcanic rock useless for potassium-argon dating . . . We have analyzed several devitrified glasses of known age, and all have yielded ages that are too young. Some gave virtually zero ages . . .[21]

The point they were making was simple: wise geochronologists don't attempt to date 'devitrified glass' rocks. But Dr Henry Morris and his associates made a different point. They used the above quotation as alleged support for their contention that 'potassium-argon dates are meaningless in so far as *true* ages are concerned.'[22] (Their italics.)

In the same context Morris quotes the famous case of lava which was erupted on to the seabed near Hawaii in 1801, but which gave potassium-argon dates of millions of years. Geochronologists learnt from this case what can and can't be done with seabed rocks. But Morris drew the false conclusion that potassium-argon dating is useless.

One of the scientists whose work was thus abused by various recent-creationist writers was Prof. John J. Naughton of the University of Hawaii. To put the record straight he wrote:

These articles . . . point out instances (ultrabasics and basalts erupted in the very deep ocean) where it is unsuitable to apply the potassium-argon method. To say that because the potassium-argon method should not be applied to such rocks, therefore it should not be applied to *any* rocks, is as logical as saying that because some plants cannot be used for human food, therefore all plants should not be used for this purpose . . . We have continued to use potassium-argon dating in our researches out here with caution, but without any hesitation as to its reliability when properly used.[23] (His italics.)

One last example. A lengthy and interesting paper on rubidium-strontium dating quotes twenty cases where flows of molten rock picked up pieces of older rock and incorporated them in the mass without completely melting them.[24] In each of these instances a sample cut from one of the incorporated rocks gave the age of this older rock, not the age of the lava flow.

My reading of this paper is that here we have another caution. Inclusions of older rock in lava flow must be watched for, or we might conceivably find ourselves accidentally dating an older rock than the one we really are interested in.

Not so with recent-creationist writer, Dr A. J. Monty White, however. In a one-page article entitled 'Rubidium-Strontium Dating'[25] he produces the data table from this paper and introduces it with the terse and misleading comment:

Does this method of dating work? The answer is No. A paper

published in *Science* in 1976 showed how useless this method of dating really is.

To some extent he atones for that incorrect statement by admitting a little later that:

The authors of the paper explain the errors(!) as being due to varying degrees of inheritance of source area radiometric age characteristics for material which has been transported by plutonic or volcanic processes.

But it is doubtful whether any of his recent-creationist readers will grasp the significance of that second statement. All they will remember is that stark simplicity of White's earlier conclusion – which is not at all what the data indicate.

An Unanswered Case

The examples I have quoted are fairly typical of recent-creationist objections to radiometric dating. Rather like debating points, they appear to be serious objections at first glance, but on further scrutiny they are seen to be of little weight. They do not really deal with the powerful evidence in favour of radiometric dating, but merely obscure the issue. When the smokescreen is blown away the case for radiometric dating remains in all its strength.

This does not mean that the ages quoted by geochronologists are necessarily as accurate as some enthusiasts assert. There is always the possibility that future discoveries will mean that the accepted ages will have to be adjusted somewhat. But there is a great weight of evidence that they are not very wide of the mark, and the idea that they all will have to be divided by about a hundred thousand is clearly absurd.

It is hard to disagree with Dr Davis Young, who is a creationist as well as a highly respected professor of geology, when he says of recent-creationist attacks on radiometric dating:

No geochronologists will ever take seriously such arguments. It is hoped that Christian lay people will not take them seriously either, for they are poor arguments.[26]

GLORY TO GOD IN THE HIGHEST

The religious implications of all this are profound. Modern science has given us a new vision of the universe – breathtakingly old, breathtakingly vast. Knowing this, Biblical passages like these can fill us with awe:

> When I look at thy heavens, the work of thy fingers, the moon and the stars which thou hast established . . . O LORD our Lord, how majestic is thy name in all the earth! (Psalm 8.4, 9.)
>
> From everlasting to everlasting thou art God . . . For a thousand years in thy sight are but as yesterday when it is past, or as a watch in the night. (Psalm 90.2, 4.)

It seems a shame to try to cut the ancient, colossal universe down in size, merely to suit one's own preconceptions about creation. Surely it is better to say: Mighty art thou, O Creation – and mightier still is thy Creator!

CHAPTER 8

'Flood Geology' and Related Fallacies

No human investigation can be called real science if it cannot be demonstrated mathematically. Leonardo da Vinci.[1]

We saw in chapter 5 that 'Flood geology', the notion that the make-up of the earth's crust is due to Noah's Flood, was a seventeenth-century idea which was dropped in the late eighteenth and early nineteenth centuries because it didn't make sense. After another 150 years of scientific discovery, it makes even less sense today. Why, then, have recent-creationists taken up such an indefensible position?

Presumably because, just as falling mountaineers will grab at an icicle, they feel that any explanation of the geological evidence is better than none at all. For their only alternative escape-route is even worse, as we shall now see.

GOSSE AGAIN

As chapter 5 mentioned, the only intellectual in the mid-nineteenth century to attempt a logical defence of recent-creationism was Philip Gosse. 'The earth is not really old,' he said, in effect. 'It just looks old, because God made it so. He even created fossils to deceive unbelieving geologists.'

Gosse received little support. The idea that God set out to deceive people was repulsive to most nineteenth-century believers. To their credit, most of today's recent-creationists also reject it, as these quotations show:

> True creation *necessarily* involves creation of an 'appearance of age' . . . We insist as emphatically as we know how that the doctrine of creation of apparent age does not in the remotest degree involve a divine deception, but is rather inherent in the very nature of creation.[2] (Henry Morris – his italics.)

> We may be assured that God did *not* create a world filled with unmistakable and essentially unnecessary testimonies to a previous history simply for the purpose of deceiving man! . . .

Creation with appearance of age is not deceptive, but glorious.[3]
(John Whitcomb – his italics.)

It seems as if we are, for once, all agreed. Our God is not a deceiver. When he created the heavens and the earth there were certain things that simply had to have an appearance of age. A newly-created man or woman is bound to look as if they had lived at least sixteen years. A sizeable oak tree on the day of its creation would have to look as if it were a hundred years old, or thereabouts. And so on.

It is a matter of logical *necessity*. As Morris put it, 'creation *necessarily* involves creation of an appearance of age.' The converse of this is, in Whitcomb's words, 'God did not create a world filled with . . . *unnecessary* testimonies to a previous history.' God does not go out of his way to deceive. He only does that which, in the nature of things, is *necessary*.

Fossils did not meet Whitcomb's and Morris's requirement of being necessary. To have created such things would evidently have been an act of deceit. Therefore, says everybody, Gosse was wrong: God did not create fossils. (Nor, says nearly everybody, did God allow the devil to create them, because God is the one and only Creator.)

This leaves recent-creationists with no alternative. Only one possible explanation of the origin of fossils is open to them: they are forced to believe that fossils are the remains of living things that perished in the Flood. Whatever its weaknesses, they must cling to 'Flood geology' like grim death – otherwise, they would have to drop the whole idea of a young earth.

Letting Gosse in the Back Door

In practice, recent-creationists find it difficult to do without Gosse's theory. Having slammed the front door in his face with their firm declaration that God does not deceive, they are under great temptation to let Gosse in through the back door.

Take the point made in the previous chapter, about the absence in nature of a great many radioactive substances with half-lives of less than fifty-million years. I showed how this must mean either that the solar system is billions of years old, or that a fantastically improbable coincidence has occurred. Some recent-creationists would say, 'Not so. There is a third alternative: God created the earth that way, to give it an appearance of age.'

But that won't do. There is no question of *necessity* here. Most

Christians find it impossible to believe that God deliberately left out all those short-lived substances at the Creation, merely to make the world look far older than it is. That surely would have been an act of deceit. Slapping fancy names on the situation, like 'appearance of age', or 'mature creation', does not turn deceit into non-deceit.

Similarly with the expanding gas clouds in chapter 7, which look precisely like the remains of supernovae that exploded tens of thousands of years ago. And those star clusters that lack all the short-lived varieties of stars. Are these things what they appear to be? Or did God create them specially to give astronomers the false impression that the universe is old? Surely not.

Recent-creationists sometimes argue thus: 'But Christ at Cana miraculously created some excellent wine (John 2.1–10), which must have looked and tasted mature. So why should not God have created a mature universe?' But this is most misleading, because the apparent maturity of that wine was *unavoidable*. There could be no parallel with what we are considering here unless Christ had created some *unnecessary* appearance of age – such as a spurious label from a Galilean wine merchant, with a vintage year written on it.

There is also a serious problem for recent-creationists who believe that God has put an 'appearance of age' on some aspects of creation but not others. They themselves spend much time in trying to find scientific evidences of a youthful creation. Why should these exist, if God has tried to make a young earth look old? As John Byrt has put it:

> A serious source of perplexity is that *if* God did in fact build an apparent age into the whole creation, one would expect that he would do it *consistently*. One would not expect evidences of youth to pop up here and there, as if God had forgotten to 'artificially age' these few aspects of his work.[4] (His italics.)

In particular, 'Flood geology' can be sustained only by falling back on Gosse whenever a problem arises. In chapter 5, for instance, we noted the seven-mile-thick layers of fossil-bearing sediments around the mouths of great rivers. Are these what they look like, deposits that those rivers have built up during millions of years? Or did the Flood, by some amazing coincidences, just happen to dump them in these places?

Some 'Flood geologists' are sorely tempted to say there is a third possibility: that God deliberately caused the Flood to do this. But such a Gossism is out of bounds. The leaders of the 'Flood geology' movement insist that God is not a deceiver – that he would not miraculously direct the Flood to produce misleading results.

We shall see more examples of this problem when we come to consider 'Flood geology' in more detail. But first it is necessary to look at two important geological questions where recent-creationists are not wholly correct.

DO GEOLOGISTS REASON IN A CIRCLE?

Geologists in the nineteenth century gave names to the various layers of sedimentary rock, and arranged them in order of age. This was not too difficult, because the oldest strata naturally occur at the bottom and the youngest on top. The only exceptions to this rule occur where some upheaval in the earth has changed the natural order, and it is nearly always evident when this has happened.

A complete list of all these layers is called 'the geologic column', and it is as fundamental to geology as the multiplication table is to arithmetic. Recent-creationists are fond of pointing out that there is nowhere in the earth's crust where a complete geological column can be seen, but it has to be built up from sections of it. For example, Morris and Parker say:

> There is only one place in all the world to see the standard geologic column. *That's in the textbook!* . . . The standard column has been built up by superposition of local columns from many different localities.[5] (Their italics.)

Despite the recent-creationist suspicions of the procedure, there is nothing illogical or unscientific about it. In one place we find layers ABCDEFG; in another, DEFGHIJ; in another, GHIJKLMN – and so on. There are so many of these fragmentary columns, and so much overlap between them, that it is quite easy to build up the complete column from A to Z (or from Archaeozoic and Proterozoic to Pleistocene and Recent, if you want to be technical).

The reasons why we never find a complete column are simple: more often than not, a layer of rock that is deposited during one period gets eroded away during a later period. The rocks we see today are the fortunate survivors. Also, sediments are mostly laid down under water; consequently, at any given location we do not expect to find sediments from those geological periods when that area was far above sea-level.

Recent-creationists are convinced that geologists are guilty of circular reasoning in building up the geologic column. They make this accusation in nearly every book they publish. This is a typical example:

> Here is obviously a powerful system of circular reasoning. Fossils are used as the only key for placing rocks in chronological order. The criterion for assigning fossils to specific places in that chronology is the assumed evolutionary progression of life; the assumed evolutionary progression is based on the fossil record so constructed. The main evidence for evolution is the assumption of evolution![6]

Professor Edgar Andrews also warns of what he calls, 'the danger of evolution relying on geology for its time, and geology relying on evolution . . . they could agree about the age of the earth and yet both be completely wrong.'[7]

But these accusations do not fit the facts, which are quite simple. William Smith, the 'father of English geology', pioneered the technique and built up the first geologic column in 1799. Evolution did not enter into the matter. Darwin then was still unborn, and Smith remained a creationist all his life. All he did was to reason, 'How do I know a Type-A stratum when I see it? By the Type-A fossils it contains. The B strata contain B-type fossils, and so on.' As the *Encyclopædia Britannica* expresses it:

> Its [palaeontology's] critical importance in geology arises from the use of fossils as time markers in stratified rocks. Near the start of the 19th century independent workers in England and in France discovered that units of sedimentary rocks can be traced over wide areas by means of distinctive fossils in each unit.
>
> . . . Some of the fossil species were found only in single beds or a few successive beds; and those ranging through somewhat greater thicknesses were seen to be replaced in higher beds by different species. Such changes seem commonplace under present concepts of evolution; *but the discoverers accepted the facts merely as a rule of thumb to aid in classifying and mapping the thick sections of sedimentary rocks.*[8] (My italics.)

Of course, any good thing can be abused. As certain writers that recent-creationists love to quote have pointed out, some misguided evolutionists have used the geologic column in an illogical way, by basing circular arguments upon it. But these are the rare exceptions and it is quite unreasonable to criticize orthodox geology because of them.

The geologic column itself was built up in a thoroughly logical way, long before the theory of evolution was invented, and many of those who contributed to its building were creationists. And there is nothing illogical or 'circular' about the way that mainstream geology uses it today.

Two Views of Uniformitarianism

The modern science of geology was born when the principle of uniformitarianism was recognised. This simply states that the same sort of geologic processes have gone on throughout the earth's geological history. Most of them are still going on, somewhere, today.

Consequently, if we want to understand how sandstone was formed in one place and shale in a nearby place, we only need to observe a river estuary. There it is easy to see how the muddy waters slow down as the estuary widens out. As the speed of flow gradually reduces, the turbulence of the water becomes less, and this makes it impossible for large particles to stay in suspension. So the coarse grains of sand settle out first, then the finer grains a little farther out to sea, and finally the fine clay.

Similarly, if we want to know how a particular kind of limestone was formed, we can go to see a coral reef where similar limestone is being formed today. And so with almost any other rock-forming process you care to name. As the cliché has it, 'The present is the key to the past.'

It goes without saying that the rates at which these processes occur must vary from time to time. In the early days of geology some uniformitarians thought that such variations would not be very great, and could therefore be ignored. They attempted to explain all past events in terms of present-day rates. Some of the other early geologists disagreed on this question of rate, though not on the actual fact of uniformitarianism, which is only commonsense.

Nowadays there is no question as to which view was right. For a long time geologists have agreed that rates of sedimentation and erosion must have varied considerably, with variations in circumstances. They have long insisted that we must also take account of occasional interruptions in these slow processes, caused by sudden major events such as giant floods, earthquakes, and volcanic eruptions. More recently they have added that even greater catastrophes, such as the fall of occasional giant meteorites, may possibly have played a part in the earth's geological history, too.

Extraordinarily, many recent-creationists seem unaware of these facts. Their view of uniformitarianism is as naïve as it is incorrect. For example, Dr D. B. Gower wrongly asserts:

> This is really the Theory of Uniformitarianism – the rate at which things are happening has been constant from the beginning.[9]

When they criticize that sort of uniformitarianism, recent-creationists are only attacking a man of straw. The real principle of uniformitarianism is so obviously sensible that it cannot be gainsaid.

Many recent-creationists are evidently aware of this, because – although they wouldn't dream of admitting it – they utilize the real principle of uniformitarianism themselves! This we shall see in what follows.

THE BASIS OF 'FLOOD GEOLOGY'

The great classic of 'Flood geology', *The Genesis Flood*,[10] is based upon a principle which has since been stated succinctly by one of its authors, Dr John Whitcomb:

> God maintains a definite *economy of miracles*. Otherwise, miracles would become commonplace and would thus lose their uniqueness and significance . . . Apart from the specific miracles mentioned in Scripture, which were necessary to begin and to terminate this period of global judgement, the Flood accomplished its work of destruction by *purely natural processes* that are capable of being studied to a certain extent in hydraulics laboratories and in local flood situations today.[11] (His italics.)

Although Whitcomb seems to be unaware of it, he is here recommending uniformitarianism. If you want to understand what the Flood must have done, don't just write it off as a miracle that we cannot possibly understand. Go and study floods occurring today, or carry out laboratory experiments on simulated floods, he advises.

The advice is excellent. The only trouble is that 'Flood geologists' have never followed it. 'Flood geology' bears all the signs of an idea that has not been properly thought through: its implications have never been carefully considered.

Let us begin with a simple example. Conglomerate is a rock that looks rather like a natural concrete. It has a matrix of sandstone or other fine-grained rock, but embedded in this are many rounded pebbles of various sizes, and even boulders. Sediments like this are brought down by rivers under extreme conditions of flood. The Institute for Creation Research textbook admits this:

> When vast region-wide blankets of conglomerate rocks are found, only region-wide floods can explain them. And such phenomena are not at all uncommon in the geologic column. The Shinarump conglomerate of the Colorado Plateau, for example, spreads over an area of 125,000 square miles.[12]

They go on to imply that Noah's Flood was responsible for this, and for all the other great concentrations of conglomerates throughout the world. But they nowhere face up to the great problems that this idea creates.

One major difficulty is that many large deposits of conglomerate lie on top of great thicknesses – often several miles – of fine-grained sedimentary rock. The great conglomerate sea cliffs near Marseilles, for instance, are hundreds of feet high and contain boulders more than a foot in diameter. What 'purely natural processes' (Whitcomb's phrase) would enable the Flood to deposit a thickness of several miles of fine-grained sediments first, and then place the boulder-laden conglomerate *on top*? Have 'Flood geologists' not heard the expression, to 'sink like a stone'?

Another problem for them is the clean, sharp line often found at the boundary between a conglomerate and an underlying sandstone. Clearly, the lower layer must already have hardened into rock when the conglomerate was dumped on top, as otherwise the stones would have sunk into it. If one Flood deposited both layers in quick succession, how could this be?

Above all, there is the fact that the boulders in conglomerates often contain fossils. How did they get there if, as 'Flood geologists' assert, fossils are the remains of creatures that died in the Flood? And these boulders are nearly always rounded, as if they had been rolled around on a river or sea bed for long periods before being dumped in their last resting place.

Of course, one can always argue that God specially created these rounded, fossil-laden boulders, and then miraculously caused the Flood to place them on top of the fine-grained deposits. But that would be to break the very rules that the leading 'Flood geologists' themselves have pronounced in the extracts quoted in this chapter: no deceit by God, and purely natural processes operating in the Flood.

MORE DIFFICULTIES OF
'FLOOD GEOLOGY'

Another problem that 'Flood geologists' have never squarely faced is the sheer volume of sedimentary rock in the earth's crust. Take just the so-called 'Phanerozoic' sedimentary rock, that is to say, the rock containing fossils, and which is therefore supposed by 'Flood geologists' to have been deposited by the Flood. This alone comes to 654 million cubic kilometres, whereas the total amount of water on earth is less than 1,400 million cubic kilometres.[13]

Try mixing water and dry soil in those proportions – or, if you don't trust the accuracy of the figures quoted above, even with double the proportion of water. The result is not just dirty water, but a rich, creamy mud, in which no fish life could possibly survive. Did Noah's ark float on water or on an earthy soup?

Now try another experiment. Borrow one of those garden fishponds where the bottom is on two different levels, to give twice the depth of water at one end as at the other. Thoroughly stir up the mud in it, and leave it to settle. Then examine the bottom of the pond. What do you find?

Where the water was twice as deep, the mud is nearly twice as thick, because there was nearly twice as much of it in suspension in the deeper water. For this reason, 'Flood geology' would lead us to expect a thick layer of sedimentary deposits at the bottom of the oceans, and a thin layer over the continents where the water was much shallower. (It only cleared the highest peaks by a mere 15 cubits – 25 feet – remember.[14])

Unfortunately for 'Flood geology', *what we actually find is the exact opposite*. The sedimentary rocks on and near the continents are in many places several miles thick, while in the deep oceans far from land they are only a small fraction of a mile thick – which is just what *orthodox* geology would lead us to expect.

Then there is the problem of the molten rock that formed the igneous intrusions. 'Flood geologists' have often spoken eloquently of the great volcanic eruptions that must have accompanied the Flood to produce these intrusions. But they never seem to have made any mathematical analysis of the consequences.

Recently, however, Robert Moore has taken the trouble to calculate the heat that would have been released within one year, if the 'Flood geologists' were right. He made it '3·65 octillion calories"[15] – which he calculated was enough to raise the temperature of the oceans by more than 2700 degrees Centigrade! Even if his result was fifty times too high, this would still have been enough to melt the pitch off the Ark and cook its precious cargo.

Strata in the Sedimentary Rocks

There is one quite astonishing example of the unwillingness of 'Flood geologists' to consider the implications of their theory. The sedimentary rocks are arranged in clearly defined layers, or strata. But floods only produce neatly stratified deposits under special circumstances, and then only in a limited total thickness.[16] Floods generate so much turbulence that they commonly mix everything up, and so deposit a gorgeous mishmash. As we saw in the previous section, 'Flood geologists' themselves have recognized this fact when discussing the origin of conglomerates.

Stratified deposits, on the other hand, are usually produced by slow, long-continued sedimentation. It is possible to see them forming slowly today, in many places where muddy rivers discharge into lakes or the sea. Consequently, the universal existence of thousands of feet of strata in the sedimentary rocks is powerful evidence that they were laid down slowly, one at a time, and not all at once by one great Flood. The response of 'Flood geologists' to this evidence is quite inadequate.

Take, for example, the standard textbook of the Institute for Creation Research[17], *Scientific Creationism*. This admits on page 112 that strata are generally quite thin: 'Each stratum may be from a fraction of an inch to several inches in thickness.' Then it goes on to claim, on page 115, that all the strata must have been laid down, one above another, during the Flood.

But it makes no attempt to explain *how* this could have happened. Nor does it pause to look at the obvious difficulties involved: it merely declares that it must have happened. In chapter 3 I quoted Hitching's criticism that Darwinists, when at a loss, use the 'Abracadabra technique'; here we see that recent-creationists are equally fond of it.

Now let us do a few sums, of the kind that recent-creationists avoid doing. We will take the average thickness of strata as 3 inches, which is really an overestimate. Consider a place where the sedimentary layer is only 20,000 feet thick. (There are some places where it is twice that thickness.) Combining these figures gives a total of 80,000 strata in a typical column of sedimentary rock.

The Flood lasted about a year, but during the first part of it the flood waters were building up, so only a portion of the year would have been available for the deposition of sediments. Let's allow 9 months, which is probably over-generous. 80,000 strata in 9 months works out at 5 minutes each.

In each 5 minutes, then, the Flood had to bring in a particular kind of sediment, distribute it fairly uniformly over a wide area – often over many tens of square miles – and deposit it on top of the previous layer. The two layers might sometimes be similar in composition, but would often be quite different. The Flood would have had to deposit the upper layer so gently that the layer deposited in the previous 5 minutes was not disturbed, so that no mixing of the two layers could occur. And it would have had to be so firmly in place at the end of the 5 minutes that the next layer could then safely descend upon it – and so on, *every 5 minutes for 9 months*.

Then there is the observation of geologists that the upper surfaces of strata often have fossil limpets or barnacles on them. This shows that those layers had time to harden into rock and attract rock-clinging shellfish before the next stratum was laid down;[18] this is hardly likely to happen in 5 minutes!

In some areas the problem would have been even more severe than I have portrayed it. The Haymond rock formation in the USA is only a portion of the sedimentary column, with other rock formations above it and below it. Yet the Haymond formation, less than a mile thick but extending over a large area, contains more than 30,000 *alternating* layers of shale and sandstone – two entirely different types of rock.[19]

Shale is made of compacted clay. As most readers will have noticed, clay consists of exceedingly fine particles which take a long time to settle in water. Turbulence keeps them in suspension, and consequently clay will only settle in quite calm water.

The 'Flood geologist' looking at the Haymond formation has a problem. How did the Flood bring in a thin layer of sand and deposit it over a large area, then bring in a thin layer of clay and allow this to settle quietly – all in a matter of minutes? And then repeat the whole performance *fifteen thousand times*?

It seems rather obvious that there is only one way in which such a series of events could possibly occur. God would have had to direct and control the whole process miraculously to achieve this result. But what of our agreed rules, that God would not use his powers to produce an effect which would mislead scientists, and that the Flood operated by Whitcomb's 'purely natural processes'?

Once more we are back at the same old dilemma. 'Flood geology' can be made to work only if we prop it up in many places with Gosse-like explanations.

Too Many Fossils

Recent-creationists are well aware that there are a great many fossils in the earth's crust. Morris and Parker, for example, state that 'the Karroo Beds in Africa contain the remains of perhaps 800 billion vertebrates.'[20] Yet they never seem to spend any time pondering the consequences if, as they assert, all these animals died in the Flood.

Robert Schadewald[21] has now carried out some of the calculations that recent-creationists have avoided. 800 billion, if spread over the entire land surface of our planet, would average 21 animals per acre. The Karroo fossils range from lizards to animals the size of cows, with the average size about that of a fox.

And that is only the fossilized animals found in one spot. By what should we multiply this figure to allow for all the other fossil deposits all over the world, and for the animals that drowned in the Flood but whose bodies putrefied instead of fossilizing? A million? A thousand? Schadewald decides to be conservative and multiplies by only a hundred, which is almost certainly far too low a figure.

But even that highly conservative estimate leads to 2100 animals per acre, which allows them each a plot the size of a hearthrug. Try feeding somebody's pet rabbit on the produce from that much ground, and see how long he survives.

That is only the beginning of the fossil problem, however. The vast majority of all fossils are shellfish. Chalk is composed almost entirely of such fossils. Many limestones also contain high proportions of fossil shellfish. To allow for other rocks which may be devoid of fossils, Schadewald estimates that on average there is at least 0·1 per cent of marine fossil material in sedimentary rock. This is undoubtedly a great underestimate, because it is known that about 20 per cent of the sedimentary rocks are chalk, limestone and similar materials.[22] We could multiply Schadewald's figure by 10 and still end up with an underestimate. From his ultra-conservative estimate Schadewald concludes:

If all the fossilized [marine] animals could be resurrected, they would cover the entire planet [land and sea] to a depth of at least 1·5 feet. What did they eat?

Schadewald may be an unbeliever, but it must be admitted that he has a point. It really does not make sense to assert that all the multitude of fossils in the earth's crust have come from a single generation of living creatures.

Coal Seams

Most recent-creationist books have a page or two on coal. They always deal with the subject in a negative manner, by showing that orthodox geology still has some unsolved problems in this area. They point out, for example, that sometimes a fossil tree trunk is found projecting through two or more coal seams, and that sometimes a coal seam will fork into two seams separated vertically by a layer of rock.

Such cases are indeed a problem for ordinary geology. But let us not exaggerate the size of the problem, as 'Flood geologists' are wont to do. Although such 'polystrate fossils' are not rare, they affect only a relatively small number – perhaps one per cent – of the world's many coal seams. They show that a small minority of coal seams must have been formed in some exceptional fashion that is not yet understood, although research into the problem continues. Large local floods may have been involved, though this is not yet proved.

The other ninety-nine percent of coal seams present no great problem to the orthodox geologist. They fit quite well the conventional explanation, of vegetation growing in a tropical swamp and then becoming deeply buried and, eventually, metamorphosed into coal.

But whilst conventional geologists cannot yet explain a few exceptional coal seams, 'Flood geologists' have a far greater problem. I have yet to see a detailed, plausible explanation of how the Flood could possibly have produced the world's store of coal. The difficulties involved are so great that the absence of an explanation is not surprising.

The first problem is, as with animal fossils, the sheer quantity existing. Well over a million million tons of coal have already been located. Nobody knows how much remains to be discovered, but one recent book puts total world reserves of coal at 15·3 million million metric tons.[23] The most pessimistic authorities would agree that there is at least 5 million million tons, if you include seams too narrow to be worth mining. That works out at 65 pounds of coal for every square yard of our planet's land surface.

Where did the vegetation come from to produce all that coal? The leading botanist Heribert Nilsson pointed out that it takes a lot of wood to produce a little coal. He wrote:

> A forest of full-grown beeches gives material only for a [coal] seam of 2 centimetres.[24]

A layer that thick would weigh about 80 pounds per square yard. At first glance it looks as if the required figure of 65 pounds is not impossible. But wait. We must take into account the following facts:

(1) Coal is not made from beech trees. The abundant fossils in coal show that it is mostly composed of the remains of large fernlike plants, which were on average a good deal smaller than beech trees and had a higher water content.

(2) Not all the earth in Noah's day would have been covered by this one kind of vegetation. Fossil plants and animals show that there always were many different kinds of habitat in the past, just as there are now.

(3) Most wood has a habit of floating, and only becomes water-logged when it has been lying in water for years. The Flood could hardly be expected to bury more than a fraction of the vegetation of Noah's day. Much of it would end up on the surface, and decompose.

When these factors are taken into account, it is evident that the Flood could not possibly have produced as much coal as there is.

Then there is what we might call the problem of mechanics. Coal seams often occur in groups, one above another, with layers of rock between. How did the Flood manage to produce these series of coal seams?

To appreciate the difficulties, imagine a group of frogmen trying to construct just such a layer cake on the seabed, while stormy currents of water surge around them. Their job is to put down a layer of woody vegetation, then a layer of mud or sand, then more vegetation, and so on. How would they achieve this?

With great difficulty, no doubt – unless they were allowed the benefit of modern technology. In that case they could use a wire cage to hold the vegetation down while they shovelled the mud on top. Without some such device the tendency of vegetation to float and wash away would defeat all their efforts.

It is hard to see how the senseless, raging waters of the Flood could have achieved such an unnatural result. Once more we have an example of the central dilemma of 'Flood geology'. Genesis portrays the Flood as *destructive*, the most destructive event in history, in fact. Yet 'Flood geologists' portray it as *constructive*, capable of creating many of the finely arranged strata in the earth's crust. Is not this almost as illogical as attributing creative powers to natural selection?

One last point about coal. The nature of the stuff is all wrong, from the 'Flood geologists'' point of view. If they were right, coal should contain plenty of fossils of modern vegetation. *But it doesn't*. Most coal was made in the Carboniferous Period from species of ferns now extinct. Such coal contains no flowering plants or trees, and none of their pollen which finds its way into practically all the more recent sediments. And radiocarbon tests on coal cut from virgin seams deep inside the earth *always* give the same result: 'Too old to give a meaningful reading.' This is so well established that radiocarbon laboratories now use coal samples to check the zero readings of their equipment.[25]

Ancient-creationists have no problem here. They accept the fossil evidence that ferns were created first and flourished during the Carboniferous ('coal-producing') Period, while flowering plants and trees were created later. But 'Flood geologists' are at a loss to explain these findings. Were there no flowering plants in Noah's day? Once more it is evident that the facts are not in accord with the theory of 'Flood geology'.

The Yellowstone Fossil Forests

In and around the Yellowstone National Park, in Wyoming, there are many square miles of fossilized forests. Petrified forests have also been found in other parts of the world, but the interesting feature of those in Yellowstone is that many of them are stacked one upon another. In one place there are as many as 44 successive forest layers in one huge stack, all buried in a kind of rock that is formed from volcanic ash. What evidently happened was this:

(1) Nearby volcanoes threw up a cloud of ash and chunks of rock, which descended on the forest and buried the trees a few feet deep. This killed the trees and eventually fossilized their lower portions, together with fallen trees and leaves on the forest floor. The tops of the trees, however, stuck up above the ash and slowly rotted away.

(2) The surface of the ash gradually weathered into soil, and a new forest grew there for a while.

(3) Then the volcano erupted again and the whole process recurred, time after time.

Because there are thousands of feet of fossil-bearing rock beneath the fossil forests, 'Flood geologists' recognize that they cannot have been formed prior to the Flood. This creates a problem for them, for there has not been nearly enough time for all those forests to grow one upon another since the Flood. The solution offered by Whitcomb and Morris[26] is that the whole formation was produced by the Flood, in the following way:

(1) First, the Flood deposited thousands of feet of sediments, complete with the living things that later became fossilized.

(2) After that, it washed up a layer of uprooted trees and left them exposed on top of the sediments, and temporarily receded.

(3) A volcano then ejected a cloud of ash, and buried these trees in it.

(4) This was followed by another great wave of water, carrying lots more floating trees. It did not wash away the freshly deposited ash, but spread out the trees on top of the ash layer as the water receded again.

(5) Then the volcano buried this second batch of trees in ash, after which the Flood surged up again with another load of trees. And so on, until many layers of alternating wood and ash had been deposited – all within a few months while the Flood was upon the earth.

Intuitively, one feels that such a suggestion is unconvincing. Such co-ordinated behaviour by the Flood and the volcano could not have occurred by mere chance. Only a miraculous operation, of the Gosse kind, could have achieved such a result. But let us see what a leading expert has to say.

Dr Richard Ritland is a palaeontologist who has done a great deal of field research on these fossil forests. He also happens to have long-standing connections with the Seventh-Day Adventists – the church that originally fostered the twentieth-century revival of 'Flood geology'. His theological background might therefore be expected to incline him to agree with the above explanation. But he does not. His field work has led him to state:

The transport theory for the origin of the fossil forests of the region as suggested by Whitcomb and Morris is not in harmony with the facts.[27]

The reasons for this conclusion are given in detail in a paper by himself and Stephen Ritland.[28] To quote just a few of them:

(1) Floods carrying trees create 'log-jams', with a tangled mass of tree trunks pointing in all directions. But the Yellowstone petrified forests are not at all like this. The majority of the fossil trunks are upright, in positions of growth, and most of the rest are horizontal, like trees that have fallen on a forest floor.

(2) The spacing of the upright trunks is generally similar to that of trees in living forests.

(3) Some of the layers contain trees of all ages, while others contain only young trees, thus representing forests that had not been growing very long when they were buried.

(4) The fossil leaves on the forest floor are not flattened like leaves that have been buried when wet, but have the surface profile of leaves that were buried in a dry condition.

(5) There are no widespread silt deposits as would be expected in any major flood.

Recently another Christian geologist, Dr William Fritz, has made a detailed study of these forests, with the 'Flood geologists' ' theory in mind. He found nothing to support such an idea, though he did find evidence that some of the upright stumps had slid down the mountainside into their final positions. Nevertheless, he concluded:

> Even though I believe transportation of upright stumps to have occurred, I argue that *many were preserved in place*.[29] (My italics.)

Thus the Yellowstone fossil forests remain what they have always been: a unique natural formation bearing evidence of many thousands of years' history. 'Flood geology' cannot possibly explain it without falling back on either an unbelievable series of coincidences, or a miracle designed to produce an entirely unnatural result.

WHY DO FOSSILS OF A FEATHER FLOCK TOGETHER?

We noted earlier that fossils of any particular kind tend to occur at one particular level in the geological column, which is why the various rock levels, or 'systems' as geologists call them, can be identified by their fossils.

Thus near the bottom of the column we find the very ancient Cambrian layer, where the animal fossils are all invertebrates (creatures without backbones). Higher up is the Carboniferous, characterized by the coal-forming ferns and by amphibians. Later comes the Jurassic, where the dinosaurs ruled; and higher still the Tertiary, with its numerous mammals.

All this points towards a series of geological 'periods': an early age of invertebrates, with a later age of amphibians, later still an age of dinosaurs, and then an age of mammals. (This is in fact a great oversimplification, because there are many more distinct periods than those four.)

'Flood geologists', of course, reject this interpretation, and say that all these fossils are of living things that died in the Flood. This leaves them with the problem of explaining how the fossils come to be arranged in such well-defined zones. How do they do it? So far as I have been able to discover they have offered only three possible explanations, none of which sounds likely.

The first might be described as the Theory of Hydraulic Sorting. If you put a handful of gravel, a handful of sand and a handful of clay in a bucket of water and stir it, a layer of gravel will settle out first, then the sand, and lastly the clay. But there will not be a clearcut division between adjacent layers; there will be quite a bit of overlap, in contrast to some of the fossil layers in the rocks, which have a sharp cut-off. Passing over this minor difficulty we soon come to a major one.

The theory proposes that the Flood swept up all the creatures that were fossilized, and allowed them to settle. The larger and denser bodies dropped to the bottom first, the smaller and less dense ones last.

It is an ingenious theory but it is in conflict with the facts. Many trilobites, for instance, are small and of low density;[30] yet they are found only at the bottom of the geological column. And they are found at exactly the same level as much larger trilobites, instead of being sorted according to size. Then there are nautiloids and ammonoids, whose beautiful spiral fossils are abundant on the cliffs at Lyme Regis in Dorset; their shells contain buoyancy chambers, and are therefore very light – yet they are never found in the upper levels. And ammonoid specimens ranging in size from a fraction of an inch to several feet across are all found together in the same deposit.[31]

On the other hand, turtles, which are both large and dense, are only found in the middle and upper layers of rock, never in the lower ones. The Hydraulic Sorting Theory is clearly a non-starter.

Next, there is what I shall call the Theory of Differential Mobility. This holds that the most mobile creatures fled to the high ground and were the last to be drowned, while the least mobile stayed where they were and so were the first to perish. Hence you find shellfish in the lowest layers; the sluggish dinosaurs were only able to make the foothills, and so are concentrated in the middle layers; and nimble human beings all fled to the mountain tops.

This sounds fine, until you stop to think. Then you begin to wonder: why is there not a single human fossil below the topmost layer? Were there no inhabitants of the coastal plains overwhelmed in their sleep? No cripples or sick folk unable to flee? And why are the pterodactyl fossils all in the middle layers? You would think that at least one or two of them would have flapped their way to the hilltops. Then there is the little problem of vegetable fossils. As R. J. Schadewald has put it:

A scenario with magnolias (a primitive plant) heading for the hills, only to be overwhelmed along with early mammals, is unconvincing. And when marine fossils are found in many places above those of land animals and plants, [this theory] loses all credibility, too.[32]

'Flood Geology's' Favourite Theory

Finally, there is the Theory of Ecological Zoning, which seems to be the one on which 'Flood geologists' currently pin their hopes. The basic idea is that the Flood deposited marine creatures at the bottom of the geological column because originally they lived in the lowest places. Creatures from the seashore would naturally come next, then those from lowland regions, and so on. In 1982, Morris and Parker spoke of the Theory like this:

According to creationists, the geological systems represent different ecological zones, the buried remains of plants and animals that once lived together in the same environment. A walk through Grand Canyon, then, is not like a walk through evolutionary time; instead, it's like a walk from the bottom of the ocean, across the tidal zone, over the shore, across the lowlands, and on into the upland regions.[33]

This also looks plausible – as long as you don't take the trouble to think about it. After a moment's thought, a huge difficulty is apparent. Morris and Parker's walk from the bottom of the ocean to the upland regions would typically cover at least a hundred miles, *horizontally*. In the wall of the Grand Canyon, however, those various ecological zones are compressed into one mile, *vertically*. How did they get there?

Orthodox geology has no problem. Hundreds of millions of years ago the site of the Canyon was under water. Later, the sea evidently receded and the region became a coastal zone, while later still the land rose higher and the Rockies were formed.

But 'Flood geologists' have not yet published any details of their Ecological Zoning Theory. How did the Flood manage to transport all those marine creatures more than four hundred miles, and spread them neatly over a great area of Arizona? And, after that, to transport layers of inter-tidal life, and life from the coastal plains, some three to four hundred miles and place them in successive layers? And then top off with layers of living things from the uplands – and all without scrambling the various layers?

When the mind has finished boggling at that thought, it is time to contemplate that the Grand Canyon is by no means the only place to present this problem. Oil company borings have revealed hundreds of sites all over the world where the same sort of vertical zoning occurs. They are found in the mountains, in the plains, and far out at sea in the offshore oil-fields. Over a large part of the earth's surface, if the Ecological Zoning Theory is correct, the Flood scooped up hundred-mile tracts of surface complete with their inhabitants, and then neatly arranged them into one-mile deep stacks – and in the right sequence, and without intermingling.

If any 'Flood geologists' know how the Flood could have achieved this, by Whitcomb's 'purely natural processes', then they should speak out. Until they do, the rest of us must be forgiven for thinking that there is only one way it could have happened in Noah's time: for God to have worked a whole series of mighty miracles beneath the waters of the Flood.

Even if the Flood could have achieved such a remarkable result in one place, it could not possibly have done so all over the world. The average thickness of fossil-bearing rock throughout the world is about a mile. Yet the precious layer of soil in and on which all life must live (except for swimming fishes and floating plants) is never more than a few feet thick. Did the Flood pick up that thin layer and with it produce sedimentary rock *one mile* thick? Because, if so, God must have multiplied that precious layer, and its quota of once-living things, like the loaves and fishes of Galilee!

Which brings us back, inexorably, to our earlier conclusion. The Flood cannot possibly have left the earth's crust the way it is – not unless God worked great miracles to produce an unnatural effect, thus leading geologists along a false trail. In other words, if the 'Flood geologists' are right, then Gosse's 'deceit theory' must have been true after all.

But if, as the 'Flood geologists' themselves assert, Gosse was wrong and our God does not deceive people, then 'Flood geology' is nothing more than a lovely pipe-dream.

They can't have it both ways.

CHAPTER 9

Some Young-Earth Arguments Examined

*The first to present his case seems right, till another comes forward
and questions him.* King Solomon.[1]

In chapters 6 and 7 we looked at some of the evidence that points
to a great age for the earth. In this chapter we shall look at the
recent-creationists' response.

While preparing the material for this book I examined a great
many of the arguments for a young earth that are scattered through
the recent-creationist literature. Some of them seemed quite
impressive at first glance, but on closer acquaintance they could be
seen to be unconvincing.

There is not room in this one chapter to look at them all, but I
shall give a representative selection. It includes those arguments
which recent-creationists seem to use most often, and so are
presumably what they regard as their strongest points.

SOME UNWISE EXTRAPOLATIONS

Many recent-creationist arguments are based upon what scientists
call 'extrapolations'. To make an extrapolation you measure a trend
over a period of time, and then assume that the trend will continue
into the future, or that you can project it back into the past.

The growth of human population is a good example. For some
years now the world's population has been increasing at a rate of
about 2 per cent a year. It is fairly safe to assume it will go on doing
so for the next few years. If you want to know how much greater
it will be in 5 years' time, a calculator will soon tell you the answer:
about 10·5 per cent more than today. This is likely to be a fairly
accurate prediction.

But if you want to know what the population will be in 350
years' time, that's another matter. This time the calculator says
that 2 per cent a year for 350 years will increase the earth's
population by a thousand times! This is obviously wrong: the earth
could not possibly support anything like that number of people.

The first extrapolation, over 5 years, was sensible and gave a believable answer. The second, over 350 years, was foolish and gave a ridiculous answer.

This illustrates the No. 1 rule of extrapolating data: short extrapolations are generally fairly safe and can be useful; but long extrapolations are fraught with danger, and should generally be avoided, except in special cases where there is good reason to think a long extrapolation is justified. (Radioactive decay is the best-known exception, because we know that atoms decay in a highly predictable way.)

Scientists generally learn this rule in their first year at college and forever after stick by it. But sometimes recent-creationists break the rule, by making enormously long extrapolations without any justification – and basing obviously unsound conclusions upon them.

In the Institute for Creation Research textbook for schools, it is argued that the rate of population increase proves the world to be young.[2] The writers of this book spend two pages showing that a growth rate of one half per cent per year could have led to the present world population in only 4,000 years. Their argument assumes that the half per cent rate can be extrapolated all the way back to Noah – a splendid example of the wrong way to extrapolate a trend.

To see how mistaken this argument is, one only has to calculate from the textbook's growth rate what its estimate of the population would have been in the time of Christ, that is after 2,100 years. The answer obtained is well under a quarter of a million for the whole world, whereas historians know that, in fact, the population of the Roman Empire alone was then many millions.

Nobody who has ever studied the population explosion would make such an unwise extrapolation. It is well known that growth rates have increased enormously in recent centuries. Population expert Paul Ehrlich gives world average yearly growth rates of 0·9 per cent between 1850 and 1930, 0·3 per cent between 1650 and 1850, and a mere 0·07 per cent in the thousand years prior to 1650.[3] And in the fourteenth century the population increase must have been very small indeed, and it may even have been turned into a big *decrease*, because of the Black Death. Ehrlich's figures are not just guesses; they are based on historical records. These facts show how misguided it is to extrapolate present population trends into the remote past.

The Earth's Magnetic Field

For reasons that are not fully understood the earth acts like a giant magnet. This is why compass needles point towards the north. Many measurements of the strength of the earth's magnetic field have been made over the past century and a half, and have shown that it is gradually growing weaker.

In 1973 the recent-creationist Dr Thomas Barnes plotted this 150 years-worth of data, and then carried out one of the most daring extrapolations in all history. He began by fitting what mathematicians call an 'exponential curve' to the plotted points. (This is a curve whose value doubles every so often, at a fixed interval – every 1400 years in the case of Barnes' curve.) Then, with breathtaking courage, he extrapolated his short curve all the way to 20,000 BC. At that date his curve indicated an impossibly high value of field strength, and so he concluded triumphantly:

> It is not very plausible that the core of the earth could have stayed together with the Joule heat that would have been associated with the currents producing such a strong field . . . (Hence) the origin of the earth's magnetic moment is much less than 20,000 years ago.[4]

Barnes' long extrapolation is not merely risky. It is totally unacceptable, on two separate counts. He did not actually publish the graph on which it is based, but this has since been published by Brush,[5] and is reproduced here as Figure 3. The solid line shows the exponential curve that Barnes fitted to the points, whilst the dotted line is a straight line fitted to the same points by Brush. It is immediately obvious that there is no justification for fitting an exponential curve. The straight line is the only one that any unbiased experimenter would think of fitting to such a scattered set of data points.

Does the difference matter, anyway? Indeed it does. Because the exponential goes on gently curving, it reaches Barnes' 'impossibly high value' at only 20,000 BC.; but the straight line takes more than *a hundred million years* to reach the same value.

The second reason for rejecting Barnes' extrapolation is even more powerful. We *know* that the magnetic field has not been getting weaker and weaker throughout the earth's history. It has reversed itself many times: it has grown weaker for a while, then stronger, then weaker again, and so on.

How do we know? Because some molten rocks carry magnetic particles which act like miniature compass needles. When the rock

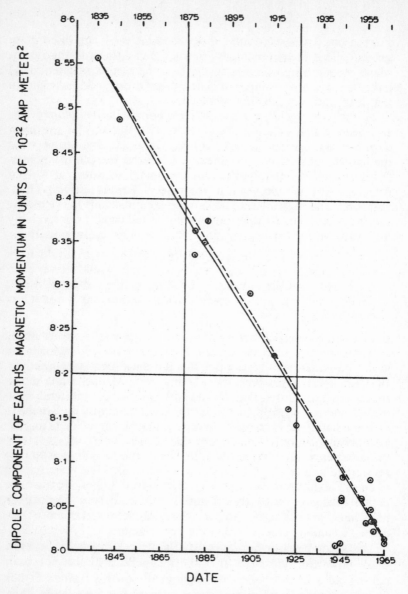

Figure 3. How the earth's magnetic field has changed over the years – curves fitted by Barnes (solid line) and Brush (dotted line).

solidifies these particles are frozen in position, like compasses whose bearings have seized.

The evidence for this was conclusive even before Barnes did his lengthy extrapolation.[6] Since then a great deal of confirmatory evidence has been obtained, including archaeological work on bricks and pottery, which also contain 'frozen' evidence of the nature of the earth's magnetism in the past.[7]

Barnes, writing in 1973, rejected this evidence. He cited as his justification a book written in 1962 by J. A. Jacobs, an authority who, at that early date, was still sceptical of the evidence for geomagnetic reversals. It seems that Barnes has not kept up with developments, because when he published another paper on the earth's magnetic field in 1981[8] he again cited Jacobs' book – despite the fact that Jacobs had long since changed his position, and had said so in the 1975 edition of his book.

The truth about Barnes' extrapolation has now been pointed out by many writers and lecturers. Yet as recently as 1982 we still find Morris and Parker citing it as 'evidence' that the earth is 10,000 years old.[9]

The Velocity of Light

Intelligent, educated Christians who have not studied science can be easily misled by recent-creationist literature. A bank manager recently said to me, 'I hear that the velocity of light is changing.'

This made me gulp, because every physicist knows that the velocity of light is one of the fundamental constants of the universe. It does not change, and, as long as the laws of physics remain what they are, it cannot change. There is a great deal of evidence for this, both experimental and theoretical. Even Harold Slusher, who is regarded by many recent-creationists as their top expert in this area, has declared that there is 'no evidence whatsoever' to suggest that such constants can vary with time.[10]

The cause of my banker friend's confusion was a pamphlet published in 1982 by the Creation Science Movement.[11] It contained a summary of a lengthy paper by an Australian creationist, Barry Setterfield.[12] The pamphlet reviews Setterfield's paper quite uncritically, and concludes, without any justification, 'There is, therefore, clear scientific evidence for accepting that the speed of light has decreased.'

What is this so-called 'clear evidence'? Setterfield gathered together some (by no means all) of the determinations of the velocity of light made by various scientists, and plotted them against the dates they were made. Because the velocity of light is extremely high (about 300,000 kilometres per second) it is difficult to measure without modern instrumentation. So it is not surprising that it is only during the past quarter of a century that the measured values have agreed closely with each other. Before that the figures become more and more inaccurate, the further back they go in time.

Setterfield, however, concluded that the velocity kept changing until 1960, and then stopped! He fitted a curve to the somewhat erratic data before that date, and then extrapolated it back all the way to infinity – a procedure so unscientific as to be ludicrous. The curve reaches a value of infinite velocity at a value quoted as '4,040 BC±20 years', which the pamphlet calls 'the time of Creation/Fall'.

The full Setterfield paper is dressed with a great deal of theoretical analysis. Lest any reader should be overly impressed by this analysis perhaps I should mention that I asked two professors of modern physics to look at it. One said it was unsound, self-contradictory, and based on an antiquated and incorrect concept of the atom.[13] The other used even stronger language.

The incredible nature of Setterfield's extrapolation can be seen from Figure 4, where I have reproduced his graph and shown how much (or rather, how little) of it is based upon data of any sort.

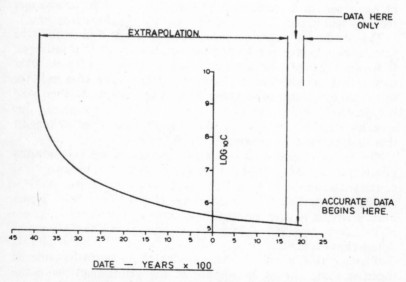

Figure 4. Setterfield's extrapolation of the velocity of light.

And only about one-tenth of even that tiny portion is based upon modern, accurate data.

Although Setterfield's data span three centuries, the first two centuries (1675-1870) are represented by only two measurements, made by Roemer in 1675 and by Bradley in 1728. Setterfield's conclusions largely depend upon the high values he attributes to these early workers (Roemer 301,300; Bradley 301,000 kilometres per second), as all results obtained after 1871 are below 300,000. *But the figures in his table are incorrect.* The true values are given in numerous scientific books and papers, and in the article, 'Light, Velocity of' in the 1973 edition of *Encyclopaedia Britannica*. They are: Roemer, 214,300; Bradley 295,000. If Setterfield had used these correct values he might have written an equally plausible paper arguing that the velocity of light has been *increasing* with time!

Finally, it must be said that Setterfield's graph is not correct, even in the very small area where there are some reliable figures. The authoritative paper on how the 'generally accepted' value of the velocity of light has changed between 1927 and 1975 was produced by the Particle Data Group of the American Physical Society.[14] (The 'generally accepted' value at a given date is the value that experts at the time regarded as the best available, taking into account *all* the data produced up to that time. It is therefore much more reliable than the result of a measurement by any one experimenter.)

This committee of thirteen leading experts showed that the value did not decrease steadily between 1927 and 1960, as Setterfield had mistakenly thought. Instead, as shown in Figure 5, it decreased from 1927 to 1935, remained roughly constant from 1935 to 1950, then rose between 1950 and 1955 to almost the original value of 1927.

And the reason for these small changes, which amounted to less than one part in ten thousand between the largest and the smallest values? Simple. It is just a matter of 'a general progression toward better understanding' of the facts, explains this distinguished group of experts.

METEORITES AND COMETS

In his book, *Age of the Cosmos*,[15] published in 1980, Harold Slusher attempts to prove from astronomical data that the universe must be young. Once again, the result is a document that looks impressive – until you examine it carefully. On close inspection, it

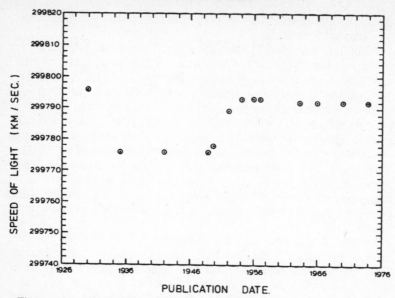

Figure 5. Accepted values for the velocity of light 1929–74; note that there is no evidence of the trend assumed by Setterfield in fig. 4.

soon becomes apparent that the arguments are no more substantial than a house of cards.

There is space here to give only a couple of examples from this book. I shall therefore choose two of Slusher's chapters that many recent-creationists regard most highly.

In the chapter entitled 'Cosmic Dust Influx', Slusher said:

Estimates of the influx of cosmic dust on Earth's surface range considerably, with different investigators (from 10,000 tons/day to 700,000 tons/day). The Swedish geophysicist, Hans Petterson, estimates 14,300,000 tons of meteoritic dust come onto the surface of the earth per year. Consequently, if Petterson's figure is used, in five billion years there should be a layer of dust approximately 54 feet to more than a 100 feet in thickness on the earth, depending on the density of matter, if it were to lie undisturbed without the various erosional agents acting on it. Using the 700,000 tons/day value, the layer should be about 965 ft. in thickness.[16]

To write like that in 1980 was inexcusable. The two sources he quotes were dated 1960 and 1967 – hopelessly out of date in a fast-changing area of science. They merely provide *estimates* of what the influx of meteoritic dust *might* possibly be.

But we no longer have to rely on estimates. A paper, published four years before Slusher's book, described how the amount of meteoritic dust in space has now been *measured*, with detectors mounted on satellites. This explained that we now know the actual amount of cosmic material falling on the earth each year:

> This value comes to 16,000 metric tonnes . . . sufficient to coat the Earth's surface with a layer of dust 4 centimetres thick during the Earth's lifetime, if the rate had remained constant.[17]

A more recent article refers to several other methods of measuring meteoritic dust influx, some of them going back to 1968, and all pointing to a value of about 1 centimetre of depth per billion years.[18] These values agree well with the actual thickness of the dust layer on the undisturbed portions of the moon's surface. Yet Slusher fills a whole chapter with arguments based on those early estimates, and ignores the many measurements that destroy his case.

In another chapter, 'Cometary Lifetimes', he points out that comets can be seen to be slowly breaking up. This shows that comets must be young, or there would be nothing left of them. How young? Although Slusher does not say so, astronomers calculate the average lifetime to be about two thousand years.[19]

Evidently there must be a steady stream of comets entering the solar system, so as to keep up the supply. Where do they come from? Astronomers have been working on that problem for several generations, and still have not solved it. The existence of a few unsolved problems in science, of course, is not necessarily an argument for the young-earth theory. But Slusher disagrees. His chapter concludes:

> The failure to find a mechanism to resupply comets or to form new comets would seem to lead to the conclusion that the age of the comets and hence the solar system is quite young, of the order of just several thousand years at most.[20]

In other words, until somebody explains exactly where comets come from, he will assume that they don't come from anywhere! The error in his logic is obvious, especially when we remember that the average lifetime of comets – and hence, on Slusher's theory, the age of the solar system – is not 'several' but *two* thousand years.

HENRY MORRIS' 'TABLE OF AGES'

The most spectacular presentation of the case for a young earth is a table compiled by Dr Henry Morris. This was first published some years ago and has reappeared, with updatings, on several occasions since then. The version before me was published in 1982,[21] with the title 'Uniformitarian Estimates – Age of the Earth'. It begins and ends like this:

Process	Indicated Age of Earth	Reference
1. Decay of earth's magnetic field	10,000 years	1
68. Influx of molybdenum into ocean via rivers	500,000 years	20

The table lists 68 processes from which an 'indicated age of earth' is supposed to have been calculated. The ages obtained range from 'too small to measure' and '100 years' to '500,000,000 years'. A casual reader would glance at this table and draw the conclusion that Dr Morris obviously wants him to draw: that uniformitarian estimates of the age of the earth are not worth the paper they are printed on.

But a more discerning reader would reach a very different conclusion. Astonishing though this may sound, it turns out that *not one* of the 68 figures in the table is a genuine uniformitarian estimate of the age of the earth!

A note at the top of the table says it is 'based on standard assumptions of (1) initial "daughter" component; (2) closed system; (3) uniform rate.' It is true that some (though not all) uniformitarian dating methods require these three assumptions. But conventional scientists only make those assumptions when they have good reasons to believe that they are correct. In most of the cases in this table, however, we *know* that the assumptions do *not* hold. And in all the others, either there is reason to be suspicious of the assumptions, or there is clear evidence that Dr Morris has made a mistake. These facts invalidate the whole table.

To be more specific, twenty-nine of the values in the table are drawn from earlier recent-creationist literature. They include three that I have already dealt with in this chapter: Thomas Barnes' figure derived from the change in the earth's magnetic field, and Harold Slusher's figures based on cosmic dust and the break-up of comets. Given enough space, it would not be difficult to point out the fallacies in the other twenty-six.

That leaves thirty-nine cases which are drawn from the conventional scientific literature. The reader who takes the trouble to track all these back to their sources makes an enlightening discovery: Dr Morris has misapplied or misunderstood *every one* of his sources!

The simplest example is his No. 29, 'Decay of natural plutonium', which he says leads to an age for the earth of 80,000,000 years. Reference to the original paper[22] shows that this does indeed quote such a figure – but not as the age of the earth. It quotes this value as *the half-life of plutonium*, which has little connection with the earth's age.

The last twenty-seven values in Morris' table all come from one source, an authoritative book on oceanography.[23] Morris' table says these values are based upon the rate of influx of twenty-seven different chemical elements to the ocean through rivers. Morris' twenty-seven 'indicated ages of earth' range from 100 years in the case of aluminium to 270,000,000 years in the case of strontium. This seems an odd set of conclusions to extract from a reputable book on oceanography.

One look at the book which he quotes is enough to show what is wrong: Dr Morris has seriously misinterpreted the data. The figures that he reproduces all come from a column in a table headed 'Residence Times' – and residence times have nothing to do with the age of the earth.

To appreciate what a residence time is, consider the hot water tank in your house. Suppose that it holds sixty gallons, and that you use thirty gallons of hot water a day. Then the residence time is given by the formula:

$$60 \text{ gallons} \div 30 \text{ gallons a day} = 2 \text{ days.}$$

This is, of course, the average time the water 'resides' in the tank before leaving it. It would be most surprising to meet someone who argued that 2 days was therefore the 'indicated age' of your house. And it is no less surprising to find Dr Morris quoting residence times of various chemical elements in the ocean as 'indicated ages' of the earth. If only he had studied the text of the book he was using he would have found the following simple definition of residence time, which might have saved him from such a woeful misunderstanding:

The residence time of an element can then be defined as the

average time which it remains in the sea water before removal by some precipitation process.[24]

There is nothing in Dr Morris' whole table that contradicts, or even casts doubt upon, the accepted methods of dating the earth or the universe. It merely serves to show the unreliability of what his book's title calls 'creation science'.

'MIOCENE MAN' AND HIS COLLEAGUES

A favourite argument for the idea of a young earth runs like this: 'You palaeontologists agree with us that *Homo sapiens* has been around for much less than a million years. Now, we can show you fossil human footprints, and even fossil human skeletons, in geological systems that you have dated at tens of millions, or hundreds of millions of years old. This shows that your geological dating is all wrong. The earth is no older than man!'

To quote a recent example, in 1983 the Creation Science Movement published a pamphlet called *Miocene Man*.[25] In its opening paragraph this accused evolutionists of 'the deliberate concealment of evidence'. It went on:

What is omitted, however, is a vast body of evidence from the fossil-record which shows that man was around millions of years before his proposed evolutionary ancestors (that is if we accept the conventional geologic timescales).

One example of this omission of evidence is found in a human skeleton that lies to this day in the basement of the British Museum of Natural History. This skeleton was dug out of the Lower Miocene deposits of Grande Terre, part of the Caribbean island of Guadeloupe . . . During the early nineteenth century, it was displayed to the public as a curiosity, namely for being the only example of fossil-man to be found embedded in a limestone mass. However, once Darwinism gained a foothold in academic circles, it seems that the specimen was quietly removed from public display. I am given to understand, in fact, that I was the first member of the public to set eyes on it since the early 1930s.

This seems like a damning indictment of orthodox geology, which says that the Lower Miocene rocks were laid down about twenty million years ago. But there are two sides to every story, and Dr Chris Stringer of the British Museum was quick to publish a note containing some sobering facts.[26] He wrote:

In a recent paper, Cooper (1983) has claimed that a human

skeleton in our collections, from the island of Guadeloupe, is of Miocene age . . . As I was the scientist who gave Mr Cooper free access to this and other specimens, I would like to point out that there has never been any restriction placed on the specimen and it has been examined by other workers from time to time. It has been mentioned in recent publications (e.g. Oakley 1972, p.70; Reader 1981, p. 20), and was actually on display to the public in the Central Hall of this Museum during the 1960's when it was seen by many thousands of people.

He went on to explain that nobody (apart from the creationist Mr Cooper) has ever said that this piece of limestone was Miocene. On the contrary, it has been recognized since 1847 as a block of what geologists call 'beachrock'. This is an exceptional kind of limestone which often forms on tropical beaches. Under favourable conditions a layer of granulated coral on a beach can turn into limestone within a few years, so that 'fossilized' beer bottles and Coke cans are sometimes found in this kind of limestone.

Stringer pointed out that the fossil shells in the limestone block are all of modern shellfish, not of Miocene ones. In the same deposits are found remains of the dog and specimens of flint, both of which are thought to have been introduced to Guadeloupe by Europeans, within the past 500 years.

Evidently the lesson to be learnt from the tale of Miocene Man is not that conventional scientists hide unpalatable facts from the public. It is that some 'creation scientists' are capable of rushing into print on the basis of hearsay, without first checking their facts.

Three More Misunderstood Men

Then there are Castenedolo Man, Olmo Man and Calaveras Man. Recent-creationists Robert Kofahl and Kelly Segraves claim that these, too, have been quietly buried in museum basements and such places:

> The Castenedolo, Olmo, and Calaveras fossils, all carefully documented, have been relegated to dusty museum closets and forgotten by the anthropologists because they do not fit into the accepted evolutionary scheme of human origins. Sir Arthur Keith, British scientist and dean of anthropologists in the first quarter of this century, in his book, *The Antiquity of Man*, described in great detail the Castenedolo, Olmo, and Calaveras fossils. He told how these fossils would have been accepted as

genuine had they not so radically contradicted the ape-to-man dogma which rules the minds of most anthropologists.[27]

Ernest Conrad[28] points out that recent-creationists are unwise to base their case on Keith's opinion, which is suspect for two good reasons. First, he lived a long time ago, when methods of identifying fossils were far less sophisticated than today. Secondly, he also accepted the spurious Piltdown Man, uncritically and with great enthusiasm.

Nowadays, says Conrad, these three 'Ancient Men' are all rejected for good reasons – nothing to do with evolution – and have been for a long time.

As early as 1899 it was pointed out that the Castenedolo skeletons, though found in a Pliocene (ancient) deposit, were all laden with salt, unlike all the other fossils in the bed. Even at that early date, this was taken by the man who made the official report on them to indicate that they were fairly recent burials. Nitrogen (collagen) tests were made in 1965 which confirmed this opinion. And in 1969 radiocarbon tests dated them at about 25,000 years ago, which is long after the Pliocene period.

The Olmo skull was found in 1863 by an Italian, Professor Cocchi, who first classified it as Lower Quaternary. (By modern reckoning, that would make it around two million years old.) But in 1897, when he was 34 years older and better informed, Cocchi changed his mind and said it was much more recent. Laboratory tests on the skull have now shown that it is probably between fifty and seventy-five thousand years old – a date which does not embarrass evolutionists at all.

Finally, Conrad explains how the Calaveras fossil has long been recognized as a nineteenth-century hoax, and is often listed in books alongside the Piltdown fraud. The main differences are that the Calaveras spoof was exposed far sooner than Piltdown, and that we know who probably did it, because he confessed to his pastor and his sister before he died.

The facts being what they are, it might be advisable for recent-creationists to stop talking of Miocene, Castenedolo, Olmo and Calaveras Man. After all, evolutionists stopped using Piltdown Man as soon as their mistake came to light. At the moment it would seem that 'the sons of this world are wiser in their own generation than the sons of light', as our Lord put it.[29]

Fossil Footprints

Recent-creationist books make much of fossil footprints, allegedly human, found in ancient rock systems. The most famous of these are near Glen Rose, Texas, where the Paluxy River flows through a limestone gorge. This limestone contains both fossil dinosaur footprints and what look like fossil human footprints – except that some of these are up to 18 inches long. But of course, as the creationists are quick to point out, Genesis says, 'There were giants in the earth in those days.'

Christopher Weber[30] and Laurie Godfrey[31] have now published a number of other facts about these footprints that the recent-creationist books are less keen to point out. Here is a summary of their findings.

(1) It is well known that there was a carnivorous dinosaur with three toes. Depending upon how it moved its feet, and how well the impressions were preserved, the tracks it left behind sometimes look quite like human footprints.

(2) The Paluxy footprints are too far apart to have been made by humans, even by long-legged giants. But they do fit the known stride of the three-toed dinosaur.

(3) Sometimes, if you follow along the line of the 'human' footprints, the tracks continue as well-defined three-toed dinosaur tracks.

(4) Some of the 'human' tracks have clear signs of a claw projecting from the 'heel'.

(5) They quote the geologist Berney Neufeld, who is a Seventh-Day Adventist and a creationist. He has made a detailed study of the Paluxy tracks, and has published his conclusions.[32] Some of the 'footprints' are random erosional markings, he says, and the rest were made by the three-toed dinosaur.

(6) They also quote recent-creationist John Morris, who seems more willing to admit problems than some of his colleagues. Morris[33] has referred to a letter written by the late Roland Bird, a palaeontologist who studied the Paluxy tracks and was regarded as a leading authority on them. He wrote:

They are definitely, repeat, definitely *not* human. I am well familiar with all the fossil footprints found in the Glen Rose (Cretaceous) of Central Texas, and have seen those purported to be 'human' by farmers lacking any geological training.

They were made by carnivorous dinosaurs wading through deep mud. When the foot was withdrawn, the sides of the resulting cavity flowed inward leaving an oblong opening only faintly suggestive of the footprint of a man in the eye of the beholder. When one followed such a trail, tracks of the dinosaur were invariably found that showed all the details of a three-toed dinosaur. (His italics.)

(7) Last but not least, they point out that the footprints are on top of fossil-bearing sedimentary rocks more than a mile deep. According to the tenets of 'Flood geology' that mile of sediment had to be laid down by the Flood, *before* the dinosaurs could walk on it. Again it is John Morris who seems to be almost the only recent-creationist writer to face the difficulty.[34] He suggests that men and dinosaurs found temporary refuge on top of the nearby Llano Uplift, while the first waves of the Flood brought in the sedimentary deposit. This is hardly plausible. Would waves big enough to deposit a mile-thick layer of sediment over a vast area be too small to cover the modest heights of the Llano? And when the water temporarily receded, would the mile-deep layer of freshly-deposited mud be firm enough to support the weight of dinosaurs, whose Paluxy tracks are only inches deep?

The 'human' footprints reported in other ancient rocks have even less likelihood of being authentic. For instance, the eminent geologist William Tanner, who is a Christian with a healthy respect for the Bible, speaks sceptically of:

> The so-called Precambrian human footprints of North Carolina (which I have examined and which are neither Precambrian nor footprints) . . . [35]

Finally, there are what the caption under a beautiful photograph in Prof. Edgar Andrews' book[36] calls 'shod human footprints in Cambrian rock, Antelope Springs, Utah'. What makes one of these prints so interesting is that it has a long-extinct trilobite fossil embedded in it. Ernest Conrad describes how recent-creationist the Reverend Boswell said to him that this footprint had been authenticated by the University of Utah.[37] So Conrad wrote to the Utah Museum of Natural History at the University of Utah, and was given written opinions by two of the authorities there:

> I have seen the specimen in question and it is nothing more than a slab of Wheeler shale that has a fragment spalled off in the

form of a footprint, which reveals a trilobite, *Erathia kingi*. To reiterate, the trilobite is genuine, the footprint is not.

I unhesitatingly assert that this is not a footprint. I have observed and collected a number of types of footprints that meet all the critical requirements, and I have had no qualms about describing these in print even though some were totally new. The Meister specimen is the result of a natural break, which happens to resemble a footprint. This type of fracture is called spalling and the part which breaks out or is detached is called a spall.

WAS THERE A VAPOUR CANOPY?

It has become almost a recent-creationist dogma that 'the waters which were above the firmament' of Genesis 1.7 formed a vast canopy of water vapour above the earth's atmosphere. This, they say, was all precipitated in the days of Noah, thus causing the Flood.

We shall look at this verse in the theological section of this book, in chapter 11. For the present I am concerned purely with the scientific aspects of the supposed canopy.

The idea was popularized by Whitcomb and Morris in their classic, *The Genesis Flood*. They have so much to say about it that there are about twenty page-references to it in their index. Yet they do not offer a single calculation in support of their idea. If they had, they would soon have discovered that it was insupportable.

They assert that the canopy's sudden collapse would have increased the volume of the ocean by 30 per cent (p. 326). This would mean that 30/100 of the original ocean volume, or something like 30/130 of the present ocean volume, came from the canopy. That amounts to about 75 million cubic miles. That quantity of water in the form of a vapour canopy would raise the pressure of our atmosphere from its usual 15 pounds per square inch to a crushing 970 pounds per square inch, which would create all sorts of problems for living things.

Worst of all, the pressure in the base of the canopy would be so high that it would need to have a temperature of over 500 degrees Fahrenheit. (Any cooler, and it would collapse into rain.) Such a temperature would have turned the earth into an oven.

Dr Joseph Dillow, a recent-creationist theologian, has appreciated these difficulties. He spent years trying to produce a detailed scientific explanation of the vapour canopy theory, and recently published his findings in a book of nearly 500 pages.[38]

He soon realized that the immense canopy proposed by Whitcomb and Morris was impossible, and settled for a much smaller canopy that would produce only a 40-foot layer of water. It would, however, still be enough to provide forty days of heavy rain as required by Genesis. Its effect would be merely psychological, since it would be nothing like enough to cause a global Flood. Such a canopy would only raise the pressure of the atmosphere to about 32 pounds per square inch, which would not be impossibly high.

Dillow spends about two hundred pages in a scientific discussion of the canopy, some of it sound, some of it not. In particular, he proposes that the phenomenon of Taylor vortices in the earth's atmosphere would somehow stabilize the canopy (pp. 250–58).

Alas, he reveals a poor understanding of Taylor vortices. These only appear under rather special conditions when a solid cylinder rotates inside a slightly larger, hollow cylinder. It is impossible for Taylor vortices to form around a rotating sphere. And, in any case, Taylor vortices are a form of turbulence; like all forms of vortices they tend to mix things up, and so could not possibly stabilize an adjacent layer of water vapour.

In all his book Dillow never really tackles the one obvious, commonsense, fatal objection to the vapour canopy theory. Canopy or no canopy, there would inevitably be winds in the pre-Flood atmosphere – a point which Dillow himself makes on page 281. Winds would soon cause the vapour to mix with the atmosphere and cease to exist as a separate canopy, just as a layer of cream floating on a cup of coffee soon disappears if you stir the drink. And once the vapour was mixed with the atmosphere the normal principles of meteorology would apply, and most of the vapour would turn into rain.

The supposed vapour canopy has been much talked about in recent-creationist circles, but very seldom thought about. A little thought soon shows there could never have been such a canopy, unless it was sustained by one long, continuing miracle. And that, of course, would be contrary to the teaching of 'Flood geologists', since they invented the canopy in the first place to explain how the Flood could have occurred by 'purely natural processes'.

SOME INCORRECT STATEMENTS

There is a common human tendency to think: 'I read such-and-such in a book, so it must be true.' To discourage this tendency, let me emphasize that all writers are fallible, so that the occasional mistake is likely to occur in all books (including my own). But in my experience incorrect statements occur more frequently in recent-creationist books than might be expected. These unfortunate errors tend to have serious consequences, since young-earth arguments are often based upon them. Though we cannot help respecting these writers' good intentions and their dedication to the cause of Christ, it is important not to take for granted the accuracy of all they say. Here are a few examples.

> *Now if the moon were four and a half thousand million years old, then such a small body should have solidified by now from its molten state.*[39] (Monty White.)

Not so. There are radioactive materials in the moon, and their decay generates enough heat to keep the moon's interior from cooling completely.

> *No dolomite sediments are being produced today at all.*[40] (Institute of Creation Research textbook for schools.)

Not so. A symposium as held in 1980 on 'Concept and Models of Dolomitization', and the published proceedings [41] contain several papers describing how dolomites have been observed forming today.

> *The relatively quiescent processes of the present day form almost no fossils.*[42] (Whitcomb and Morris.)

Not so. Numerous publications[43] have described how, under certain conditions which are now well understood, large numbers of fossils are being formed today. The Black Sea is just one place where this is happening, because its bed is free of oxygen and practically sterile.

> *The second law of thermodynamics (which states that disorder in a closed system increases with time) forces us to the conclusion that the earth was once more organized and integrated and beautiful than it is now.*[44] (John Whitcomb.)

What he says about the second law is true of *thermodynamic* disorder, but not of disorder in general. More seriously, the earth is not a closed system, because it receives energy from the sun. Consequently his conclusion, which is the really important part of his statement, is incorrect.

> *Analysis of the various proposed models for the original matter-energy fireball by the principles of classical physics (non-relativistic physics) reveals that the ball would collapse rather than expand.*[45] (Kofahl and Segraves).

Of course! Nobody knowing the first thing about the 'Big Bang' would dream of applying classical physics to it. The laws of classical physics break down before you get within a million miles of the Big Bang. You simply have to apply the high-powered mathematics of modern, relativistic physics if you want to get a meaningful answer to this problem. Having used an inappropriate method of analysis, Kofahl and Segraves naturally obtain a wrong answer.

The Big-Bang Theory flatly contradicts the Second Law of Thermodynamics.[46] (Morris & Parker.)

Not so. An article published by the American Institute of Physics says:

> However, standard big-bang cosmology recognizes that the Universe was at a low entropy at its outset and undergoes entropy increases globally through each step of its evolution. When a star condenses or when a galaxy forms, there is a local ordering and a great release of heat. The second law is not violated because the decrease of entropy in one place is offset by a far greater increase somewhere else.[47]

The Second Law of Thermodynamics says that all natural processes are deteriorative or degenerative.[48] (Harold Slusher.)

It says nothing of the kind. It is not concerned with '*all* natural processes', but only with *thermodynamic* processes – hence the name of the law. (See any textbook on thermodynamics, or ask any thermodynamicist what he thinks of Slusher's definition.) And note that Isaac Asimov has warned: 'Unfortunately the second law is a subtle concept that most people are not accustomed to dealing with, and it is not easy to see the fallacy in the creationist distortion.'[49]

This method [carbon-14 dating] is quite unreliable for ages over 3,000 years.[50] (Malcolm Bowden.)

Not so. Carbon-14 dating has shown to agree remarkably well with dates derived from (1) historical and archaeological studies of Egyptian and other ancient civilizations, and (2) tree-ring dating. Both these methods take us back far beyond 3,000 years. They establish the accuracy of carbon-14 dating beyond any reasonable doubt to at least 4,000 years ago. And provided that it is properly used, there is no reason to suspect the method of being unreliable at much greater ages.

CARELESS QUOTATIONS

Recent-creationists frequently quote the writings of scientists in support of their case. There is nothing wrong with this: I have done it myself extensively in Part I. But such quotations have to be made with great care, as otherwise it is possible to misrepresent the views of the writers being quoted.

Unfortunately, recent-creationists frequently do not take enough care with their quotations. Occasionally they quote on the basis of hearsay, without actually checking the exact words of the person they are quoting. More frequently, they seize enthusiastically upon a few words that seem to support them, without studying the context to see whether those words on their own are a fair representation of the writer's opinion. Here are four examples from among many that have come to my notice.

> In 1929, Woolley was digging some pits at the site of the Biblical Ur of Chaldea when at the forty-foot level he came upon an eight-foot layer of clay free from all the usual signs of civilization. He concluded that this alluvial deposit of clay, obviously laid down by a tremendous flood, was a direct confirmation of the Genesis Flood account.[51]

One would think from this that Woolley supported the biblical record. But such is not the case. What he actually wrote in his famous book, *Ur of the Chaldees*, is as follows:

> There could be no doubt that the flood of which we had thus found the only possible evidence was the Flood of Sumerian history and legend, the Flood on which is based the story of Noah.
>
> . . . The discovery that there was a real deluge to which the Sumerian and the Hebrew stories alike go back does not of course prove any single detail in either of those stories . . . The older inhabitants of the country were wiped out by the Flood, and the Sumerians who survived it were able not only to develop their own civilization . . . but also to advance northward.[52]

Another example comes from page 187 of *The Genesis Flood*, where Whitcomb and Morris are discussing the Lewis overthrust. This is an area in the Canadian Rockies where the strata are in the wrong order. Geologists explain this by pointing to evidence of huge rock movements in the area, which evidently heaved up the lower strata and slid them on top of the upper ones. Whitcomb and Morris deny that there is any evidence of such movements, and quote two orthodox geologists as supporting them. They state:

Ross and Rezak say: 'Most visitors, especially those who stay on the roads, get the impression that the Belt strata are undisturbed and lie almost as flat today as they did when deposited in the sea which vanished so many years ago' (op. cit., p. 420).

However, C. G. Weber has pointed out that if Whitcomb and Morris had continued this quotation a very different picture would have emerged. The next sentence in the Ross and Rezak text is: 'Actually, they are folded, and in certain places they are intensely so.'[53] Ross and Rezak go on to pile up masses of evidence that folding and sliding really has taken place. By carelessly quoting just one sentence out of context, Whitcomb and Morris have made an opponent sound like an ally!

Orthodox Scientists React

It is understandable that scientists who have suffered from this sort of carelessness should be angry. Nobody likes to see his own views misrepresented in print. The evolutionist Stephen Jay Gould has protested that he resents being quoted as a supporter of creation when he is nothing of the kind:

> It is infuriating to be quoted again and again by creationists – whether through design or stupidity, I do not know – as admitting that the fossil record includes no transitional forms. Transitional forms are generally lacking at the species level but are abundant between larger groups. The evolution from reptiles to mammals . . . is well documented. Yet a pamphlet entitled 'Harvard Scientists Agree Evolution Is a Hoax' state: 'The facts of punctuated equilibrium, which Gould and Eldredge . . . are forcing Darwinists to swallow, fit the picture that . . . God has revealed to us in the Bible.'[54]

Evolutionist Richard Lewontin is even more furious. He writes:

> Several examples of falsification can be found in a recent issue of *Acts & Facts*, published by the Institute for Creation Research, in an article written by Gary E. Parker, a member of the Institute and a teacher at Christian Heritage College in El Cajon, California . . . The past tense of my article ('It *was* the marvelous fit of organisms to the environment . . . that *was* the chief evidence of "Supreme Designer" ') has been conveniently dropped by creationist Parker in his attempt to pass off this ancient doctrine as modern science.[55] (His italics.)

THE IMPLICATIONS

We saw in Part I that there is a strong case for creation, despite what diehard Darwinists may say. Now we have seen in Part II that the case for a young earth is extremely weak. Through mixing the strong and the weak together, the recent-creationists have made their entire case as vulnerable as the mighty idol in Nebuchadnezzar's dream, with its feet that were 'partly iron and partly clay'.[56]

By this, and by their carelessness in handling both scientific data and quotations from scientific writings, recent-creationists have lost their credibility and antagonized the whole scientific world.

Have they made these great sacrifices because Genesis demands it? Or because they have mistaken their own *interpretation* of Genesis for revealed Truth? We shall look at that question in Part III.

Part III

BIBLE TEACHING ON CREATION

CHAPTER 10

The Days of Creation

====

*People who demand to have Creation explained from beginning
to end are asking the impossible . . . We are limited creatures.
How can any one of us encompass infinity?*   Morris West[1]

How are we to regard the six days of Genesis 1, in which the entire
work of creation was performed? That question is of crucial
importance. *If* they were ordinary days, then man must be only
three or four days younger than all the other species of the living
world. And in that case, since all are agreed that the creation of
man was a fairly recent event, it would follow that the rest of
creation took place recently, too.

This is the principal reason why recent-creationists enter into
their confrontation with science. They believe that the only honest
way to understand Genesis is to take those days literally, and thus
they are led to contend that the earth is young.

Prof. Edgar Andrews went even further when he expressed his
recent-creationist viewpoint in these words:

I do not accept the . . . idea that the six days were millions of
years long because the only reason for accepting this is to make
the Bible agree with evolution.[2]

Extreme statements like that are not justified. They are a slur on
numerous Christians who accept the evidence that the earth is very
old, but who are just as Bible-minded and just as strongly opposed
to evolution as Andrews is. Moreover, the idea of long days of
creation was introduced, as we saw in chapter 5, by *creationists*, of
the early nineteenth century. They were concerned about the facts
of geology and not about the theory of evolution.

The revulsion that Andrews evidently feels for the idea of age-
long days of creation shows how strongly recent-creationists feel
about the subject. Despite their over-reaction I have a measure of
sympathy for them. Those six days do present a problem for the
Biblical expositor, and we must face it squarely.

In this chapter I shall review the main solutions to this problem
that have been proposed. The last of these is the one that appeals

to me as being perhaps the most helpful. It has never received the publicity that it seems to deserve and will probably be new to most readers. I shall therefore set it out at greater length than the others, without claiming that it is necessarily correct.

THE FIVE WELL-KNOWN THEORIES

So much has been written about the days of creation that it is impossible in a few pages to do justice to every idea on the subject. By leaving out many of the minor variations, however, it is possible to narrow the field to six main theories, of which five are well known.

Theory No. 1: Literal Days of (Recent) Creation

This is the only theory that recent-creationists will tolerate. Indeed, they hold that it is not a theory but a fact. Consider these emphatic words of Dr Henry Morris:

> The only way we can determine the true age of the earth is for God to tell us what it is. And since he *has* told us, very plainly, in the Holy Scriptures that it is several thousand years in age, and no more, that ought to settle all basic questions of terrestrial chronology.[3] (His italics.)

This attitude is not only simplistic, it is without any factual basis. Dr Stephen Brush, who is not a creationist but a moderate and fair-minded critic, has commented on Morris' words:

> I have not yet found a creationist who can point out such a statement in the Bible, other than Bishop Ussher's seventeenth-century addition to the King James version.[4]

There is no denying that the theory of six 24-hour days of creation has its problems. It is not only that it is, as we have seen, in head-on collision with an enormous collection of scientific discoveries. It also creates a number of *Biblical* difficulties.

The first of these is that the Hebrew word *yom* (day) is used in three different ways in the creation narrative, thus:

> And God saw that the light was good; and God separated the light from the darkness. God called the light *Day*, and the darkness he called Night. And there was evening and there was morning, one *day*. (Genesis 1.4, 5.)

These are the generations of the heavens and the earth when

they were created. In the *day* that the LORD God made the earth and the heavens . . . (Genesis 2.4.)

The first 'day' mentioned above appears to be about 12 hours long, the second is evidently 24 hours, and the third refers to the whole period of creation. This being so, it is hardly wise to be dogmatic about the length of the days in Genesis 1.

It is also worth noting that the expression 'a (the) day of the Lord' is used many times in both Old and New Testaments as a figure of speech. It means 'an occasion when God acts'[5] and gives no indication of how long that action by God will last.

Now let us examine the Biblical grounds for the recent-creationist dogma about the days of creation.

The strongest point is based on Exodus 20, verses 9–11:

Six days you shall labour, and do all your work; but the seventh day is a sabbath to the LORD your God; in it you shall not do any work, you, or your son, or your daughter, your manservant, or your maidservant, or your cattle, or the sojourner who is within your gates; for in six days the LORD made heaven and earth, the sea, and all that is in them, and rested the seventh day; therefore the LORD blessed the sabbath day and hallowed it.

The recent-creationist argument runs like this. If the days of creation were of the normal length, then that would give point to the commandment in Exodus 20. God worked for six ordinary days and rested on the seventh, and therefore Israel should do likewise. But, the recent-creationists say, it would not make sense for Exodus to declare, 'God worked for six vast periods of unspecified length, and then rested on a seventh period – and therefore Israel should work for six days and rest on the seventh.'

I can appreciate that argument. It does carry some weight, though not nearly as much weight as its advocates imagine. But it is open to two significant objections based on Scripture.

First of all, the sabbath commandment is repeated in Exodus 31.12–17. This gives the same reason as the passage quoted above, but it adds three significant words: '. . . in six days the LORD made heaven and earth, and on the seventh day he rested, *and was refreshed.*'

God does not grow tired as men and women do. 'The Creator of the ends of the earth . . . does not faint or grow weary.' (Isaiah 40.28.) Those words in italics are obviously figurative. That being so, it is hardly reasonable to insist that the word 'days' in the same sentence are unquestionably literal days. They might be, or they might not.

Next, there is an interesting parallel to Exodus 20.9–11 in the First Epistle of John, chapter 3, verse 16:

> By this we know love, that he laid down his life for us; and we ought to lay down our lives for the brethren.

Does anyone believe that the two layings-down of life in this verse must be the same? Obviously not. Christ laid down his life in agony as a perfect atonement for our sins – and therefore, says John, we must dedicate our lives to serving our fellow men. The greater sacrifice forms a pattern for the lesser.

Similarly, Exodus 20 indicates that the greater activity of God in creation forms a pattern for Israel's weekly calendar. To reason that God's days must necessarily be of the same length as ours is on a par with deducing from 1 John 3.16 that our sacrifices must be of the same magnitude as our Lord's.

The other recent-creationist argument in support of literal days goes like this. Wherever else in the Old Testament we meet the Hebrew word *yom* (day) preceded by an ordinal number (first, second, third, etc.), it refers to a real 24-hour day. And therefore, they say, it must also refer to a 24-hour day in Genesis 1.

But this simply does not follow. Elsewhere, the passages tell us about days on which human beings did things. Naturally those are 24-hour days, the only days available to mankind for work. But Genesis 1 is unique, as being the only passage that describes how God once worked on a cosmic scale. It is hardly wise to derive a rule about *human* days of work, and then insist on applying that rule to *divine* days of work.

And in any case, there is at least one exception which shatters the so-called rule. In Hosea 6:2 it says that 'on the third day he [God] will raise us [Israel] up.' Long before the present controversy, commentators were pointing out that this 'third day' was evidently figurative, and was quite possibly a reference to the events described in 2 Kings 19.29, in which case it would represent a year. Some expositors even equated Hosea's 'third day' with the Millennium.

There is also Luke 13.32, where the Lord Jesus says, 'I cast out demons and perform cures today and tomorrow, and *the third day* I finish my course.' This was spoken many weeks before he was crucified, so that these three 'days' were undoubtedly not literal days.

Finally, there is strong evidence that the sixth day of creation must have lasted more than 24 hours. Look how much took place in that sixth day!

To begin with, God created the higher animals, and then created Adam. After that:

> And the LORD God planted a garden in Eden . . . And out of the ground the LORD God *made to grow* every tree . . . (Genesis 2.8, 9.) Then *every* animal and *every* bird was brought to Adam for naming.

In all that long procession of living things, Adam saw that 'there was not found a helper fit for him'. (Genesis 2.20.) So God put Adam to sleep, created Eve, and presented her to Adam, who joyfully declared:

> This *at last* is bone of my bones and flesh of my flesh; she shall be called Woman, because she was taken out of Man. (Verse 23.)

All commentators are agreed that the expression translated 'at last' in the RSV means just that. They usually express the literal meaning of the Hebrew as 'now, at length', and some of them quote numerous other passages in the Old Testament where this Hebrew word carried the same sort of meaning. Thus the Hebrew indicates that Adam had been kept waiting a long time for his wife to appear – and all on the sixth day.

Dogmatism about the length of the days of creation is therefore not justified. This is one of the many areas where it is wise to recognize the limitations of our own knowledge, and to respect alternative points of view.

Theory No. 2: Literal Days of Re-creation

Although none of the usual versions of the Bible does so, it is possible to translate the opening passage of Genesis 1 like this:

> In the beginning God created the heaven and the earth. And the earth *became* [usual translation, 'was'] without form and void.

Some of the nineteenth-century geologists mentioned in chapter 5 chose to retranslate Genesis like that. They then harmonized Genesis with geology by proposing that Genesis 1, verse 1, referred to a *previous* creation of our planet, complete with life. Because of sin, this previous creation was supposed to have been wrecked only a few thousand years ago, thus allowing the earth to 'become without form and void'.

On this hypothesis, practically all the earth's rocks with their fossils were formed during the previous creation, while present forms of life were formed during the six literal days of re-creation. Although this would provide a delightfully simple solution to the problem it is not much in favour today,[6] because it is open to objection on both Biblical and geological grounds.

Biblically, it is dubious because it involves hanging an important assumption on one ambiguous Hebrew expression, with little support from the rest of Scripture. And geological evidence for a recent global catastrophe followed by the creation of a new world is lacking.

Theory No. 3: Days = Geological Ages

Others of the nineteenth-century geologists chose to regard the days of creation as vast geological ages, of unspecified length. They pointed out that there were no men on earth to measure time on the first five-and-a-bit days, so that these days must have been 'divine days', not man-sized days. ('Elements of eternity', as a modern writer has called them.[7]) These nineteenth-century writers quoted 2 Peter 3.8 and Psalm 90.4 as evidence that 'days' on God's timescale are a great deal longer than our days.[8]

Again, we have here a simple solution that presents difficulties. On the Biblical side, the six days of Genesis 1 certainly sound like 'real' days: the first day was produced by the separation of light from darkness, and each one was rounded off with an evening and a morning. And geologically there is a problem in the order of creation. The record of the rocks is broadly in line with the sequence in Genesis, but not wholly so.

For instance, fruit trees were created on the third day, birds[9] on the fifth, and 'creeping things' on the sixth. Yet fossils of reptiles are found lower down in the geological column than those of birds and fruit trees. So Genesis 1 does not appear to be a precise summary of geological history, as this theory would seem to require.

Theory No. 4: Intermittent Days of Creation

The idea that the days of creation might not have been consecutive days goes back at least to the middle of the last century.[10] Robert Newman[11] has recently worked out a detailed scheme in which there are six 24-hour days of creation, but which are not consecutive days. He sees the six days as separated by vast periods of geological time, during which other acts of creation were going on. To him, the days are days when God *initiated* new phases of his creative work, and not the days when he did it all.

This idea is attractive from a scientific point of view. It is so flexible that it can accommodate any amount of geological data. But it is less attractive from a biblical standpoint. Its opponents argue that it is not reasonable for a 'creative week', with a sabbath at the end of it, to consist of six separate days with millions of years between them. The parallel with the Jewish calendar week seems to call for consecutive days.

Theory No. 5: Days of Revelation

In the middle of the last century J. H. Kurtz suggested that the days of Genesis 1 were not the actual days when God did the work, but were the days when God *revealed* to Moses what he had done.[12] More recently, a variation on this theme has been expounded in great depth by P. J. Wiseman, who makes quite a strong case for it.[13]

The idea appeals to many creationists because it solves the geological problem as neatly as the previous theory, and at the same time accepts the six days as consecutive, literal 24-hour days. Its main disadvantage is that it is based upon a somewhat questionable assumption: there is nothing in Genesis 1 to show conclusively that the six days were days of revelation, and the arguments drawn from later chapters are also inconclusive. Nevertheless, the idea merits careful consideration.

THE NEGLECTED THEORY: DAYS OF DIVINE FIAT

This theory suggests that Genesis does not intend us to take the six days of creation as the days on which God did the actual work. Instead, they could be the days in which God issued his creative commands, or 'fiats' as they are usually called.

The idea was first suggested to me by the late Peter Watkins, who evidently thought of it himself some thirty years ago. Unfortunately, he failed to convince many people that the idea was worth considering. Dallas Cain has recently discovered[14] that the idea actually goes back at least to 1902. In that year F. H. Capron published it, tucked away in the middle of a massive book on other matters.[15] It made little impact, and lay forgotten until Cain's recent rediscovery of Capron's suggestion.

Many readers may find this theory strange, at a first reading. But this is only because of its novelty. When it is once grasped the theory has much in its favour, as the following pages will attempt to show.

The Physical Reality of God's Fiats

If we are not careful we can easily overlook the importance of God's fiats. Scripture warns us not to do this. In at least four different places, Bible writers remind us that creation took place because God commanded it.

(1) By *the word of the* LORD the heavens were made, and all their host by the breath of *his mouth*.
For *he spoke*, and it came to be;
he commanded, and it stood forth. (Psalm 33.6, 9.)
(2) *He commanded* and they were created, (Psalm 148.5.)
(3) By faith we understand that the world was created by *the word of God*. (Hebrews 11.3.)
(4) By *the word of God* heavens existed long ago, and an earth formed out of water. (2 Peter 3.5.)

We must not confuse these fiats of God with fiats uttered by a human ruler. The latter may be put into effect, or they may not. It is over a hundred years since the British and French governments proclaimed, 'Let there be a Channel Tunnel!' The work was started in the nineteenth century, but was soon abandoned, and for a hundred years it was uncertain whether it would ever be completed.

But God's pronouncements *always* come to pass.[16] When he promises something, the deed is as good as done. Consequently, God can (and sometimes does) speak of his future plans *as if* they were already accomplished.

In accordance with this principle, Paul was able to say that God 'chose us in him before the foundation of the world' (Ephesians 1.4.), even though, in literal fact, we did not then exist. In similar vein, Revelation 13.8 speaks of our names being 'written before the foundation of the world'. Again, God told the prophet Jeremiah, 'Before I formed you in the womb I knew you, and before you were born I consecrated you.' (Jeremiah 1.5.)

Thus we must not think of the great fiats of Genesis 1 as if they were mere statements. The future is as real to God as the past is to us. To him, those fiats were as actual as the creative actions which followed. The fiats are the most vital part of Genesis 1, for the creative acts and processes themselves were only the outcome of those fiats: they were absolutely bound to follow. It appears that from God's point of view – which is very different from ours – creation was virtually completed as soon as he had uttered his infallible fiats.

The importance of this profound fact cannot be over-emphasized.

Parenthesis in Scripture

Another fact that impinges on our understanding of Genesis 1 is this: the writers of the Bible were much given to the use of parentheses. That is to say, they would often insert a secondary thought into the middle of their primary message. Here is an example from the New Testament:

> In those days Peter stood up among the brethren (the company of persons was in all about a hundred and twenty), and said, 'Brethren . . .' (Acts 1.15.)

Observe how the main sentence makes perfect sense if we read it on its own, ignoring the bit in brackets, as a separate but related thought.

There is no mistaking a parenthesis in modern English writing, because we usually enclose it in brackets, although sometimes we allow a pair of dashes, or even a pair of commas, to do the work of brackets. But punctuation marks were not invented in Bible times, and so there are no brackets, dashes or commas in the Greek and Hebrew manuscripts to guide our translators. They have to rely upon the sense of the words to show them where parentheses occur.

And it is evident that they do occur very frequently in the Bible. The translators of our King James Version were well aware of this. As Bullinger said of the first edition of the KJV:

> The Edition of 1611 abounded in parentheses. In the subsequent editions there has been an increasing tendency to discard them; and to supply their place by commas; or to ignore them altogether.[17]

The fact remains that in the original text of the Bible there are a great many parentheses. Some of them are marked as such in modern translations, others are not. And they go right back to the creation narrative. The earliest one marked in the RSV is in Genesis 2, where a pair of dashes encloses a lengthy parenthesis:

> In the day that the LORD God made the earth and the heavens, when no plant of the field was yet in the earth and no herb of the

field had yet sprung up – for the LORD God had not caused it to rain upon the earth, and there was no man to till the ground; but a mist went up from the earth and watered the whole face of the ground – then the LORD God formed man of dust from the ground, and breathed into his nostrils the breath of life; and man became a living being. (Genesis 2.4-7.)

The NIV also has a parenthesis in Genesis 2:

A river watering the garden flowed from Eden, and from there it divided; it had four headstreams. The name of the first is the Pishon; it winds through the entire land of Havilah, where there is gold. (The gold of that land is good; aromatic resin and onyx are also there.) The name of the second river is the Gihon; it winds through the entire land of Cush. (Genesis 2.10-13.)

Genesis 1 Repunctuated

We have now noted two important facts about the Bible: the absolute reality of God's fiats; and the fondness of the Biblical writers for inserting parentheses. With these two points in mind, we can now consider the nature of Genesis 1.

The very first verse evidently summarizes the early stages of creation. If it were not for the majesty of its contents, it might be likened to the little note headed, 'The Story So Far', which a magazine editor uses to introduce the latest instalment of a serial. It tells us:

In the beginning God created the heavens and the earth. (Genesis 1.1.)

The next verse tells us to imagine the curtain rising on an already-created planet, but a shapeless and empty one. God's Spirit is about to start fashioning it and then populating it:

The earth was without form and void, and darkness was upon the face of the deep; and the Spirit of God was moving over the face of the waters. (Genesis 1.2.)

At this point, God begins to speak. According to the Fiat Theory, the rest of the chapter is basically an account of the great creative fiats, which were uttered upon the six (presumably literal and consecutive) days. Inserted into this primary narrative is a whole series of parentheses, which describe the subsequent fulfilments of the fiats. These out-workings of the fiats, of course, could have taken any amount of time to occur. The fiats of God are uttered swiftly, but his mills grind slowly.

To make the point clearly there follows a repunctuated version of the whole passage up to Genesis 2.3, with the parentheses printed in italics.

And God said, 'Let there be light.' (*And there was light. And God saw that the light was good; and God separated the light from the darkness. God called the light Day, and the darkness he called Night.*) And there was evening and there was morning, one day.

And God said, 'Let there be a firmament in the midst of the waters, and let it separate the waters from the waters.' (*And God made the firmament and separated the waters which were under the firmament from the waters which were above the firmament. And it was so. And God called the firmament Heaven.*) And there was evening and there was morning, a second day.

And God said, 'Let the waters under the heavens be gathered together into one place, and let the dry land appear.' (*And it was so. God called the dry land Earth, and the waters that were gathered together he called Seas. And God saw that it was good.*) And God said, 'Let the earth put forth vegetation, plants yielding seed, and fruit trees bearing fruit in which is their seed, each according to its kind, upon the earth.' (*And it was so. The earth brought forth vegetation, plants yielding seed according to their own kinds, and trees bearing fruit in which is their seed, each according to its kind. And God saw that it was good.*) And there was evening and there was morning, a third day.

And God said, 'Let there be lights in the firmament of the heavens to separate the day from the night; and let them be for signs and for seasons and for days and years, and let them be lights in the firmament of the heavens to give light upon the earth.' (*And it was so. And God made the two great lights, the greater light to rule the day, and the lesser light to rule the night; he made the stars also. And God set them in the firmament of the heavens to give light upon the earth, to rule over the day and over the night, and to separate the light from the darkness. And God saw that it was good.*) And there was evening and there was morning, a fourth day.

And God said, 'Let the waters bring forth swarms of living creatures, and let birds fly above the earth across the firmament of the heavens.' (*So God created the great sea monsters and every living creature that moves, with which the waters swarm, according to their kinds, and every winged bird according to its kind. And God saw that it was good. And God blessed them, saying, 'Be fruitful and multiply and fill the waters in the seas, and let birds multiply on the earth.'*) And there was evening and there was morning, a fifth day.

And God said, 'Let the earth bring forth living creatures according to their kinds: cattle and creeping things and beasts of the earth according to their kinds.' (*And it was so. And God made the beasts of the earth according to their kinds and the cattle according to their kinds, and everything that creeps upon the ground according to its kind. And God saw that it was good.*)

Then God said, 'Let us make man in our image, after our likeness; and let them have dominion over the fish of the sea, and over the birds of the air, and over the cattle, and over all the earth, and over every creeping thing that creeps upon the earth.' (*So God created man in his own image, in the image of God he created him; male and female he created them. And God blessed them, and God said to them, 'Be fruitful and multiply, and fill the earth and subdue it; and have dominion over the fish of the sea and over the birds of the air and over every living thing that moves upon the earth.' And God said, 'Behold, I have given you every plant yielding seed which is upon the face of all the earth, and every tree with seed in its fruit; you shall have them for food. And to every beast of the earth, and to every bird of the air, and to everything that creeps on the earth, everything that has the breath of life, I have given every green plant for food.' And it was so. And God saw everything that he had made, and behold, it was very good.*) And there was evening and there was morning, a sixth day.

Thus the heavens and the earth were finished, and all the host of them. And on the seventh day God finished his work which he had done, and he rested on the seventh day from all his work which he had done. So God blessed the seventh day and hallowed it, because on it God rested from all his work which he had done in creation. (Genesis 1.3—2.3.)

WHAT REALLY HAPPENED AT CREATION?

We are now ready to gather together the threads from all that has gone before.

In Parts I and II we saw some of the evidence that our planet has been maturing for several billion years. But not maturing haphazardly, under the influence of natural laws alone; we saw also that no theory of natural evolution can explain the origin and development of life. It seems clear that some kind of creative power must have been directing events.

Is it possible to dovetail the observed facts with Genesis 1, using the Fiat Theory to help us? The question sounds almost impertinent. Our present knowledge, both scientific and biblical, is still so limited.

It is true that mankind has come a long way since Newton said he felt like a child, playing on the seashore while the great ocean of truth rolled away beyond his sight. We have climbed the cliffs behind Newton's beach and can now see vistas beyond his wildest dreams. But even so, we still see only the inshore waters. Ultimate truth continues to elude us, as surely as it did Newton when he died in 1727.

This being so, it behoves us all to tread warily. The whole subject of creation is awe-inspiring in its majesty, and we must approach it with reverent humility. The reconstruction that follows is offered as a tentative suggestion of the way things might have been. After the Day of Judgement perhaps we shall know just how much of it is mistaken.

The Prologue to Creation

If modern cosmological dating is anything like correct, it appears that the greater part of the universe's history is passed over in those few words, 'In the beginning God created the heavens and the earth.'

This raises some profound questions. Why did God omit so much of the story? Why did he not give us a truly cosmic description of creation? Why did he, instead, portray creation as it would have appeared to an observer stationed on our planet?

Since the Lord has not seen fit to tell us, we must first admit that no one really knows. All we can do is to seek for possible reasons, of which there are several.

To begin with, God evidently wished to provide information that would make sense in all ages. If he had given an account of the Big Bang, nobody would have understood a word of it until the twentieth century. As it is, he has given us an account of creation that enlightened the ancient Israelites and is still of immense value today. That this should be so is little short of a miracle, and is evidence of the inspired nature of Genesis.

There may perhaps be a deeper reason why the detailed creation narrative starts where it does. It rather looks as if the Spirit of God began 'moving over the face of the waters' (Genesis 1.2) at the moment when direct intervention in the affairs of Planet Earth by its Creator became necessary. This remarkable conclusion appears to follow from the results of resent research into the origin of the universe.

It now seems clear that when God began to 'create the heavens and the earth', he miraculously produced a gigantic concentration of energy and provoked a Big Bang. Because he had designed the properties of matter with great precision; the outcome of this was, in general terms, quite predictable. Without any further miraculous intervention by the Creator, the great expansion would inevitably produce gas clouds, galaxies of stars, planets. But they would all form *at random*, and randomness, we now know, is inhospitable to life.

The great majority of stars appear to be incapable of supporting an inhabited planet. The other eight major planets in our solar system are all totally unsuited to life, in several ways at once. Mercury and Venus are far too hot, and the other six are far too cold. Some are too big, and the rest are too small. All have chemical compositions that rule out the existence of any advanced forms of life. In each of many important respects, Earth alone is 'just right' for living beings.[18]

Our planet, it seems, began as a fireball of hot gases, orbiting an even hotter sun. As it cooled, some of these gases condensed to form a core of molten minerals, surrounded by a great envelope of gas so dense that it must have obscured the sun's light completely. It was at this stage, apparently, that God saw fit to intervene on Planet Earth. It could no longer be left to the random forces of Nature. *This* planet needed skilful preparation; it must one day become fit to support intelligent life. So his Spirit was moving over the face of the 'waters', ready to start moulding it for its great future.

The Uttering of the Fiats

Then the Creator spoke. 'Let there be light' – light that was to be 'separated from the darkness', so as to produce the alternation of day and night.

Had there been an observer present, he might have had to wait many millions of years for the gases to thin sufficiently for the first gleams of light to penetrate to the liquid surface. But God does not see things as men see them. To him, remember, the fiats are real: once the word is spoken, the deed is certain to follow. He commanded, and at once he saw – in his mind's eye, so to speak –

the light of day, followed by darkness. 'And there was evening and there was morning, one day.'

For ever after, in God's own eternal framework of heavenly glory (which is so different from the petty continuum of space-time in which we dwell) the endless succession of day and night continued – even though, to our imaginary observer, the dawn of the first material day was yet to come. In each of the next five of those 'divinely-real' days, God spoke. And on the seventh day he rested, for all the work was then as good as done.

Thus it was that on the second day he ordained an open 'firmament' – a sky – with waters below it and clouds above. Our imaginary observer would have had to wait further millions of years for this to occur, but to God it was as if it happened as soon as he had spoken. And so on each succeeding day, fiat followed fiat until all was accomplished.

Those last four words, of course, describe the situation in divine terms. To put it into human terms we should have to say 'until all was *foreordained*', instead of 'accomplished'. We humans have to make this distinction because our earth-bound minds are too puny to grasp the realities of eternity. But from the perspective of Heaven it seems that foreordaining something is tantamount to creating it.

To Whom Were the Fiats Uttered?

Genesis does not tell us whom God was addressing when he uttered his fiats. But there is a suggestion in a later book of the Bible that God's audience may have been the angels. God asked Job:

Where were you when I laid the foundation of the earth?
    Tell me, if you have understanding.
Who determined its measurements – surely you know.
Or who stretched the line upon it?
On what were its bases sunk,
    or who laid its cornerstone,
when the morning stars sang together,
    and all the sons of God shouted for joy? (Job 38.4–7.)

The passage is poetry, and it would be unwise to base too firm a conclusion upon it. But there does seem to be a hint here that the heavenly 'sons of God' were involved in the Creation. After all, they are God's 'ministering spirits sent forth to serve' (Hebrews 1.14), and they might well have taken part in the detailed work of creation.

It may be, therefore, that God made a preliminary disclosure to his angels, telling them what he required them to do. If so, then the fiats would have been a summary of the work before them. They were evidently delighted with what they heard, for as God said to Job, the angels 'shouted for joy'.

Advantages of the 'Days of Fiat' Approach

To recap: the suggested approach is that we should regard the days of creation as the days in which God uttered his creative fiats, with a number of parentheses inserted to show some of the consequences of those fiats. There are quite a number of advantages attaching to this way of looking at Genesis 1. (Several of them apply also to the theory of 'Days of Revelation', which appeals to me as the next most helpful theory.)

First of all, the suggestion is not just speculation. It is based upon two well-established Biblical principles: the fact that when God has foreordained something he regards it as if it already existed, and the widespread use of parentheses in Scripture.

Secondly, it allows the days to be viewed as consecutive literal days, making up a 'divine week'; yet it allows any amount of time for the physical processes that were the consequence of those days of fiat.

A third advantage is that it helps us to understand why the days of creation are arranged in a formal manner. They fall into two related groups of three, thus:

Day 1   LIGHT appears.
Day 2   WATERS are divided.
Day 3   LAND appears, with vegetation.
Day 4   LIGHTS [plural] appear.
Day 5   WATERS bring forth living creatures.
Day 6   LAND is populated.

To an ancient Hebrew, this sort of arrangement would appear poetical. The most obvious characteristic of Hebrew poetry is 'parallelism', that is to say, repetition at measured intervals, with modifications – and that is the way that Genesis 1 is structured. Poetry was originally intended for saying out loud; what could be more natural than that God's six great fiats should be proclaimed in a poetic form?

Fourthly, it explains why the order of events in Genesis 1 is similar to, but not identical with, the order in which fossils appear in the geological record. The broad similarity is because the creative processes were presumably *started* in much the same order as the daily fiats. The discrepancies are because those creative processes took varying lengths of time to complete, so that there would be a great deal of overlapping in the periods of active creation.

Fifthly, it throws light on Genesis 2.4–25, which unbelievers criticize as being a second (and contradictory) account of creation. Genesis 2 is nothing of the kind. It can be regarded as the last, and greatest, of God's descriptions of the way one of his fiats was brought to pass. It is a detailed account of how God first fulfilled, 'Let us make man in our image.'

The sixth point is that it also throws light on Genesis 2:2, which says that God took a sabbath rest after the six days. Yet Genesis does not attribute an evening and a morning to that seventh day, as if to imply that it did not possess the boundaries of an ordinary sabbath. This hint is taken up in Hebrews, which tells us that the real 'sabbath' of God is still future:

> For he has somewhere spoken of the seventh day in this way, 'And God rested [in the past] on the seventh day from all his works' . . . So then, there remains [in the future] a sabbath rest for the people of God; for whoever enters God's rest also ceases from his labours as God did from his. (Hebrews 4.4, 9, 10.)

We are now able to see that the parallel drawn in this Hebrews passage has a literal basis. The sabbath rest after the days of uttering fiats is long since over; but the sabbath rest after the long periods of outworking will be in the age to come.

Finally, and perhaps most important of all, this suggested approach makes it easier to understand why the New Testament is so insistent that Genesis 1 is a prophecy of Christ. For example, the first fiat, 'Let there be Light', had its primary fulfilment when God brought light to the surface of a dark planet; but there was also another fulfilment, according to Paul, which occurred when Christ came into our sin-darkened world:

> For it is the God who said, 'Let light shine out of darkness' [the first fiat], who has shone in our hearts to give the light of the knowledge of the glory of God in the face of Christ. (2 Corinthians 4.6.)

Again, Paul calls Christ 'the last Adam . . . the second man' (1 Corinthians 15.45, 47). He says in two places that Christ is 'the image of God', just as Adam was (2 Corinthians 4.4, KJV; Colossians 1.15). So also does Hebrews 1.3 (KJV). And Paul promises that all

Christ's faithful followers shall one day carry that heavenly image in themselves (1 Corinthians 15.49).

Evidently Paul saw the sinful Adam as only the beginning of what God had in mind when he decreed, 'Let us make man in our image.' The greater fulfilment was the coming of the sinless Christ. And the outworking of the fiat will not be complete until all God's people have received immortality, and so been stamped with the image of God in all its glory.

Thus it is possible to view all the rest of the Bible as one giant parenthesis, describing in fine detail the outworking of God's last and greatest creative fiat. And God's eternal kingdom is the sabbath rest which will follow.

CHAPTER 11

Some other Biblical Questions

We pick out a text here and there to make it serve our turn; whereas, if we take it all together, and consider what went before and what followed after, we should find it meant no such thing.
John Selden.[1]

The intentions of recent-creationists are admirable. They have a burning desire to give God's Word the honour and respect due to it – a desire to which every sincere believer is bound to say 'Amen'. Their whole position takes the absolute authority of Scripture as its starting point – and rightly so.

But they go further than this. They claim to be the *only* true defenders of the Biblical account of creation. Unfortunately, like so many of their claims, this one does not stand up to close examination. On the one hand, there are many ancient-creationists who are equally concerned to defend the Bible. And on the other hand, there are a number of areas where the biblical expositions of recent-creationists are questionable, as we shall now see.

THE 'WATERS ABOVE'

We saw in chapter 9 that the notion of a pre-Flood vapour canopy around the earth is scientifically indefensible. Here we shall see that their scriptural justification for such a belief is also dubious.

The idea is based upon the following two texts:

And God said, 'Let there be a firmament [sky] in the midst of the waters, and let it separate the waters from the waters.' And God made the firmament and separated the waters which were under the firmament from the waters which were above the firmament. (Genesis 1.6, 7.)

In the six hundredth year of Noah's life, in the second month, on the seventeenth day of the month, on that day all the fountains of the great deep burst forth, and the windows of the heavens were opened. And rain fell upon the earth forty days and forty nights. (Genesis 7.11, 12.)

The recent-creationist claim is that the first of these passages teaches the creation of a vast canopy of water or water vapour, and that the second indicates the canopy collapsed to cause the Flood.

This, however, is a new interpretation of those passages. Even the great canopy enthusiast Joseph Dillow admits that 'The usual and oldest view is that the reference is to the clouds in the sky.'[2] He mentions that Calvin's commentary on Genesis teaches this. To forsake this well-established and obvious explanation of the passage in favour of a new and exotic one needs some justification. What other Scriptures are there which can be brought in as evidence?

The fact is that there do not seem to be any. Dillow does call on 2 Peter 3.5, 6 for support, but this appears to support the idea of clouds at least as well as that of a canopy.

On the other hand the great biblical hymn on creation, Psalm 104, strongly indicates that the waters above are the clouds. In the verses that reflect on the work of the second day we read:

> Thou art clothed with honour and majesty,
> who coverest thyself with light as with a garment,
> who hast stretched out the heavens like a tent,
> *who hast laid the beams of thy chambers on the waters,*
> *who makest the clouds thy chariot,*
> who ridest on the wings of the wind. (Verses 1–3.)

The words in italics are somewhat obscure, but they seem to suggest that God's 'chambers' and 'waters' are nothing more nor less than the clouds. We are not left in doubt, however, because this idea is positively confirmed in verse 13. This says that it is those 'chambers' (the same Hebrew word as in verse 3, above) which God uses in our day to water the hills.

Another Biblical poem, Psalm 148.3–4, clinches the matter when it declares:

> Praise him, sun and moon,
> Praise him, all you shining stars!
> Praise him, you highest heavens,
>   *and you waters above the heavens!*

From these two Psalms it is evident that the 'waters above the firmament' were not a canopy that collapsed and ceased to exist in Noah's day. They are waters that were still in the sky in King David's day, and provided rain as a blessing for mankind.

Hence, if we follow the time-honoured rule of letting Scripture interpret Scripture, there is only one conclusion we can come to. The orthodox view is right, and the recent-creationists are mistaken: the 'waters above the firmament' are the ordinary clouds.

The expression in the Flood narrative, 'the windows of the heavens were opened' (Genesis 7.11), does not help the case for a canopy, either. Later Bible passages assure us that the windows of the heavens were still capable of opening in the days of Elisha (2 Kings 7.2), of Isaiah (24.18) and of Malachi (3.10). The expression merely indicates a miraculous outpouring of *something* by God: of rain in the case of the Flood, of judgement in the Isaiah passage, and of material wealth and food in the other two cases.

Clearly, there is a lack of biblical support for the idea of a vapour canopy prior to the Flood.

THE FALL OF MAN

In the last verse of Genesis 1 we are told that God was well pleased with the whole of his creation: 'Behold, it was very good.' Genesis 3 tells how Adam spoilt things by disobeying his maker, and how God then sentenced him to death. Paul comments on this event:

Sin came into the world through one man and death through sin, and so death spread *to all men* because all men sinned. (Romans 5.12.)

Many recent-creationists go a great deal further than Paul. It is fast becoming a dogma with them that animal death, as well as human death, began at the time of the Fall of man.

They justify this belief with some very dubious exposition. I have heard one of them in a public meeting quote *the first half* of the above passage from Romans to make his point about animal death. Most of his audience were probably unaware that the rest of Paul's sentence expressly referred to the death of human beings. Such a flagrant misuse of Paul's words is not typical of the best recent-creationist expositors, but it is not unusual, either.

The following passages are also quoted to the same end:

And to Adam he [God] said,

Because you have listened to the voice of your wife,
    and have eaten of the tree
of which I commanded you,
    'You shall not eat of it',

> cursed is the ground because of you;
>   in toil you shall eat of it all the days of your life;
> thorns and thistles it shall bring forth to you . . .
>   (Genesis 3.17, 18.)

I consider that the sufferings of this present time are not worth comparing with the glory that is to be revealed to us. For the creation waits with eager longing for the revealing of the sons of God; for the creation was subjected to futility, not of its own will but by the will of him who subjected it in hope; because the creation itself will be set free from its bondage to decay and obtain the glorious liberty of the children of God. We know that the whole creation has been groaning in travail together until now. (Romans 8.18–22.)

These texts are a flimsy foundation on which to build such a dogma. The Genesis passage speaks only of the curse falling upon man and upon the vegetable kingdom – which is very odd if, as is alleged, its main effect was to introduce death into the animal kingdom.

And the Romans passage has always been subject to a variety of interpretations, as anyone who consults several commentaries on Romans will soon see. To insist on one particular interpretation is risky, especially when that interpretation leads to the conclusion that in the age to come the earth will be filled with immortal plants, immortal animals, and even immortal bacteria!

In any case, we know that death existed in the vegetable kingdom before Adam sinned, because plants were created as food for man and beast (Genesis 1.29, 30). If the death of plants was a good and necessary part of the balance of nature in Eden, why should not the death of animals serve the same useful purpose? Without animal death, reproduction would rapidly cause overpopulation and chaos. And it is no use speculating that reproduction also might not have started until the Fall, because on the fifth day of creation God commanded the birds and fishes to 'be fruitful and multiply'. Moreover, before he sinned Adam was warned, 'In the day that you eat of it you shall die.' (Genesis 2.17.) How could Adam understand such a warning unless he had seen at least one dead animal?

So we need to look for a better and more Scriptural explanation of Romans 8. Of several that have been suggested, the following is perhaps the most reasonable. Before the Fall, God commanded man to exercise a wise stewardship over the whole of creation, thus:

So God created man in his own image . . . and God said to them, 'Be fruitful and multiply, and fill the earth and subdue it; and *have dominion* over the fish of the sea and over the birds of the air and over every living thing that moves upon the earth.' (Genesis 1.27–28.)

After the Fall, God used a very different form of words. He knew that fallen mankind would abuse their position of power, and ruthlessly exploit the rest of creation. Compare the italicized words in the passage above with those in the passage below.

'Be fruitful and multiply, and fill the earth. *The fear of you and the dread of you* shall be upon every beast of the earth, and upon every bird of the air, upon everything that creeps on the ground and all the fish of the sea; into your hand they are delivered.' (Genesis 9.1, 2.)

This grim prophecy in Genesis 9 has been amply fulfilled. The presence of our race has proved to be an ecological disaster for Planet Earth. Scattered over the world there are many man-made deserts, where once there was fruitful soil teeming with life. Thousands of species have been made extinct as a direct consequence of man's selfish exploitation of Nature, and thousands more are threatened. Ecologists warn us that if we go on like this for another century we shall ruin the earth completely.

No wonder, then, that 'the whole creation has been groaning' under the 'futility' of man's behaviour, as Paul put it.

The Fall and the Second Law

A closely related dogma, for which there is not a particle of evidence, is that the Second Law of Thermodynamics did not operate before the Fall. Henry Morris expresses the idea like this:

The universal validity of the second law of thermodynamics is demonstrated, but no one knows why it is true . . . But the Biblical explanation is that it is involved in the curse of God upon this world and its whole system, because of Adam's sin . . . Therefore, we conclude that the Bible teaches that, originally, there was no disorder, no decay, no aging process, no suffering, and above all, no death, in the world when the creation was completed. All was *'very good'*.[3] (His italics.)

Those words suggest that Dr Morris does not really understand either the Second Law, or the scientific concept of 'disorder', or the biblical expression, 'very good'. Properly understood, the three terms are quite compatible.

Take the notion of disorder first. This may be a bad thing, or it may be good; it all depends on circumstances. If a vandal breaks into a house, goes to the food store, and tips the contents of various packages in a heap on the floor, then the resulting disorder is bad.

But if the housewife tips four ounces of flour, two of fat, one of sugar, a couple of eggs and a handful of raisins into a bowl and mixes them together, what then? A scientist would say she has created disorder – but a lover of home-made cake would insist that this particular form of disorder was 'very good'. Disorder in the wrong place is bad, but in the right place it can be highly desirable.

Nature abounds with processes where disorder increases. The leaves that fall to the forest floor are highly ordered objects. But not for long. In a year or two they decay into a disorderly mixture of simple chemicals. *And a 'very good' job they do, too*, since those chemicals are needed as food for the next generation – as gardeners who prize leaf-mould are well aware.

The assumption that the Second Law of Thermodynamics is somehow 'not very good' is equally naive. The Law is concerned with the running down of sources of available energy. But what of it? Am I to tell my aunt, whose antique grandfather clock is her pride and joy, that it is not a 'very good' clock because (in accordance with the Second Law) it stops if she forgets to wind it once a week? The one 'winding' that God first gave his Creation is evidently enough to keep it ticking away for many millions of years before it would demand any further input from him.

The Second Law does not denote a universe where things have gone wrong. It characterizes a universe where energy transfers can occur, and consequently one where things can *happen* – in other words, a 'very good' universe. A world where the Second Law did not operate would stagnate.

Moreover, it can be shown from Genesis that the Second Law must have been in operation before Adam sinned. We need to eat as a consequence of the Second Law, because the available energy in our bodies decreases and must be replenished from an external source. And both man and the animals needed food before man fell, according to Genesis 1.29, 30. This implies that they were subject to the Second Law of Thermodynamics from the moment of their creation.

THE FLOOD

'Flood geology' was invented with the best of motives. It was a brave attempt to reconcile science with Scripture. Unfortunately it fails to meet its objective for two reasons: it does not square with the scientific data, as we saw in chapter 8; and it is hard to reconcile with a number of Biblical passages, as we shall now see.

To start with a simple example, 'Flood geologists' assert that the earth's fossil fuels, coal and petroleum, were formed from organic material buried by the Flood. Consequently, if their theory is right there should have been no petroleum in existence prior to the Flood.

Yet it seems from the Bible that there was already an abundance of it. Pitch is a petroleum residue which is found on the earth's surface in some areas where there is a liberal supply of petroleum under the ground. And before the Flood there was already enough pitch available for Noah to plaster it all over his enormous vessel, inside and outside, according to Genesis 6.14.

Mountain Building

A more important clash arises when 'Flood geologists' claim that the Flood completely altered the earth's geography. They assert that the Flood deposited great layers of sediment, up to several miles thick; that after the Flood was over, low hills were heaved up to become high mountains; and that there were 'drifting and colliding continents also triggered by the Flood', according to the ICR textbook.[4]

But Genesis knows none of this. It depicts the waters as receding to reveal a landscape that was pretty much the same as before. Mount Ararat is portrayed as an existing mountain that was uncovered by the receding waters, not a new one that was freshly heaved up after the Flood was over. Even some of the rivers were still recognizable, for the Tigris and the Euphrates which are mentioned in Genesis 2.14 are still in existence today.

Ignoring all this, 'Flood geologists' rest their case[5] on the following text:

Thou didst cover it [the earth] with the deep as with a garment;
the waters stood above the mountains.
At thy rebuke they fled;
at the sound of thy thunder they took to flight.

The mountains rose, the valleys sank down
 to the place which thou didst appoint for them.

(Psalm 104.6-8.)

This is obviously poetry. It is not wise to take an expression out of its context in a Biblical poem, and then use it to establish a doctrine that does not appear in the historical narrative of Genesis. And in any case, most Hebrew scholars think that the passage needs translating idiomatically: five of the six versions I keep on my desk[6] do not say 'the mountains rose, the valleys sank', but *'the waters* flowed over the mountains and down into the valleys', or words to that effect.

What Creatures Died in the Flood?

I have never collected fossils seriously, but I do keep my eyes open for them when in the country or on the seashore. In that way I have found many hundreds of fossils in my time. One of them was the horn of an extinct mammal, but all the others were fossil shellfish.

This illustrates a highly significant fact: although, given the right conditions, the shells or skeletons of land animals fossilize readily, it so happens that fossils of land animals are in a very tiny minority. The overwhelming majority of fossils[7] are of marine or freshwater creatures.

The number of extinct species of such creatures is enormous. Although there are more than 30,000 species of brachiopods known to science, less than 300 of them are alive today; all the rest are only known from their fossils. Among the aquatic molluscs there are about 40,000 extinct species; among the sea lilies over 5,000 extinct species, compared with only a few hundred living ones.

Now let us suppose for the sake of argument that the 'Flood geologists' are right, and practically all the earth's fossils were formed by the Flood. In that case, the Flood must have killed many times more underwater creatures than land creatures. And it must have caused *many tens of thousands* of underwater species to become extinct.

But there is not a hint of this in Genesis, which emphasizes repeatedly that it was the land animals that died:

And all flesh died *that moved upon the earth,* birds, cattle, beasts, all swarming creatures *that swarm upon the earth,* and every man; *everything on the dry land in whose nostrils was the breath of life* died. He blotted out every living thing *that was upon the face of the ground*, man and animals and creeping things and birds of the air; they were blotted out *from the earth*. Only Noah was left, and those that were with him in the ark. (Genesis 7.21–23.)

If the 'Flood geologists' are right, then why does Genesis give such a misleading picture? If the Flood really did turn the earth's oceans into a gigantic mud-bath, where most species of fish life would have been wiped out, why was God only concerned to save the land animals and birds from extinction? Why was Noah not told to include an aquarium in the ark?

There seems only one possible answer for a reverent Bible reader. Genesis does not give a misleading impression. Most of the casualties in the Flood were land-dwelling creatures. The marine species were well able to survive the Flood and so were not in danger of being made extinct by it.

And that means that 'Flood geology' is not only in a head-on collision with science. It is also in conflict with the Genesis account of the Flood.

IS IT POSSIBLE TO DATE NOAH AND ADAM?

In Genesis 5 we are given a genealogy (line of descent) from Adam to Noah. Genesis 11 follows with another, from Noah to Abraham. The first one begins like this:

> When Adam had lived a hundred and thirty years, he became the father of a son in his own likeness, after his image, and named him Seth . . . When Seth had lived a hundred and five years, he became the father of Enosh . . . (Genesis 5.3, 6.)

At one time it used to be thought that the date of Adam's creation could be worked out, by adding the figures in these genealogies, and by using other information in the Old Testament to cover the period from Abraham to Christ. More than three hundred years ago Archbishop Ussher did this. He dated Adam at 4004 BC, and the Flood at 2349 BC.

Some recent-creationist writers still hold to these dates, but the majority do not. Whitcomb and Morris,[8] for instance, explain at some length why they think creation occurred about 10,000 years ago, not 6,000. The Flood cannot have occurred in 2349 BC, or anywhere near it, because there are historical records in Egypt going back centuries before that date. In some areas of the Middle East archaeologists have found a fairly continuous record of civilization back to 3000 BC and earlier.

Where, then, did Archbishop Ussher go wrong? He overlooked an important point that later scholars have discovered.[9] *Biblical genealogies are not intended to provide a complete record*. They have an unknown number of gaps in them.

To give just a few examples, Matthew 1.8 lists King Joram as the father of King Uzziah. But Old Testament history shows that Joram was actually the great-great-grandfather of Uzziah. Matthew deliberately skips three generations – presumably because the kings concerned were not fit to be included in Christ's genealogy.

Then there is Ezra 7.1–5, which traces Ezra's line back about a thousand years, to Aaron. But there are only sixteen generations in the line. Evidently Ezra misses out many of his ancestors who were unworthy of mention.

Most relevant of all, we are told in Luke 3.35–36 that Arphaxad was the grandfather of Shelah.[10] This evidently points to a gap in the genealogy of Genesis 11, which lists Arphaxad as the *father* of Shelah.

It is clear that the Hebrews did not attempt to keep complete lists of ancestors. Their genealogies only listed those names that were deemed worthy of inclusion.

Because of this, there is no way that we can calculate the dates of Noah and Adam. The Bible never even hints that the genealogies in Genesis were given us for that purpose. If we try to use them in such a fashion we shall certainly obtain the wrong answer.

We must accept the fact that nobody knows how long ago Noah and Adam lived. The Bible does not tell us, and it is pointless making guesses. Even if we did know, the information would not take us one inch along the road to eternal life. That, no doubt, is why God leaves us in ignorance.

CHAPTER 12

Some Biblical Objections to Theistic Evolution

Darwinian Man, though well-behaved,
At best is only a monkey shaved.
                                                    W. S. Gilbert[1]

We have seen how two great revolutions in theology were forced upon mainstream Christianity in the nineteenth century by science. First, the findings of geologists and astronomers made it necessary to rethink Ussher's chronology and the meaning of the Days of Creation. As was shown in earlier chapters, this necessary adjustment was made without doing violence to the teaching of Scripture.

But what of the second great adjustment, made when the triumph of Darwinism caused most theologians to drop their belief in a series of miraculous, creative acts by God? Is it equally simple to reconcile Scripture with theistic evolution – that is, with the belief that God used the natural process of evolution to create all forms of life?

The question is complicated because there are two distinct versions of theistic evolution, one taught by liberal theologians and the other by conservatives. These are so different that they need separate treatment.

THE LIBERAL VERSION OF THEISTIC EVOLUTION

In the late nineteenth century a great wave of liberalism overwhelmed the church. Many laymen were highly suspicious of it, but numerous theologians seem to have welcomed it as the best thing since George Stephenson's *Rocket*.

The beauty of it was that it enabled them to cut a whole tangle of Gordian knots. If the Bible was not wholly true, there was no longer any need to bother about the impact of science. Did some scientists say that miracles were impossible? Never mind: just write off the Biblical miracles as wishful thinking by the men who wrote the Bible. Did the stories of Creation, the Flood and the Tower of Babel present a problem? Not to worry: just say the first eleven chapters of Genesis are a collection of Hebrew myths.

Naturally, this approach to the Bible meant that certain Biblical doctrines were affected. In particular, the notion of the Fall of man had to be dropped overboard. Genesis may have said that man was created in the image of God and then fell; but Darwin (who sounded much more convincing than Genesis to liberal ears) said that man was a creature newly evolved from the apes. So the imperfections of human nature could no longer be regarded as a legacy from Adam – they were seen as a hangover from our animal ancestry.

Some of the greatest Christian preachers and writers of the day – including Henry Ward Beecher in America, and Henry Drummond and Archbishop Frederick Temple in Britain – expounded the new evolutionary Christianity. God, they said, had created things with the potential to evolve; then all he needed to do was to stand back and let nature take its course. On this basis, the advent of Christianity could be viewed as a major milestone on man's evolutionary road from the slime to the stars.

A recent historical study by James Moore[2] has shown that this liberal approach had one surprising consequence. The new evolutionary gospel changed or soft-pedalled much of orthodox theology. But it did not stop at that: it also made drastic alterations to Darwinism! This was because its advocates wanted to place their main emphasis on Christian love. But Darwinism was too unloving for their liking, since the essence of natural selection is, 'Make war, not love.' So the liberals modified Darwin in the same cavalier fashion as they reassessed the biblical writers.

Their version of the theory of evolution, in fact, was so different from Darwin's that Moore refuses to dignify it with the name Darwinism. Instead, he insists that we should call it 'Christian Darwinisticism'.

But this name is altogether too good for it. If it is necessary to add the suffix '-isticism' to Darwin's name, to indicate that his teaching has been perverted, it is not logical to stop at that. To be consistent, this palatable cocktail of liberal theology and liberal science should surely be termed 'Christianistic Darwinisticism'.

Where Liberal Theistic Evolution Leads

Dismissing the first eleven chapters of Genesis as myths might seem a good idea at first. On reflection a serious snag appears: the New Testament always refers to the early characters of Genesis, including Adam and Eve, as historical figures.

Luke, for instance, traces one line of descent of the Lord Jesus Christ,[3] generation by generation, right back to Adam. Our confidence in Luke as an accurate historian need not be disturbed by the evidence given in the previous chapter that Luke deliberately skipped over some generations. He did this for good reasons, and was acting in accordance with the accepted Hebrew method of compiling genealogies.

But it would be hard to place much reliance in the accuracy of Luke – to say nothing of the doctrine that he is an *inspired* historian – if his genealogy starts with a line of historical characters and then slides without a break into a line of mythical people. To take a modern parallel, what credibility should we give to a present-day historian who traced the pedigree of Prince Philip and the Greek royal family back to Hercules and other shadowy figures drawn from Greek mythology?

Worse still, if we treat the Fall of Adam as a piece of religious fiction[4] we strike at the very heart of the Christian gospel. The liberal is forced to reinterpret Paul's teaching about salvation through Christ's Cross in this fashion:

> For as in [the fictitious] Adam all die, so also in [the real] Christ shall all be made alive . . . Just as we have borne the image of the [fictitious] man of dust, we shall also bear the image of the [real] man of heaven. (1 Corinthians 15.22, 49.)

> If, because of one [fictitious] man's trespass, death reigned through that one [fictitious] man, much more will those who receive the abundance of grace and the [real] free gift of righteousness [truly] reign in life through the one [real] man Jesus Christ. (Romans 5.17.)

Such a blend of fact and fiction is a flimsy foundation on which to build a doctrine of eternal life. Observe how Paul weaves Adam's sin and Christ's righteous death together into the very fabric of salvation. Paul evidently regarded Adam and Christ as the two key characters in human history, each playing a vital role in the destiny of mankind. But if Paul was mistaken, and Adam's fall is actually little more than a touching tale for tiny tots, then why should we believe Paul when he tells us that Christ rose miraculously from the dead? And 'if Christ has not been raised, your faith is futile', Paul warns us. (1 Corinthians 15.17.)

It is not surprising that liberal evolutionary theology has been a stepping-stone to unbelief for some of its advocates.

THE CONSERVATIVE VERSION OF THEISTIC EVOLUTION

By the middle of the twentieth century many Christians had become aware of the perils of liberalism. The resulting evangelical revival has led directly to the upsurge of creationism in recent years. But many evangelicals grew up in the days when Darwinism reigned securely, and they considered that it would be intellectual suicide to doubt Darwin. So they turned to a conservative form of theistic evolution, based upon the conviction that somewhere in the evolutionary history of man there must have been a real Adam and a real Fall.

This was no new idea. Moore[5] tells us that there were plenty of conservative theologians in the late nineteenth century who embraced Darwinism. Interestingly, he says that whilst the liberal theologians played as fast and loose with *On the Origin of Species* as they did with Genesis, most of the conservatives were as orthodox in their Darwinism as in their theology.

The same tendency exists today. Whilst many liberal Christians and agnostics in the scientific community pick holes in Darwinism, we find one of Britain's foremost evangelical writers in this area, Professor R. J. Berry, trying to reassure his fellow biologists in 1982:

> Evolution is *fact*, not theory . . . It is a *fact* that all living things come from previous living forms . . . To paraphrase Archbishop Ramsey's reply to a young radical who asserted that God was dead: far from being dead, there is no firm evidence that Darwinism is even ill.[6] (His italics.)

In the light of the evidence presented in Part I, this is a remarkably dogmatic statement. It is also interesting to find Berry, in the same scientific paper, confessing his evangelical faith and describing himself as a 'theistic creationist'. As Moore remarked, the attitudes of theistic evolutionists are 'paradoxical'.

A Typical Conservative View

Despite making a fairly extensive literature search on both sides of the Atlantic, I have failed to find an adequate statement of belief by any contemporary theistic evolutionist of the conservative school. By piecing together statements by a number of writers[7-11] it is, however, possible to build up a composite picture of the mainstream conservative view, of which the following is a brief summary.

> The first three chapters of Genesis are a mixture of history and allegory. We cannot take the creation narrative literally, but the New Testament insists on a historical Adam and Eve, and a real Fall. So we must proceed as follows. All forms of life, including *Homo sapiens*, evolved along Darwinian lines. But these naturally-evolved human beings still lacked one vital attribute of true humanity: they were unable to commune with God – they were not yet 'religious animals'. So God selected one chosen pair from this species, and gave them this missing element of spirituality and a moral law. He remained in close touch with these two for a while, but they failed to keep his commands. God therefore withdrew his presence from them, thus sentencing them to 'spiritual death'. This punishment has been extended to embrace the whole of mankind, thus making necessary the atoning sacrifice of Christ.

This summary contains the essential features of the conservative approach to theistic evolution. Its main difference from the liberal version is that it accepts the Bible as inspired and authoritative, and the fall of Adam and Eve as an historical fact.

PROBLEMS IN RECONCILING GENESIS

It is not easy to reconcile the conservative form of theistic evolution with Genesis. Quite a formidable case against any kind of theistic evolution can be mounted on Genesis. Unfortunately, creationists (both young-earth and old-earth advocates) sometimes use a mixture of strong and weak arguments to oppose theistic evolution.

One weak argument which is often heard is based upon the expression 'according to their kinds' in Genesis 1. It seems to have become almost a creationist dogma that this phrase teaches what used to be called, 'the fixity of species' – or, if not of species, of biological groupings somewhat larger than species. In other words, it is argued that God created a cat-kind, and a dog-kind, and a horse-kind, and all the other 'kinds' (groupings) of living things; that these 'kinds' never interbreed; and that although small-scale evolution *within* a 'kind' is possible, larger-scale evolution across the boundaries of any 'kind' is impossible.

Now, I am not disputing the truth of that last sentence. The biological evidence indicates that it may well be correct. But it does seem to me that there is insufficient reason to argue that *Genesis* teaches any such thing. To read such a complex idea into an ambiguous little phrase of three or four words – 'according to their kinds' in the RSV, 'after his kind' in the KJV – is unsound exposition.

The convinced creationist will demand to know what else the phrase could possibly mean. There is no difficulty about that. If we can but free our minds from preconceived ideas, the natural meaning of the phrase is rather obvious. Take the passage where it first occurs:

> And God said, 'Let the earth put forth vegetation, plants yielding seed, and fruit trees bearing fruit in which is their seed, each according to its kind, upon the earth.' And it was so. The earth brought forth vegetation, plants yielding seed according to their own kinds, and trees bearing fruit in which is their seed, each according to its kind. (Genesis 1.11, 12.)

This evidently tells us that God created almond trees to produce their particular kind of nuts, vines to yield grapes, and so forth. We are expected to draw from these verses the same conclusion as our Lord, when he told his disciples, 'You will know them by their fruits. Are grapes gathered from thorns, or figs from thistles?' (Matthew 7.16.) We are not entitled to make unprovable claims that the passage is a cryptic denial-in-advance of the theory of evolution.

Later in Genesis 1 the phrase crops up several times in connection with the animal kingdom, for instance, 'Let the earth bring forth living creatures according to their kinds' (v. 24). Evolutionists often argue that the expression in this context is simply a Hebrew way of saying 'all kinds of', and I know of no way to prove them wrong. The Good News Bible supports them, translating the above passage, 'Let the earth produce all kinds of animal life.' The same Hebrew expression crops up again in Genesis 6.20, where several versions, including the NEB and the NIV, render it 'all kinds of'.

Creationists would be wise to oppose theistic evolution with arguments that are not so easy to shoot down. Genesis 1 emphasizes that God created the plants and the lower animals, but it does not tell us what method he used to create them. We may, if we wish, humbly speculate about God's methods – but we must not pretend that we *know* about things that God has not revealed. It is only when we come to Genesis 2 and 3 that we are given any details of the creative process, and those are concerned only with Adam and Eve. This is where we must turn for some sound biblical arguments against theistic evolution.

The Creation of Adam

Genesis 2.7 describes the creation of Adam in a series of three simple statements:

(1) The Lord God formed man of dust from the ground,
   (2) and breathed into his nostrils the breath of life;
      (3) and man became a living being.

According to the conservative theistic evolutionist this means that God took a living specimen of 'super-ape', the recently evolved *Homo sapiens*, and imparted to him a spark of the divine. It is difficult to see how such a meaning can logically be derived from this verse. Let us take the three statements, one at a time, and paraphrase them to fit (a) the conservative evolutionist view, and (b) a moderate expression of the creationist view.

(1)(a) The Lord God caused a mortal man to appear (through a long process of evolution).	(1)(b) The Lord God fashioned the lifeless body of a man from non-living matter (by an act of special creation).

Thus far the honours are about even. Genesis does say, 'God formed *man*', and the evolutionist takes this literally, whilst the creationist has to interpret it to mean 'the man's lifeless *body*'. On the other hand, the creationist, who equates 'dust' with 'non-living matter', is being much more literal than the evolutionist, who uses figurative verses in later books of the Bible to justify saying that 'dust' means 'living, but mortal'. The bits in brackets, on both sides, merely express the prejudices of the readers.

(2)(a) Then God miraculously imparted spirituality to this particular man (who, like the rest of his race, had previously lacked it).	(2)(b) Then God miraculously imparted life to that lifeless body.

This time there is no doubt that the creationists have the better case. There appear to be no Biblical grounds for interpreting 'breath of life' as 'spirituality', or anything like it. The same phrase 'breath of life' occurs several times in the story of the Flood (Genesis 6 and 7), and each time it is made clear that it is possessed by both man *and the animals*.[12] Genesis uses 'breath of life' to mean 'that which gives physical life to air-breathing creatures of all kinds'. The creationist reading of Genesis 2.7 agrees with this usage, but the evolutionist reading appears to be in sharp conflict with it.

(3)(a) And thus this live man was transformed into a unique spiritually-minded specimen of *Homo sapiens*.

(3)(b) And thus this lifeless body of a man was transformed into a living creature.

Here also the creationist's paraphrase is obviously more in line with the natural meaning of Scripture. The 'living being' (KJV 'living soul') that man became means simply a 'living creature'. Indeed, the identical Hebrew phrase is translated that way in Genesis 1.20, 'Let the waters bring forth swarms of living creatures', and again in verses 21 and 24.[13] The evolutionist interpretation of 'living creature' to mean '*spiritually-minded* creature' seems to be unjustified.

If we let the Bible speak for itself there appears to be only one natural way to read Genesis 2.7: the verse informs us that God miraculously created Adam from non-living matter (though without telling us precisely how he did it).[14] The idea of God stamping his image upon a living super-ape can hardly be read into Genesis 2.7 without distorting it.

The Creation of Woman

Genesis 2 describes how a succession of animals was brought to Adam, so that he might name them. None of them was suitable to be a companion for Adam, and so God provided him with a wife. He rendered Adam unconscious, removed a portion of his body, and from it made a woman. There was a purpose in this curious process. When Adam saw her he rejoiced that, unlike all the animals, Eve was 'bone of my bones and flesh of my flesh'.

There is no way of squaring this sequence of events with theistic evolution. Consequently, the conservatives take a leaf from the liberals' book and regard this portion of Genesis 2 as a myth or an allegory.

But is this a reasonable way to treat Genesis? We may not agree with the liberals, but at least they are consistent. They make no claim to accept the verbal inspiration of all Scripture, and dismiss the entire creation narrative as myth. The conservative theistic evolutionist takes up a curious position, when he asks us to believe that the inspired narrative in Genesis 2 and 3 switches without warning from history to myth (or allegory), and back again to history.

The story reads like a continuous historical account. Its author even takes pains to pinpoint the location of Eden, by naming the four rivers that watered it. He evidently thought he was writing history. How much reliance could we place on the words of a historian who cannot distinguish between historical events and mythical ones? The theistic evolutionist appears to fall between two stools, when he reasons that God inspired Moses to compile a mixture of history and myth, and then left it to us to sort out for ourselves which is which.

The Problem of Pre-Adamic Man

The creationist position is not without its problems, but how to explain pre-Adamic Man is not one of them. To the creationist, Adam was in every sense the first member of the human race. Because, as we saw in chapter 11, the Bible does not tell us how long ago Adam lived, we have no idea where to fit him into the succession of fossils unearthed by the anthropologists. (And in any case, as chapter 3 showed, there are many unanswered scientific questions relating to those fossils.) All we can say for sure is that any ape-like creatures existing before Adam cannot have been human, and must have belonged to some advanced species of animal.

This is not so to the evolutionist, however. He sees *Homo sapiens* as having evolved fully, before Adam was selected to be turned into the first 'spiritual man'. This presents the conservative evolutionists with a problem for which they offer various solutions, none of them very convincing.

The anthropologist Victor Pearce[15] suggests that the pre-Adamites were Old Stone Age men, and that Adam was the first of the New Stone Age farmers. He proposes that we should regard the 'man in God's image' of Genesis 1 as referring to the pre-Adamites. But it is doubtful whether Genesis permits us to do any such thing. Genesis 5 begins thus:

> This is the book of the generations of Adam. *When God created man, he made him in the likeness of God. Male and female he created them*, and he blessed them and named them Man when they were created. When Adam had lived . . .

The words printed in italics are a reference to Genesis 1.26–7. Yet the preceding sentence and the following sentence both speak of

Adam by name. This is quite a strong hint that Genesis 1.26–7 is
about Adam. More decisively, Psalm 8 refers to Genesis 1.26–7
and applies it to our own race – Adam's race – and not to an extinct
race of pre-Adamic men.

Berry[16] visualizes the pre-Adamites living on and intermingling
with the race of Adam, and sees references to them in Genesis
4.14, 17 and 6.2. He implies that Christ might have been descended
from these pre-Adamites, and says explicitly that he was not
necessarily a physical descendant of Adam[17] – a view which
evidently contradicts Luke 3.23–38. Berry recognizes that Genesis
3.20 presents a problem, with its reference to Eve as 'the mother
of all living', and suggests that it might be possible to give a
figurative meaning to the verse.[18] But that would certainly distort
its natural meaning.

There are also later Scriptures, especially Acts 17.26 and Malachi
2.10,[19] which seem to emphasize that the entire human race is
descended physically from Adam. It is not easy to reconcile such
passages with the notion that *Homo sapiens* evolved from ape-like
ancestors before Adam was personally selected for upgrading to
Homo spiritualis.

The Fall and Its Consequences

The conservative theory of theistic evolution is at its weakest where
it touches the Fall. Conservatives quite rightly take their lead from
the New Testament and insist that the Fall was a real historical
event, and not just a myth or an allegory. Yet they always seem to
gloss over the Biblical details of the Fall, which are exceedingly
difficult to fit into any sort of evolutionary picture.

Genesis 1 ends upon a triumphant note. When God had finished
the entire creation, including the man who was in his image, he
'saw everything that he had made, and behold, it was very good'.

After Adam and Eve sinned, this 'very good' creation was
cursed. We saw in the previous chapter that extreme creationists
go far beyond what the Bible says, in asserting that the curse
introduced death to the animal kingdom. Theistic evolutionists go
to the opposite extreme, and suggest that the curse had little or no
physical effect upon the world.

What Genesis 3 actually tells us is that the Fall had four main
consequences. (1) It brought punishment to the creature that
tempted Eve to sin. (2) It affected the physical nature of woman,
so that childbearing became more painful than it otherwise would
have been. (3) Agriculture was adversely affected, so that man's

life became more of a struggle than it need have been. (4) Above all, it caused the human race to be alienated from God and subjected to death.

It is obviously difficult for an evolutionist to take much of this literally. He sees the world as having already evolved with 'thorns and thistles' to make the farmer's life a hard one, and with gynaecological problems to make life tough for women, too. Above all, he sees Adam as being *already* a mortal man, when God took him and stamped his own image upon him.

Consequently, conservative evolutionists generally treat the story of the serpent, and the record of the curses upon the land and upon woman, as pure allegory. They regard the sentence on Adam as 'spiritual death',[20] instead of physical death. This they justify by noting that God had warned Adam, '*In the day* that you eat of it you shall die' – whereas Adam did not die physically until long after.

But this is very questionable exposition. The New Testament concept of spiritual death is never found in the early books of the Old Testament. The only kind of death the ancient Hebrews spoke of was physical death. Even in the New Testament the death that Adam brought into the world is treated primarily as physical death; in I Corinthians 15, for example, it is contrasted with Christ's resurrection, which all conservatives agree was a physical fact.

Moreover, we saw in chapter 10 how God often speaks of the future in the present tense, or even the past tense, because to him the future is real. To God, on the very day that Adam sinned he was as good as dead – physically. Also, various Hebrew scholars translate 'you shall die' as 'you shall be doomed to death', or something similar.[21]

The conservative evolutionist's theology of the Fall is clearly an uncomfortable one. He begins by accepting that the Fall must be taken as a real event, but ends by abandoning most of the historical details, to make Genesis fit his evolutionary views. We are left with a lingering doubt: can such an approach reasonably be called 'conservative'?

WEIGHING THE ALTERNATIVES

Most readers of this book will probably agree that the authority of the Bible must be respected. For them, this will rule out the liberal version of theistic evolution. Bible-believers will probably agree that there are only two possible views about the origin of man. For them, the choice will lie between the conservative version of theistic evolution and the older view that man was miraculously created from non-living matter.

The evolutionary view is the only one that is acceptable to a majority of scientists. But there is a heavy price to pay for this scientific respectability. As we have now seen, there are weighty theological difficulties associated with this view. The biblical problems are so grave, in fact, that evolutionary writers make little attempt to deal with them seriously. It is probably fair to say that they tend to dispose of these problems superficially, by clouding over the biblical record with such words as 'allegory', 'metaphor' and 'spiritual'.

Admittedly, there are many allegories, and even more metaphors, in the Bible, as well as many passages that are obviously meant to be taken spiritually and not literally. The question is, do the second and third chapters of Genesis largely consist of such non-literal passages? If it were not for the theory of evolution it is doubtful whether anyone would think so. And even those who are motivated by that theory have not yet produced a convincing detailed exposition of Genesis 2 and 3 along those lines.

It is obviously more satisfactory to take those chapters at their face value. We need to remember that the whole Bible abounds in figures of speech, and it would be foolish to deny that they existed in these chapters, too. Nevertheless, the narrative seems to demand of us that we regard it as essentially historical. Adam, it tells us, was created out of non-living matter – 'dust'; afterwards, Eve was made from material taken from his body; eventually the two of them broke God's law, and so were sentenced to live for a while in a sin-cursed world, and finally to die.

What is to stop us from believing this simple message of Genesis, forming as it does the foundation for the New Testament doctrine of salvation in Christ? Nothing but prejudice – and Darwin's theory of evolution.

Yet that theory, as we have seen, is now reeling under a massive onslaught – mounted not by theologians, but by a steadily increasing army of scientists, who assert that it simply does not fit the observed facts. Even some agnostics are rejecting Darwinism today. Is it really necessary for believers to let such a dubious scientific theory push them into an unsatisfactory theological position?

CHAPTER 13

CONCLUSIONS

===========

No rain, no mushrooms.
No God, no world. An African chief.

Part I lies a long way behind now, but it is essential that its message should not be forgotten. We must not allow the follies of some creationists to blind us to the true position. For the fact is that the evidence for creation is stronger now than at any time this century.

It was Darwin who spoilt the case for creation, by saying, 'Here is an alternative explanation for all the wonders of the living world.' But nowadays there are many biologists who think Darwin's explanation just doesn't work. For years, some of them have been searching for a better explanation of evolution than Darwin's – but without much sign of success. They think the evidence points to a mysterious 'something' in Nature that has produced the marvellous complexity of living things. Yet they have no idea what that 'something' might be.

Recently a great many physicists have started to think along similar lines. By combining the data from nuclear physics with those from astronomy, an astonishing conclusion has been reached. The universe is held together by a whole series of physical properties that happen to be 'just right' for the job. The chances against this being a mere coincidence are many *billions* to one.

Paul Davies, though an unbeliever, has recently summed up the position like this:

The temptation to believe that the Universe is the product of some sort of *design*, a manifestation of subtle aesthetic and mathematical judgement, is overwhelming.

The belief that there is 'something behind it all' is one that I personally share with, I suspect, a majority of physicists. This rather diffuse feeling could, I suppose, be termed theism in its widest sense.[1] (His italics.)

STIRRING UP THE OPPOSITION NEEDLESSLY

Davies adds that it is a far cry from this to accepting Jesus as the Son of God. No doubt it is. That is why many anti-Darwinists and awe-struck physicists are not Christians. But the fact remains that belief in some kind of a creation – of a creative 'something' behind Nature – has suddenly become scientifically respectable again.

This being so, you might expect that scientists would regard Christian creationists with more respect than formerly. Do they? Not a bit of it. In the corridors of science, the stock of creationists is at an all-time low. Consider these scathing remarks by Michael Ruse, a philosopher of science:

> I believe Creationism is wrong, utterly and absolutely wrong. I would go further. There are degrees of being wrong. The Creationists are at the bottom of the scale.[2]
>
> What we must do – and here I speak to scientists, humanists and educators – is show scientific creationism for the wicked, sterile fraud it is.[3]

Ruse was talking specifically about *recent*-creationism, and in particular the version of it proclaimed by the Institute for Creation Research. In the first quotation he was referring to their school textbook, *Scientific Creationism*. In the second he was reporting on the Little Rock court case, where he appeared as a witness. Unfortunately, he makes little attempt to differentiate: all shades of creationist are tarred alike with his savagely-wielded brush.

In a way his anger is understandable. We saw in Part II that there is a tremendous weight of evidence for the great age of the earth, drawn from many branches of science. The recent-creationists sweep all this aside for no good reason. And their own case for a young earth appears to be without foundation.

Shakespeare's observation, that the devil can cite Scripture for his purpose, has become a cliché. Some of us have had experience of doorstep missionaries doing just that. The worst of these quote only those passages that suit them, ignoring all the rest; they take biblical verses out of their context and apply them in a way that the writers obviously did not intend. And they are remarkably successful with many listeners. It takes someone with a good knowledge of the Bible to see the fallacies in their arguments. The tragedy of it all is that these are sincere, well-meaning folk, who deceive others only because they themselves have been deceived.

It is not only the Bible that can be misused in this way. Recent-creationists appear to do much the same with the literature of science. By partial and selective quotations, by disregarding context, and by ignoring the great mass of evidence that does not suit them, they build up a picture of modern science that is altogether misleading.

Yet they are just as sincere and well-meaning as the doorstep evangelists. It is merely that their zeal for their cause has overridden their scientific judgement.

Thus it is that they stir up the wrath of the whole scientific community. In doing so they bring a bad name upon all forms of creationism, not just their own extreme version. The strong case for creation is brought crashing down, when it is tied rigidly to the hopeless case for a young earth.

Let those who wish to go on believing in a young earth do so. But they would do the cause of Christ a service if they would treat it as an issue that is quite distinct from the question of creation. It is sad to see them forgetting that for a hundred years prior to 1961 (the year *The Genesis Flood* was published), the great majority of the world's leading creationists believed in an ancient earth. Many in those earlier days mounted some formidable opposition to evolution upon that basis. And many continue to do so today.

Two Simple Tests

A Christian friend once confessed to me that he was thoroughly confused by the whole creation/evolution debate. 'Recent-creation, ancient-creation, theistic evolution – how am I supposed to choose between them? I'm no scientist, I'm just an ordinary chap trying to follow Christ. How can I possibly tell what's right?'

I told him the situation was not as hopeless as he seemd to think. Sometimes in a murder trial the prosecution relies mainly upon scientific evidence. Yet many, perhaps all, the members of the jury have no scientific education. How do they manage to make up their minds?

Fortunately, they are able to come to a decision by asking a few searching questions. Two of these are particularly important, and it is helpful to pose them about the matters discussed in this book.

The first question is: Do the experts agree among themselves? Where evolution is concerned, the answer is an emphatic, 'No!' There always have been eminent biologists who have argued vigorously against Darwin's theory of evolution, and more of them are doing it today than at any time for a hundred years. Clearly, the theory of evolution is still a very long way from being proved.

But when it comes to the question of the age of the earth, it has to be recognized that the real experts are all in agreement. Despite many years of extensive reading in this area I have never come across a single example of an eminent geologist rejecting the geological evidence for an ancient earth; nor of an eminent astronomer rejecting the astronomical evidence for an ancient universe; nor of an eminent nuclear physicist rejecting the evidence from radio-active dating. Clearly, the evidence for an ancient earth must be very much stronger than the evidence for evolution.

The second question is this: Can the experts provide simple but convincing experimental proof that their views are correct? Once again, the answer concerning evolution seems to be 'No'. An enormous amount of experimental work has been aimed at creating life from ordinary chemicals – all with negative results. An equally vast amount of effort has been spent in laboratories trying to make one sort of creature evolve into a fundamentally different sort of creature – again, with negative results. This all seems to show that large-scale evolution does not and cannot occur.

But there is an abundance of experimental evidence in favour of geology. Oil companies employ thousands of geologists to tell them where to look for oil. Lots more are employed in the mining industries. Orthodox geologists have a remarkably successful record of predicting what, on the basis of normal geological theory, is likely to lie a mile below the surface at any given spot. In other words, conventional geology *works*. On the other hand, 'Flood geology' can give no useful guidance at all to oil companies or mineral prospectors. Thus the experimental facts prove that it is the orthodox geologists, and not the 'Flood geologists', who are on the right lines.

Having asked those two questions and heard them answered, the ordinary men and women in the jury box would not find it difficult to reach a verdict. Evolution is not proven; the biblical doctrine of creation still stands; but the evidence for an ancient earth is unshakable.

THE WAY AHEAD

Just over nineteen centuries ago the church at Corinth was in turmoil. The members had grouped themselves into several disputing factions. They were arguing about several issues: about resurrection; about the way to run their equivalent of a communion service; about the way to handle a brother who was living in sin; above all, about whether it was right for a Christian to eat meat from animals that had been used in pagan religious ceremonies.

Their spiritual father was Paul the apostle. He wrote to beg them to cease their squabbling and to pull together. At the heart of his long letter was the following advice:

> 'All things are lawful', but not all things are helpful. 'All things are lawful', but not all things build up. Let no one seek his own good, but *the good of his neighbour . . . Give no offence* to Jews or to Greeks or to the church of God, just as I try to please all men in everything I do, not seeking my own advantage, but that of many, that they may be saved. (1 Corinthians 10.23, 24, 32, 33.)

In other words, Paul told them to get their priorities right. 'It is not what *you* like', he said, in effect, 'but what attracts *other people* that matters. Consider how your views and your conduct will affect unbelievers: will they be brought nearer to God by you, or repelled? And existing members of the church – will your actions help them along the road to eternal life; or hinder them?'

The apostle's wise counsel is highly relevant to the creation controversy today. Unsound arguments for a young universe have stirred up a hornet's nest, and turned many scientists into bitter opponents of evangelical Christianity. Recent-creationism has given a great deal of unnecessary offence to the modern equivalent of 'Jews and Greeks'.

It has also done a lot of harm amongst believers. Many have reacted so violently against the unscientific nature of young-earth theories that they have moved to the opposite extreme, and embraced theistic evolution. And, as was shown in chapter 12, that is a position with grave implications for biblical theology.

The middle position, ancient-creationism, is not a compromise. It is a position of strength, because it accepts both the teaching of Scripture and the facts of science. And it is a position of love, because it avoids giving needless offence to scientists and Bible-believers alike.

Moreover, it enables us to make good use of the astonishing evidence for design, and hence for a great Designer, that astronomers and physicists have produced in recent years. It is sad to see recent-creationists throwing all that valuable evidence down the drain, by claiming that there never was a Big Bang.

The Science that Is Not

It is a pity that the term 'Creation Science' was ever invented. Creation is not a branch of science, and never can be. Creation is a matter of faith, one of the fundamental beliefs of Christianity.

The Apostles' Creed begins, 'I *believe* in God the Father almighty, maker of heaven and earth.' Hebrews 11.3 asserts, '*By faith* we understand that the world was created.'

It is legitimate enough to argue that creationism is not in conflict with modern science. That is precisely what I have tried to do in this book. But recent-creationists go further than this. They claim that their version of creationism is a scientific model which can compete on equal terms with Darwinism. Then, when atheists shoot the so-called 'creation science' full of holes, the result is tragic: it looks as if atheism has triumphed over Bible-based Christianity.

It is high time that creation was restored in the eyes of the world to its proper status: a Christian doctrine that we hold in faith. It is encouraging to note that modern science is not in conflict with our faith. But we must not pretend that our belief in creation depends upon science for its support.

The result of trying to sustain creationism by unsound arguments is plain to see. Recent-creationists, in their misguided enthusiasm, have brought the very idea of divine creation into disrepute. The mass media, as quick as ever to seize on sensations, highlight the most extreme creationist follies they can discover. To many people the very word 'creationism' conjures up a vision of wild-eyed fanatics. Somehow this image must be changed, by improving the standard of creationist scholarship.

It will not be easy to effect such a change. The Christian bookshops are flooded with recent-creationist literature. Most of the younger generation have never seen any other form of creationism advocated. Even many of their elders have forgotten that in their youth creationists accepted geology. Far too many Bible-believers have soaked up the propaganda which falsely claims that only evolutionists believe the earth to be old.

To redress the balance, a great deal of new creationist literature is urgently needed. There are still many creationists who respect both the Bible and the physical sciences. But their voices have been muted for too long. It is time for them to speak out, from pulpit and from lecture platform, in magazine articles and in books.

There is still time for a return to commonsense, and for creationism to be kept from sliding into the eccentric fringe of

Christianity. If only it can be divorced from the fallacy of a young earth, the case for creation is stronger than ever today.

If we can but present it with moderation and good sense, the world may yet come to see the truth of physicist Sir William Bragg's famous dictum:

> Religion and science are opposed . . . but only in the same sense as that in which my thumb and forefinger are opposed – and between the two, one can grasp everything.[4]

Notes and References

Introduction

(1) *Faith and Thought*, 1975, *102* (3), p. 182.
(2) Quoted in *New Scientist*, 23/30 December 1982, p. 864.
(3) Richard Dawkins, 'Against alternative history'. *Times Literary Supplement*, November 1983.
(4) 'The Survival of Charles Darwin', Thursday, April 22, 1982.
(5) Monday, April 19, 1982.
(6) Irving Stone, 'The death of Darwin'. *New Scientist*, 8 April 1982, p. 91
(7) Richard Dawkins, 'The necessity of Darwinism'. *New Scientist*, 15 April 1982, p. 130.
(8) Tract: *The Big Lie – Exposed!* BM Box 6155 London WC1V 6XX.
(9 Lamarck lived about half a century before Darwin. His theory of evolution was based on the assumption that acquired characteristics could be passed on – for example, that athletes would have well-muscled children. The facts do not fit Lamarck's theory, however, and it has always languished, although it obstinately refuses to die altogether.
(10) See, for example, Douglas Dewar, *The Transformist Illusion*. Dehoff Publications, Murfreesboro, Tennessee, 1957. This is one of the most scholarly and effective exposures of the weaknesses of Darwinism ever written.

Chapter 1   Wind of Change, p. 13

(1) *The Merchant of Venice*, II.i.94.
(2) The correct term is the 'British Museum (Natural History)'.
(3) *Nature*, 289, 26 February 1981, p. 735.
(4) *New Scientist*, 15 April 1982, p. 149.
(5) Oxford University Press, London, 1982 (p. 63).
(6) *New Scientist*, 15 April 1982, p. 133.
(7) E. G. Conklin, *Man, Real and Ideal* (Scribner, New York, 1943) p. 147.
(8) Dent, London, 1971.
(9) *Nature*, 255 (1975) p. 8.
(10) *New Scientist*, 15 April 1982, p. 130.
(11) Julian Huxley, ed., *The Humanist Frame*. Allen & Unwin, London, 1965.

(12) *New Scientist*, 9 August 1979, p. 456, quoting from Darwin's *Life &* *Letters*.

(13) *Bulletin of the Field Museum of Natural History*, 50, January 1979.

(14) *Biologist*, 25 (4) (1978) p. 163.

(15) This is strictly true of the theory of punctuated equilibria (or punctuated equilibri*um*, as it is sometimes called). It is only loosely true of cladistics, which is not a theory but a scheme of classification. In principle cladistics is neither for nor against Darwinism, but is separate from it; but in practice it calls into question many of the assumptions made by orthodox Darwinists.

(16) N. Eldredge, *The Monkey Business: a Scientist Looks at Creationism*. Washington Square Press, 1982.

(17) *Nature*, 8 April 1982, *296*, p. 508.

(18) Quoted by Roger Lewin in *Science*, *210*, 21 November 1980, p. 883.

(19) Stephen Jay Gould, 'Species are not specious'. *New Scientist*, 2 August 1979, p. 374.

(20) This remark refers to cladistics in its modern form, which is sometimes termed 'transformed cladism'. See M. Ridley, 'Can classification do without evolution?' *New Scientist*, 1 December 1983, pp. 647-51.

(21) Colin Patterson, 'Cladistics and classification'. *New Scientist*, 29 April 1982, p. 303.

(22) Ibid.

(23) Colin Patterson, 'Are the reports of Darwin's death exaggerated?' Radio 4, October 1981. Cited by B. Leith, *The Descent of Darwin*. Collins, London, 1982, p. 109.

Chapter 2 Biologists who Reject Darwinism, p. 21

(1) From a previously unpublished preface to *Animal Farm*, published posthumously in *Times Literary Supplement*. Quoted by W. H. Thorpe, *Purpose in a World of Chance*. Oxford University Press, London, 1978.

(2) E. Nordenskiöld, *The History of Biology: A Survey*. (Transl. L. B. Eyre.) Kegan Paul, London, 1929.

(3) *New Scientist*, 20 January 1983, p. 184.

(4) *A General History of the Sciences*, *volume 4*. Thames & Hudson, London, 1966, p. 446. Originally published as *La Science Contemporaine II* ed. René Taton. Presses Universitaires de France, Paris, 1964.

(5) P. Gavaudan, 'L'Evolution considérée par un Botaniste–Cytologiste.' (English translation by Aletheia Services.) In: P. S. Moorhead and M. M. Kaplan, *Mathematical Challenges to the neo-Darwinian Interpretation of Evolution*. Wistar Institute Press, Philadelphia, 1967.

(6) T. Dobzhansky, in a review of the first (French) edition of Grassé's book. *Evolution*, *29 (2)*, June 1975, p. 376.

(7) P. P. Grassé, *Evolution of Living Organisms*. Academic Press, New York & London, 1977.

(8) S. Ohno, *Evolution by Gene Duplication*. Springer-Verlag, Berlin & New York, 1970.

(9) C. P. Martin, 'A non-geneticist looks at evolution'. *American Scientist*, January 1953, p. 100.

(10) G. A. Kerkut, *Implications of Evolution*. Pergamon Press, Oxford, 1960, p. 155.

(11) W. R. Thompson, in the Centenary Edition of Darwin's *Origin of Species*, Everyman Library No. 811, Dent, London, 1956.

(12) Cambridge, 1940.

(13) Gavaudan, op. cit.

(14) Other species, that is, in the same genus, or maybe the same family.

(15) F. Jenkin in *North British Review*, June 1867.

(16) Readers with sufficient scientific background to follow the argument (O-level botany and maths, plus a determined spirit, is probably enough) will find this part of Willis' book fascinating, and are strongly recommended to study it.

(17) Op. cit. pp. 187, 188.

(18) A. M. MacLeod and L. S. Cobley, *Contemporary Botanical Thought*. Oliver & Boyd, Edinburgh & London, 1961.

Chapter 3   Other Evolutionists with Serious Doubts, p. 33

(1) *Helen.*

(2) S. J. Gould, 'The chance that shapes our ends'. *New Scientist*, 5 February 1981, p. 347.

(3) A virus is a simpler living thing, but it is not self-sufficient. It cannot live without enzymes, and it can only obtain these from other, more complex, living creatures. So the virus can only live as a kind of mini-parasite, inside the cells of some other and much more complex organism.

(4) See, for example, F. B. Salisbury, 'Natural selection and the complexity of the gene.' *Nature*, 224, 1969, p. 342. Also L. M. Spetner, 'Natural selection versus gene uniqueness.' *Nature*, 226, 1970, p. 948.

(5) F. Hoyle. *The Universe: Past and Present Reflections*. University College, Cardiff, 1981. (Also, *Steady-State Cosmology Revisited*, University College, Cardiff, 1980.)

(6) M. Ridley, 'Extraterrestrial genes.' *New Scientist*, 15 October 1981, p. 188.

(7) H. N. V. Temperley, 'Could life have happened by accident?' *New Scientist*, 19 August 1982, p. 505.

(8) F. Hoyle, 'The big bang in astronomy.' *New Scientist*, 19 November 1981, p. 521.

(9) Page 28 of Reference 5, above.

(10) 'Threats on life of controversial astronomer.' *New Scientist*, 21 January 1982, p. 140. (The anonymous writer argued that this statement might have so infuriated conservative Darwinists that they threatened Wickramasinghe's life.)

(11) F. Hoyle & N. C. Wickramasinghe, *Evolution from Space*. Dent, London, 1981.

(12) That is to say, genes with fundamentally different functions, not

counting the myriads of minor differences between the genes of different individuals in the same species.

(13) *30*, p. 140; *31*, p. 138; *31*, p. 337.

(14) *New Scientist*, 14 May 1981, p. 452.

(15) Wistar Institute Press, Philadelphia, 1967. Editors P. S. Moorhead and M. M. Kaplan.

(16) Geneticists will, I hope, forgive this gross oversimplification.

(17) A. Koestler, *The Case of the Midwife Toad*. Hutchinson, London, 1971.

(18) A. Koestler, 'Nothing but.' In: R. Duncan and M. Weston-Smith, *Lying Truths*. Pergamon, Oxford, 1979, p. 200.

(19) Editors, R. Duncan and M. Weston-Smith. Pergamon, London and New York 1977, p. 227.

(20) F. Hitching, *The Neck of the Giraffe*. Pan, London & Sydney, 1982.

(21) The tiny handful of slightly more advanced pre-Cambrian fossils are still the subject of controversy. Even if they should eventually be proved genuine they do not affect the fact that ancestors of the wide variety of Cambrian flora and fauna are almost entirely absent from the fossil record.

(22) Oxford University Press, London, 1955.

(23) Collins, London, 1979.

(24) Secker & Warburg, London, 1983.

(25) R. J. Andrew in *Nature*, *236*, April 1972, p. 292.

(26) *Financial Times*, 6 May 1981.

(27) J. Cherfas and J. Gribbin, 'The molecular making of mankind.' *New Scientist*, 27 August 1981, p. 518.

(28) J. Cherfas, 'Leakey changes his mind about Man's age.' *New Scientist*, 18 March 1982, p. 695.

(29) From the opening sentence of G. E. Kennedy, 'Early Man in the New World.' *Nature*, *255*, May 1975, p. 274.

(30) *New Scientist*, 20 May 1982, p. 491. News item: 'Equality in all things – even teeth.' (Although this writer did not say so explicitly, he may have been referring to pre-Homo specimens, not early human remains.)

(31) J. Reader, 'Whatever happened to Zinjanthropus?' *New Scientist*, 26 March 1981, p. 802.

(32) R. Martin, 'Man is not an onion.' *New Scientist*, 4 August 1977, p. 283.

(33) Op. cit.

(34) R. Lewin and A. Marshack, 'An ancient cultural revolution.' *New Scientist*, 2 August 1979, p. 352.

(35) Reported by J. Cherfas, 'Trees have made man upright.' *New Scientist*, 20 January 1983, pp. 172–8. (The series of quotations from *New Scientist* in references 27 to 34 is especially weighty, because this is a journal whose editors make a policy of staunchly supporting Darwinism and opposing – or even ridiculing – religion.)

Chapter 4   The Design Argument Stages a Comeback, p. 54

(1) Inscription beneath her bust in the Hall of Fame for Great Americans, New York University.

(2) F. Hoyle & N. C. Wickramasinghe, *Evolution from Space.* Dent, London, 1981, p. 96.

(3) E. J. Ambrose, *The Nature & Origin of the Biological World.* Wiley, Chichester and New York, 1982.

(4) Op. cit.

(5) Op. cit.

(6) Op. cit.

(7) Op. cit.

(8) Op. cit.

(9) Op. cit.

(10) Op. cit.

(11) F. Crick, *Life Itself.* Macdonald, London & Sydney, 1981.

(12) Op. cit.

(13) B. Leith, *The Descent of Darwin.* Collins, London, 1982, p. 107.

(14) P. C. W. Davies, 'The great conundrum in the sky.' *The Guardian,* London, 2 September 1982, p. 17.

(15) B. Lovell, *In the Centre of Immensities.* Hutchinson, London, 1979, p. 122.

(16) P. C. W. Davies, *The Accidental Universe.* Cambridge University Press, London, 1982, p. 95.

(17) We are not concerned here with the value that gravity happens to have at the earth's surface, which is a particular property of our planet. The generalized gravitational force is expressed numerically as the universal gravitational constant, G, which enables the gravitational force between any two bodies in the universe to be calculated from the equation, $F = G\, M_1\, M_2/d^2$.

(18) To be precise, it is the mass we are measuring, and to obtain the required degree of precision from the weighing operation it would be necessary to apply a small correction for the buoyancy of the atmosphere.

(19) This illustration is taken from real life. I actually did make a sphere like this once, for a novel experiment in physics. See *Journal of Scientific Instruments,* 37, April 1960, p. 113.

(20) Op. cit. pp. 107-9.

(21) P. C. W. Davies, *God and the New Physics.* Dent, London, 1983, p. 179.

(22) More precisely, the universe seems to be – within the limits of observation, anyway – almost perfectly homogeneous and almost perfectly isotropic, when viewed on a scale greater than that of the galactic clusters. This is remarkable, in view of its marked heterogeneity and anisotropy when viewed on a smaller scale.

(23) In Reference 16, p. 110.

(24) Op. cit., p. 125.

(25) When astronomers observe this happening they call the exploding star a supernova.

(26) Op. cit., p. 140.

(27) Quoted by P. C. W. Davies (Reference 16), p. 118.

(28) Ibid., p. 68.

(29) 15 March 1979, p. 864 (anonymous).

(30) For a detailed analysis of the many 'lucky coincidences' that render our planet fit for life, see my book *Does God Exist? Science Says Yes*, Lakeland Paperbacks, Basingstoke, 1983. (Previously published in hardback by Marshall, Morgan & Scott, London, 1978, with the title, *God Is* and by Thomas Nelson, Nashville, Tennessee, 1981, as *God Is*.)

(31) In Reference 16, p. 73.

(32) This unprovable speculation, when dressed up in philosophical jargon, to make it sound much more profound than it really is, has been termed 'The Weak Anthropic Principle.' (Another version of it, in a form that greatly flatters mankind, is sometimes called 'The Strong Anthropic Principle.')

Chapter 5   Another Wind of Change, p. 69

(1) *Cosmos*. Random House, New York, 1980, p. 91.

(2) Presbyterian & Reformed, Philadelphia.

(3) For a good elementary summary of Greek scientific discoveries, see chapter 11 of A. C. Bouquet, *Everyday Life in New Testament Times*, Carousel, London, 1974.

(4) Augustine, *The City of God*, in *Nicene and Post-Nicene Fathers*, Eerdmans, Grand Rapids, 1956, vol. 2, p. 315.

(5) This remark by Luther, along with similar statements by Calvin and Melanchthon, are cited by A. D. White in his *A History of the Warfare of Science with Theology in Christendom*, 1896, republished Appleton, New York & London 1932, vol. 1, p. 126.

(6) Joshua 10.12, 13, NIV.

(7) Psalm 19.4–6, NIV.

(8) Cited by C. R. Longwell, *Encyclopaedia Britannica*, 1973, article 'Geology', vol. 10, p. 178B.

(9) E. H. Andrews, *From Nothing to Nature* (Evangelical Press, Welwyn, 1978) p. 63.

(10) The early geologists inferred these great thicknesses from what they could see, and especially from measurements of tilted or folded strata where these outcrop. Modern measurements have shown that their deductions were essentially correct.

(11) E. Hitchcock, *Elementary Geology*, 1847, p. 292.

(12) *Creation/Evolution*, Issue 3, Winter 1981, p. 9. (In November 1983 the secretary of the Society claimed in a personal communication that the membership had reached the two-thousand mark.)

(13) The launching of the quarterly, *Creation/Evolution*, is an example of atheistic opposition to the recent-creationist movement in the USA.

(14) The combined weight of a dozen leading churchmen, including Pope John Paul II, is thrown into the attack on recent-creationism in *Is God a Creationist?* (ed. R. M. Frye), Scribner, New York, 1983.

(15) See Esther 4.14.

(16) P. H. Abelson, in *Science*, 8 January 1982, vol. 215, p. 119.

(17) In H. M. Morris and G. E. Parker, *What is Creation Science?* Creation-Life Publishers, San Diego, California, 1982, pp. 219, 195–6.

(18) Jeremy Cherfas, *New Scientist*, 14 January 1982, p. 59.

(19) N. L. Geisler, *The Creator in the Courtroom*. Mott Media, Milford, Michigan, 1982, p. 20.

Chapter 6   The Witness of the Sedimentary Rocks, p. 82

(1) *Heaven.*

(2) In: Morris & Parker (ref. 17 of ch. 5), pp. 220, 239.

(3) Ibid., p. 221.

(4) *Encyclopædia Britannica*, 1973, vol. 10, p. 170.

(5) D. E. Wonderly, 'Coral reefs and related carbonate structures as indicators of great age'. Paper presented at the Baltimore Creation Fellowship Symposium, March 1981, and subsequently published as Research Report No. 16 of the IBRI (see address in Reference 7, below); it has an extensive bibliography.

(6) For a brief treatment of these reefs, see D. A. Young, *Christianity and the Age of the Earth*. Zondervan, Grand Rapids, 1982, pp. 84–6.

(7) For a more detailed treatment, with extensive bibliography, see D. E. Wonderly, *God's Time-Records in Ancient Sediments*. This was published in 1977 by Crystal Press, Michigan, but is now distributed by the Interdisciplinary Biblical Research Institute, P.O. Box 423, Hatfield, Pennsylvania. This is a book I can particularly recommend, being written in language that a layman can understand, by a Bible-believing creationist with a profound understanding of sedimentary geology. It is hard to imagine how any open-minded creationist could read it without being convinced that the earth is millions of years old. The above Institute also publishes Wonderly's more recent (and more technical) book, *Neglect of Geologic Data: Sedimentary Strata Compared with Young-Earth Creationist Writings* (1987).

(8) Geologists make a technical distinction between dolomite and its less pure form, dolostone, but I shall here use the more familiar word for both forms. Both of these are calcium carbonate which has been converted *in situ* to calcium magnesium carbonate, by a slow process of ion exchange from seawater.

(9) See pages 113–26 of Reference 7, above.

(10) This is an oversimplification of a complex subject. There is a world of difference, for example, between glacial lakes and tropical lakes. Some lakes give only two annual layers, others provide several. Sometimes varves cannot be detected by eye since there is no colour change – the alternations in such cases are of chemical composition only.

(11) Similar varves are forming today in Lake Zurich (Switzerland), Lake McKay (Ottawa), and elsewhere. For a detailed treatment of the Green

River varves, see Wilmot H. Bradley, *The Varves and Climate of the Green River Epoch.* U.S. Geological Survey Professional Paper 158 (1929), pp. 87ff. Also: Thomas H. Clark and Colin H. Stearn, *The Geological Evolution of North America.* Ronald Press, New York, 1958. Recent-creationist writers attempt to sweep all this evidence under the carpet by pointing out that there are fish fossils in these shales. Some of these extend through a hundred varves or more, and these creationists argue that a fish could not spend a hundred years being fossilized, as it would rot. But this is not so. Chemical analysis of the varves shows that the water at the bottom of the ancient Green River lake was extremely alkaline. Dead fish dropping into this natural pickling fluid could have been preserved indefinitely. See F. Press and R. Siever, *Earth.* W. H. Freeman, San Francisco, 1974. (Cited by C. G. Weber, in 'The Fatal Flaws of Flood Geology'. *Creation/Evolution*, Issue 1, Summer 1980, pp. 24–37.)

(12) See pp. 77–112 of Reference 7, above, for a thorough treatment of these evaporite varves.
(13) The principal source of data for this section is chapter 9 of Reference 7, above.
(14) D. A. Young, *Creation and the Flood* (Baker, Grand Rapids, 1977), pp. 183, 184.
(15) Ibid., pp. 193–8.
(16) D. E. Wonderly, in an appendix to R. C. Newman and H. J. Eckelmann, *Genesis One and the Origin of the Earth.* Baker, Grand Rapids, 1981, p. 96.
(17) C. T. Scrutton, 'Periodicity in Devonian coral growth.' *Paleontology*, 1965, vol. 7, pp. 552–8.
(18) S. J. Mazzullo, 'Length of the year during the Silurian and Devonian periods – new values.' *Geol. Soc. Amer. Bull.* vol. 82, 1971, pp. 1085–6.
(19) p. 65 in Reference 7, above.

Chapter 7   More Evidence of Age, p. 97

(1) Job 22.12 KJV.
(2) Cited from *The Scientific Papers of Sir William Herschel* by D. J. Krause, 'Astronomical distances, the speed of light, and the age of the universe.' *Journal of the American Scientific Affiliation*, December 1981, pp. 235–9.
(3) Cited from *Life & Letters of Thomas Campbell* by D. J. Krause, op. cit.
(4) Cited by D. J. Krause, op. cit.
(5) H. M. Morris, *The Remarkable Birth of Planet Earth.* Dimension Books, Minneapolis, 1972, p. 61.
(6) H. S. Slusher, *Age of the Cosmos.* Institute for Creation Research, San Diego, California 1980, pp. 33–7.
(7) P. Moon and D. E. Spencer, 'Binary Stars and the velocity of light.' *Journal of the Optical Society of America*, 1953, vol. V–43, pp. 635–41.
(8) Op. cit.
(9) P. G. Phillips, 'A 15.7 light-year universe?' (Publication pending.)
(10) This applies only to main-sequence stars, and not to exceptional stars

such as white dwarfs and red giants. The estimates of age of star clusters are therefore based upon main-sequence stars alone. The clusters of interest in this study are those of the galactic type, since globular clusters all tend to be much the same age.

(11) For this argument and that in the next two sections I am indebted mainly to S. Freske's article, 'Evidence supporting a great age for the universe', in *Creation/Evolution*, Issue 2, Fall 1980, pp. 34–9. Additional information was drawn from D. N. Schramm, 'The Age of the Elements', in *Scientific American*, 1974, 230, pp. 69–77. See also J. Byrt, 'Creation', in *Faith and Thought*, 1976, *103 (3)*, pp. 158–88.

(12) Ibid.

(13) G. R. Morton, 'Electromagnetics and the appearance of age.' *Creation Research Society Quarterly*, *18* (March 1982), p. 227.

(14) The most important exception to this rule is that carbon-14 dating can be applied to some very recent sedimentary rocks. Because of its relatively short half-life, however, this gives reasonably accurate results only with rocks younger than about 30,000 years, and is of no use at all beyond about 50,000 years, when the tiny residue of radioactivity from the carbon-14 is swamped by the ever-present background radiation.

(15) For a brief but adequate treatment, see pp. 93–116 of Reference 6 of chapter 6.

(16) The experimental procedure is complicated, because the air we breathe contains a little argon. This atmospheric argon usually contaminates both rock samples and laboratory apparatus. Fortunately it is easy to distinguish it from radiogenic (radioactively generated) argon-40, because atmospheric argon is a mixture of argon-40 and argon-36, in the ratio of 295·5 parts to 1. This enables the geochronologist to determine the amount of atmospheric argon present, and to allow for it.

(17) A. T. J. Hayward, *Repeatability and Accuracy*. Mechanical Engineering Publications, London and New York, 1977.

(18) H. S. Slusher, *Critique of Radiometric Dating*. I.C.R. Technical Monograph No. 2, second edition (Institute for Creation Research, San Diego, California, 1981) pp. 20–3.

(19) Private communication to S. G. Brush. Cited by Brush in 'Finding the age of the earth by physics or by faith?' *Journal of Geological Education*, 1982, vol. 30, pp. 34–58.

(20) The usual recent-creationist response to this objection is to suggest that God might have changed other properties of matter, such as heat capacity, by a factor of a hundred-thousand also, so as to absorb the excess energy from increased decay rates. But this cannot have happened, because these other changes would themselves have a disastrous effect upon life. Another natural consequence of the increase in decay rates would be to increase radiation levels by a hundred-thousandfold, thus destroying by radiation any higher form of life that managed to escape the heat.

(21) J. F. Evernden, D. E. Savage, G. H. Curtis, and G. T. James, 'K/A dates and the Cenozoic Mammalian Chronology of North America.' *American Journal of Science*, vol. 262, (February 1964) p. 154.

(22) H. Morris (editor), *Scientific Creationism*. Creation-Life Publishers, San Diego, California, 1974, pp. 145-6, 148.

(23) Private letter to S. G. Brush, cited by him (see Reference 19, above).

(24) C. Brooks, D. E. James and S. R. Hart, 'Ancient lithosphere: its role in young continental volcanism.' *Science*, vol. 193 (September 1976), pp. 1086-94.

(25) *Creation News*, No. 33 (Spring 1979).

(26) In Reference 6 of chapter 6, pp. 115-16.

Chapter 8 *'Flood Geology', and Related Fallacies, p. 114*

(1) Cited by P. C. W. Davies in Reference 21 of chapter 4, p. 221.

(2) H. Morris, *The Twilight of Evolution* (Presbyterian & Reformed Publishing Co, Philadelphia, 1963), pp. 56, 57.

(3) J. C. Whitcomb, *The Early Earth*. Evangelical Press, London, 1972, pp. 32, 37. (L. H. Worrad, Jn. makes a similar point in an article in *Creation Research Society Quarterly*, *13* (March 1977), pp. 199-201, entitled 'God Does Not Deceive Men.' He points out that 'the essence of deceitfulness lies in the intent'; God undoubtedly did not *intend* to deceive us.)

(4) J. Byrt, 'The roles of the Bible and of science in understanding creation.' *Faith and Thought*, *103 (3)*, 1976, pp. 158-88.

(5) In Reference 17 of chapter 5, pp. 196-8.

(6) In Reference 22 of chapter 7, p. 136.

(7) In Reference 9 of chapter 5, p. 58.

(8) C. R. Longwell, article, 'Geology'. *Encyclopædia Britannica*, 1973, vol. 10, p. 175.

(9) D. B. Gower, *Radiometric Dating Methods*. Pamphlet No. 207 of the Creation Science Movement, Worthing, Sussex (formerly the Evolution Protest Movement).

(10) J. C. Whitcomb and H. M. Morris, *The Genesis Flood*. Presbyterian & Reformed, Philadelphia, 1961.

(11) J. C. Whitcomb, *The World that Perished*. Baker, Grand Rapids, 1973, p. 67.

(12) In Reference 22 of chapter 7, p. 103.

(13) R. A. Moore, 'The impossible voyage of Noah's ark.' *Creation/Evolution*, 11 (Winter 1983), pp. 1-43.

(14) Genesis 7.20.

(15) R. A. Moore, op. cit.

(16) This is because in a thick deposit, containing many strata, the lower strata need time to harden before the upper layers are deposited. A single flood provides only enough time for a limited number of strata to be laid down.

(17) Reference 22 of chapter 7.

(18) D. E. Wonderly, in Reference 7 of chapter 6, p. 130.

(19) E. F. McBride, 'Flysch sedimentation in the Marathon region.' In: J. Lajoie, ed., *Flysch Sedimentology in North America.* Geological Association of Canada 1970, pp. 67–83.

(20) In Reference 17 of chapter 5, p. 138.

(21) R. J. Schadewald, 'Six "Flood" arguments creationists can't answer.' *Creation/Evolution* (9), Summer 1982, p. 12.

(22) J. E. Sanders & G. M. Friedman, 'Origin and occurrence of limestones', in *Developments in Sedimentology, No. 9A, Carbonate Rocks,* 1967, p. 193. Also B. B. Hanshaw, 'Inorganic geochemistry of carbonate shelf rocks', *American Assoc. of Petroleum Geologists Bulletin* (abstract), *53* (1969), p. 720. (Cited by D. E. Wonderly in Reference 7 of chapter 6.)

(23) G. Foley, *The Energy Question.* Penguin, London, 1976, p. 115. (Cited by Hitching, in Reference 20 of chapter 3.)

(24) H. Nilsson, *Synthetische Artbildung,* Lund University, Gleerup, Sweden, 1954, p. 1198. (Cited by Hitching, in Reference 20 of chapter 3.)

(25) Living things derive freshly-generated carbon-14 from the air. When they die, this store of carbon-14 gradually decays. When their remains are more than 40,000 years old, less than one per cent of the original carbon-14 is left. The radiation emitted by this minute amount then becomes practically impossible to detect, because it is swamped by the background radiation that is always with us. Occasional reports by amateur geologists that they have found radiocarbon dates of (say) 50,000 years on coal are undoubtedly the consequence of their inexperience with background radiation. A few early measurements on coal contaminated with recent material have given young ages, as would be expected. But all authentic measurements on ordinary coal can be relied upon to give a result of 'no carbon-14 left'. On the other hand, meaningful radiocarbon dates have been obtained on various frozen Siberian mammoth carcases, ranging from 11,450 to 39,000 years old, according to C. G. Weber. ('Common creationist attacks on geology.' *Creation/Evolution,* 2 (Fall 1980), p. 10.) This provides one more problem for 'Flood geologists,' who assert that coal and the mammoths are the same age.

(26) In Reference 10, above, pp. 418–21.

(27) R. M. Ritland, private communication, 1983.

(28) R. M. Ritland and S. L. Ritland, 'The fossil forests of the Yellowstone region.' *Spectrum* (a Quarterly Journal of the Association of Adventist Forums), 1974, (1 and 2), pp. 19–65.

(29) W. J. Fritz, 'Geology of the Lamar River formation, Northeast Yellowstone National Park.' *Proceedings of the Thirty-Third Annual Field Conference of the Wyoming Geological Association,* 1972, pp. 73–101.

(30) This is because their skeletons are composed of both calcium carbonate and chitin. The statement on p. 274 of *The Genesis Flood* (Reference 10, above) attributing high density to trilobites is erroneous. (Based on a private communication from D. E. Wonderly.)

(31) *The Observer's Book of British Geology*. Frederick Warne, London & New York, 1949, pp. 151–3.

(32) Op. cit.

(33) In Reference 17 of chapter 5, p. 131.

Chapter 9 Some Young-Earth Arguments Examined, p. 135

(1) Proverbs 18.17, NIV.

(2) In Reference 22 of chapter 7, pp. 167–9.

(3) P. R. Ehrlich, *The Population Bomb*. Pan Books, London, 1971, pp. 2 and 3. He quotes doubling times, which I have converted to average annual rates of growth, using the mathematical law which relates the two.

(4) T. G. Barnes, *Origin and Destiny of the Earth's Magnetic Field*. Creation-Life Publishers, San Diego, 1973, p. 38. Cited by Brush in Reference 19 of chapter 7.

(5) In Reference 19 of chapter 7, p. 54. Reproduced by permission.

(6) See A. Cox, G. B. Dalrymple, and R. R. Doell, 'Reversals of the earth's magnetic field.' *Scientific American*; (February 1967), pp. 44–54.

(7) Various recent papers on the archaeological evidence are cited by Brush, in Reference 19 of chapter 7.

(8) T. G. Barnes, *Depletion of the earth's magnetic field* (I.C.R. Impact Series, No. 100). Institute of Creation Research, San Diego, 1981. It is worth noting that Barnes appears not to understand the strength of the case against him. In the 1983 edition of his book (Reference 4, above) he has added a section entitled 'Answers to the Critics'. In this he has dealt briefly with two side-issues in Brush's paper but he ignores the main thrust of Brush's argument, which completely destroys Barnes' case. (Based on a private communication from Dr Brush.)

(9) In Reference 17 of chapter 5, p. 254.

(10) H. S. Slusher, *Age of the Cosmos* (ICR Technical Monograph No. 9). Institute for Creation Research, San Diego, 1980, pp. 22, 23.

(11) Pamphlet No. 230, *Decrease in the Speed of Light*. Creation Science Movement, Worthing, 1982.

(12) B. Setterfield, *The Velocity of Light and the Age of the Universe*. A reprint from *Ex Nihilo*, Creation Science Publishing, Brisbane, 1981.

(13) Private communication from Prof. John Bilello, of the State University of New York at Stony Brook.

(14) T. G. Trippe, and others. 'Review of particle properties.' *Reviews of Modern Physics*, *48 (2)* Part II, April 1976, pp. S1–S20. A recent article by G. W. E. Beekman, 'Hunt for the speed of light' (*New Scientist*, 13 October 1983, pp. 100, 101) leads to the same conclusion.

(15) Reference (10), above.

(16) Op. cit., p. 40.

(17) D. W. Hughes, 'Earth – an interplanetary dustbin.' *New Scientist*, 8 July 1976, pp. 64–6.

(18) D. G. (initials only given), 'Mainstream scientists respond to creationists.' *Physics Today*, February 1982, pp. 53-5.
(19) The value given by Hughes in Reference 17, above.
(20) Op. cit., pp. 53, 54.
(21) In Reference 17 of chapter 5, pp. 254-7.
(22) 'Natural plutonium' (unsigned). *Chemical and Engineering News*, 49 (1971), p. 29.
(23) J. P. Riley and G. Skirrow (eds.), *Chemical Oceanography*, Vol. 1. Academic Press, New York, 1965, tables by E. D. Goldberg on pp. 164-73.
(24) Ibid, p. 172.
(25) W. R. Cooper, *Miocene Man* (Pamphlet No. 234). Creation Science Movement, Worthing, 1983. (Also published as an article in *Ex Nihilo*.)
(26) C. B. Stringer, *A Note on the Guadeloupe Skeleton*. British Museum (Natural History), London, 1983.
(27) R. E. Kofahl and K. L. Segraves, *The Creation Explanation*. Harold Shaw, Wheaton, Illinois, 1975, p. 125. Cited by Conrad in Reference 28, below.
(28) E. C. Conrad, 'Are there human fossils in the "wrong place" for evolution?' *Creation/Evolution*, 8 (Spring 1982), pp. 14-22. His paper, upon which my summary is based, contains a thoroughly documented account of the evidence that the Castenedolo, Olmo and Calaveras fossils are not in the wrong places.
(29) Luke 16.8, RSV.
(30) C. G. Weber, 'Paluxy Man – the creationist Piltdown.' *Creation/Evolution*, 6, pp. 16-22.
(31) L. R. Godfrey, 'An analysis of the creationist film, *Footprints in Stone*.' *Creation/Evolution*, 6, (Fall 1981), pp. 23-30.
(32) B. Neufeld, 'Dinosaur tracks and giant men.' *Origins*, 2 (2) (1975), pp. 64-76.
(33) J. Morris, *Tracking those Incredible Dinosaurs: And the People Who Knew Them*. Creation-Life Publishers, San Diego, 1980, p. 93.
(34) Ibid, pp. 182-5.
(35) W. F. Tanner, 'Time and the rock record.' *Journal of the American Scientific Affiliation*, 33 (2) (June 1981), pp. 100-5.
(36) Plate II, in Reference 9 of chapter 5.
(37) E. C. Conrad, 'Tripping over a trilobite: a study of the Meister tracks.' *Creation/Evolution*, 6, (Fall 1981), pp. 30-3.
(38) J. C. Dillow, *The Waters Above – Earth's Pre-Flood Vapour Canopy*. Moody Press, Chicago, 1981.
(39) A. J. M. White, *What About Origins?* Dunestone Printers, 1978, p. 58.
(40) In Reference 22 of chapter 7, p. 104.
(41) D. H. Zenger, J. B. Dunham and R. L. Ethington (eds.) *Special Publication No. 28*. Society of Economic Paleontologists and Mineralogists, Tulsa, Oklahoma, 1980. See papers by J. A. McKenzie *et. al.* (pp. 11-30), M. Muir *et.al.* (pp. 51-67), G. M. Friedman (pp. 69-80).

(42) In Reference 10 of chapter 8, p. 130.
(43) See, for example: W. Schäfer, *Ecology and Paleoecology of Marine Environments*. University of Chicago, Chicago, 1972; R. H. Dott & R. L. Batten, *Evolution of the Earth*, McGraw Hill, New York, 1976; C. W. Stearn, R. L. Carroll and T. H. Clark, *Geological Evolution of North America*, 3rd edn., John Wiley, New York, 1979.
(44) In Reference 3 of chapter 8, Preface.
(45) R. E. Kofahl and K. L. Segraves, *The Creation Explanation*. Harold Shaw, Wheaton, Illinois, p. 155. Cited by White in Reference 39, above, p. 65.
(46) In Reference 17 of chapter 5, p. 226.
(47) In Reference 18, above, p. 54.
(48) In Reference 10, above, p. 6.
(49) *Creation/Evolution*, 6 (Fall 1981), pp. 41, 42.
(50) M. Bowden, *The Rise of the Evolution Fraud*. Sovereign Publications, Bromley, Kent, 1982, p. 200.
(51) R. P. Benedict, *Journey Away from God*. Fleming H. Revell, Old Tappan, New Jersey, 1972, pp. 110, 111.
(52) C. L. Woolley, *Ur of the Chaldees*. 1929, Penguin 1938, pp. 23–5.
(53) Cited by C. G. Weber in 'Common creationist attacks on geology.' *Creation/Evolution*, 2, pp. 10–25.
(54) *Creation/Evolution*, 6 (Fall 1981), p. 38.
(55) Ibid., pp. 34–6.
(56) Daniel 2.42.

Chapter 10   The Days of Creation, p. 161

(1) *The Shoes of the Fisherman*.
(2) In Reference 9 of chapter 5, p. 73.
(3) From *The Remarkable Birth of Planet Earth*, cited by S. G. Brush in 'Finding the age of the earth by physics or by faith?' *Journal of Geological Education*, 30 (1982), pp. 34–58.
(4) S. G. Brush, see Reference 3, above.
(5) For example, Isaiah 13.6; Jeremiah 46.10; Ezekiel 30.2, 3; Joel 1.15; Amos 5.18; Obadiah 15;2 Peter 3.10 – and many others.
(6) Its best-known modern exponent is probably Dr Arthur Custance. See his *Evolution or Creation?* Zondervan, Grand Rapids, 1976, pp. 92–108.
(7) D. C. Spanner, *Creation and Evolution*. Falcon Books, London, 1965, pp. 35–7.
(8) It is my impression that this became the most widely accepted view in Britain in the early twentieth century. Its popularity may have been partly due to the way this view was advocated in the best-selling Bible Commentary of Ellicott.

(9) Creationists sometimes argue that the Hebrew word *'oph* can refer to flying insects. This statement is true, but misleading. The word occurs 71 times; in 68 of these the KJV translates it 'bird' or 'fowl'. In the other 3 places it is translated 'flying' or 'that flieth', and is related to the phrase 'creeping things' – in other words, it then becomes *part* of a phrase meaning 'flying insect(s)'. When used on its own (as in Genesis 1) the word never refers to insects, but is always translated 'bird' or 'fowl'. All authorities seem to agree that the correct translation in Genesis 1 is 'birds'.

(10) J. O. Means, 'Narrative of the Creation in Genesis'. *Bibliotheca Sacra*, March–April 1855, pp. 116–17.

(11) In Reference 16 of chapter 6, pp. 64 and 74.

(12) J. H. Kurtz, *Bible and Astronomy* (third German edition, 1857), cited by B. Ramm in *The Christian View of Science and Scripture*. Paternoster, Exeter, 1964 edn., pp. 150–4.

(13) P. J. Wiseman, *Clues to Creation in Genesis*. Marshall, Morgan & Scott, London, 1977. He suggests that the revelation might have been made to one of the early characters of Genesis, in the form of a series of six daily visions. This person could have been inspired by God to write on clay tablets a summary of what he saw. These tablets could subsequently have been used by Moses as source material for the Book of Genesis.

(14) D. E. Cain, *Creation and Capron's Explanatory Interpretation*. Paper published by the author at 18 Edmel Rd, Scotia, NY 12302, USA, 1982.

(15) *The Conflict of Truth*. Hodder & Stoughton, London, 1902, pp. 169–99.

(16) Except, of course, when there is a stated or implied condition: 'Such-and-such shall come to pass, unless . . .'

(17) E. W. Bullinger, *How to Enjoy the Bible*. Bagster, London, reprint of 1974, p. 56.

(18) For a full exposition of the subject of this paragraph, see 'The Just-So World', chapter 4 of my book *God Is*. (Reference 30 of chapter 4.)

Chapter 11   Some other Biblical Questions, p. 179

(1) 'The Scriptures', in *Table Talk*, 1689.

(2) In Reference 38 of chapter 9, p. 48.

(3) In Reference 2 of chapter 8, p. 37.

(4) In Reference 22 of chapter 7, p. 126.

(5) See, for example, p. 66 in Reference 3 of chapter 8, and p. 70 in Reference 2 of chapter 8.

(6) KJV, RV, RAV (known in USA as NKJV), GNB, and NIV.

(7) I am not counting micro-fossils here, nor fossilized vegetation.

(8) Appendix 2, in Reference 10 of chapter 8.

(9) See W. H. Green, 'Primeval chronology.' *Bibliotheca Sacra*, 47, 1890, pp. 285–303. (Reprinted as an appendix in Reference 16 of chapter

6.) For a more detailed exposition, see J. Urquhart, *How Old is Man?* Nisbet, London, 1904.

(10) Luke agrees here with the Septuagint translation of Genesis.

Chapter 12   Some Biblical Objections to Theistic Evolution, p. 189

(1) *Princess Ida.*

(2) J. R. Moore, *The Post-Darwinian Controversies*. Cambridge University Press, Cambridge, 1979.

(3) Matthew gives another, totally different, genealogy. This can, however, be harmonized with Luke's by assuming that Luke gives Mary's line (whilst putting her husband's name instead of her own), and that Matthew gives Joseph's line. See any good conservative commentary for details.

(4) It is sometimes argued that a myth or an allegory is not really fiction, because it is a portrayal of truth in the guise of a story. Be that as it may, the people in such stories are wholly fictitious; nobody would claim that Screwtape or Mr Worldly Wiseman were not fictitious characters. If Genesis 1–11 are treated as myth or allegory, Adam becomes like a character in a parable: meaningful, but fictional. (*Chambers Twentieth Century Dictionary* defines 'allegory' as 'a narrative to be understood symbolically'.)

(5) Op. cit., pp. 305, 307.

(6) R. J. Berry, 'Darwin cleared.' *Biologist*, 29(2), 1982, pp. 100–4. The first half of this extract was a quotation from another biologist, but Berry quotes it as an eloquent expression of his own views.

(7) R. J. Berry, *Adam and the Ape* (Falcon, London, 1975), is my principal source. Additional information was derived from personal correspondence with Prof. Berry, from his *Biologist* paper cited above, from publications by various evangelical writers, and especially references 8–11, below.

(8) D. C. Spanner, *Creation and Evolution*. Falcon, London, 1965.

(9) E. K. V. Pearce, *Who was Adam?* Paternoster, Exeter, 1969.

(10) R. H. Bube, 'Creation: (A) How should Genesis be interpreted? (B) Understanding creation and evolution.' *Journal of the American Scientific Affiliation*, March 1980, pp. 34–9, and September 1980, pp. 174–8.

(11) John Stott, *Church of England Newspaper*, 17 June, 1968. Cited in N. M. de S. Cameron, *Evolution and the Authority of the Bible*. Paternoster, Exeter, 1983, p. 63.

(12) Two synonymous Hebrew words for 'breath' are used in these 'breath of life' passages in Genesis 6 and 7, one of which is the word used in Genesis 2.7.

(13) J. O. Buswell III, 'A creationist interpretation of prehistoric man.' In R. L. Mister (ed.), *Evolution and Christian Thought Today*. Eerdmans, Grand Rapids, 1959, pp. 165–89.

(14) The words of Genesis do not necessarily mean that God (or his angel) built a man-shaped heap of dust, and then bent down and gave it a

kind of 'kiss of life'. It seems more likely that the words are meant to inform us that God miraculously produced a human body from non-living material in some unspecified way, and then animated it by his creative power.

(15) Op. cit., pp. 21, 33–8.
(16) In Reference 7, above, pp. 43, 50.
(17) Ibid, p. 42.
(18) Ibid, p. 43 (footnote).
(19) It is possible that Malachi is referring here to the descent of the children of Israel from one man, Jacob; but the reference in the same verse to creation suggests rather that he has in mind mankind's descent from Adam.
(20) Ibid, p. 51, and Spanner, op. cit., p. 57.
(21) The words quoted are the translation of Speiser in the Anchor Bible, *Genesis* (1964), p. 17, as cited by D. Watts, in 'Creation by Evolution', *Biblical Creation*, *14* (1983), pp. 15–25. A similar interpretation was placed upon the verse by the Jewish scholar, U. Cassuto, in, *A Commentary on the Book of Genesis – Part I, Adam to Noah*: English trans. Oxford University Press, London, 1961, p. 125.

Chapter 13   Conclusions, p. 201

(1) P. Davies, 'The Christian perspective of a scientist.' (Book review.) *New Scientist*. 2 June 1983, p. 638.
(2) M. Ruse. *Darwinism Defended: A Guide to the Evolution Controversies*; Addison–Wesley, 1982. Cited by R. J. Berry in *Christian Graduate*. 1983.
(3) M. Ruse, 'A philosopher at the monkey trial.' *New Scientist*, 4 February 1982, pp. 317–19.
(4) Reputedly uttered during a lecture on Sound, at the Royal Institution.

Index of Names

Index of Subjects

man, creation of, 165, 195–7,
223–4nn; origin of, 50–3;
pre-Adamic, 197–8
mature creation, 116
metamorphic rocks, definition
of, 83; formation of, 94–5
meteorites, 141
meteoritic dust, 142–3
micro-evolution, 4
Millennium, 164
Miocene Man, 146–7
missing links, 52
Mississippi, sedimentation by,
83–4
molluscs, 186
moon, cooling of, 153
mountain building, 185
Muskox intrusion, 93
mutation, 22, 24–31, 33–4, 38,
40–1, 47, 55
myth, nature of, 223n

Natural History Museum, 13
natural selection, 5, 18, 23–6,
29–30, 33, 38, 40–1, 49, 55,
190
nautiloids, 131
Nebuchadnezzar's dream, 157
neo-Darwinism, 5
'new biology', 57–8
New Stone Age, 197
Noah, 187–8
nuclear force, 60
nucleotides, origin of, 39
nuclides, 105

Old Stone Age, 197
Ohno Man, 147–8
over-development, 46
oxygen, origin of, 63

Palaeontology, 17
Palisades sill, 93
Paluxy River, 149
parallax, 97–8

parallelism, Hebrew, 176
parasitic plants, 30
parentheses in Scripture,
169–72
peacock, 46–7
petrified forests, 128–30
petroleum, 185
Piltdown Man, 148
pitch, 185
Planet Earth, uniqueness of,
174
plant distribution, 31
plutonium, half-life of, 145
polystrate fossils, origin of, 215
population of world, 135–6
potassium-argon dating, 107,
110, 216n
prebiotic evolution, 15, 34
pre-Cambrian fossils, 211n
probability theory, 34
progressive creation, 4
punctuated equilibria, 18, 55

Radioactive decay rates, 216n
radioactive nuclides,
distribution of, 105–6
radiocarbon dating, 128, 148,
154, 216n, 218n
Radiolaria, 91
radiometric dating, 106–12
Ramapithecus, 50
recent-creationism, definition
of, 6
recent-creation theory, 165–6
red dwarfs, 64
residence times, 145
resurrection of Christ, 191, 199
revelation-day theory, 167,
176, 222n
Riemannian space, 100–2
rock-forming processes, 119
rubidium-strontium dating,
111

Sabbath, 163, 177–8